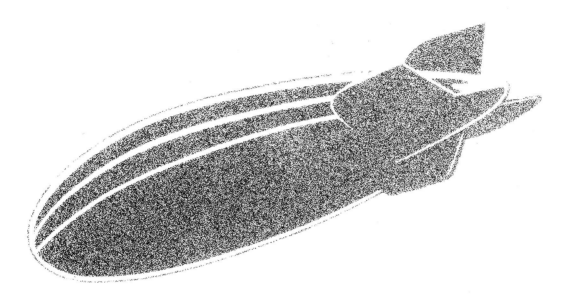

Copyright © 1991 Omnibus Press
(A Division of Book Sales Limited)

Edited by
CHRIS CHARLESWORTH

Book designed by
LISA PETTIBONE
FOUR CORNERS DESIGN

Picture research by
PAUL GIBLIN, DAVE LEWIS & DAVID BROLAN

ISBN 0.7119.2416.3
Order No. OP 46135

Exclusive distributors:

BOOK SALES LIMITED
8/9 Frith Street
London W1V 5TZ, UK

MUSIC SALES CORPORATION
225 Park Avenue South
New York, NY 10003, USA

MUSIC SALES PTY LTD.
120 Rothschild Avenue
Rosebery, NSW 2018, Australia

To the Music Trade only:
MUSIC SALES LIMITED
8/9 Frith Street
London W1V 5TZ, UK

Photo credits:
Beer Davis: 16. George Bodnar: 38(3), 72. Camera Press: 29(3), 32(3). Carl Dunn:
introduction, 4, 5(centre & bottom), 11(bottom), 13(left & right), 20, 24, 30(2&3),
31(6&7), 33(4&5), 42, 77(bottom), 119. Bob Gruen: 11(left), 44. Kobal: 18. LFI: vi,
opposite 1, 6, 7, 8, 22, 26, 29(2), 30(4&5), 31(8&10), 33(7&8), 34/5, 36, 37(1-6),
38(1&2&4), 43, 76, 78, 88(b), 89, 115, 118, 120. Dave Lewis: 1, 3(bottom). Pic
Photos: 74. Pictorial Press: 2, 3(top), 11(centre), 15, 19, 23, 25, 27, 28, 33(4),
39(5&6), 73(top & bottom), 80, 81, 82. Chuck Pulin: 63. Redfearns: 29(4), 30(1),
32(1), 33(6), 79. Relay: 12, 14, 17, 75(top), 83(bottom), 88(top), 93. Retna: 31(9),
77(top). Rex Features: 29(1), 32(2), 39(7&8), 73(centre), 83(top). Angelica
Strilmothe: 70. M. Taylor: 37(7). Tyne Tees Television: 71. Chris Walter: 5(top).

Typeset by
Saxon Printing Ltd., Derby, England

Printed and bound in Singapore

LED-ZEPPELIN

— A·CELEBRATION —

DAVE·LEWIS

OMNIBUS PRESS
LONDON · NEW YORK · SYDNEY

CONTENTS

CREDITS &
ACKNOWLEDGEMENTS

This celebration would be a whole lot less complete without the invaluable assistance, advice and inspiration of the following people: Gary Foy, for his continued interest, Mary Hooton at Atlantic, Lee Ellen Newman at East West, Martyn Robinson and Roy Dougan at Warner Music, Peter Doggett at *Record Collector*, Phil Carson for his time and assistance, Howard Mylett and Robert Godwin for some sterling previous Zepp chronicles, Taylor at *Zoso* magazine for keeping it together every month (well worth a read), Matt Brown and Paul Brandreth for all their Mission info, Colin Davey, Nigel Glazier and Lee Sargent out in the field, Neil Boote in the office and all at OPM 163, Paul, Andrew, Caroline, Hilary and Sally at Omnibus, Terry Boud for guiding me through a night of Directors ale at the Nirvana celebration (cheers Terry!), Dave Collins for his computer knowhow and some torrid running battles on the soccer field, the music of Nick Drake and Led Zeppelin for accompanying me during many late nights writing all this, all past *Tight But Loose* readers for sharing the original platform of communication.

And to my wife Janet for constant support and encouragement. To my family and close friends for sharing in my enthusiasm, especially my late mother Edith.

Very special thanks to Andy Adams. His vast Zepp archive and knowledge benefited this project greatly.

And to my editor Chris Charlesworth for making all this possible and realising that their popularity has obviously not waned!

Finally to a little girl whose timely arrival on the afternoon of June 4, 1990, coincided with the first 'Manic Nirvana' tour date at Hammersmith. The only act I've ever seen upstage Robert Plant.

Samantha Elizabeth Lewis – this is for you.

DAVE LEWIS
December 1990.

INTRODUCTION

I n a stuffy London rehearsal room in the early autumn of 1968, Jimmy Page called out a chord sequence of G to A to his new found musical colleagues Robert Plant, John Paul Jones and John Bonham. Seconds later the walls reverberated to the sound of 'The Train Kept A Rollin'' and the foundations were laid for what would become one of the most influential forces in the history of rock music.

Led Zeppelin were airborne and destined for a memorable 12-year flight.

A decade after their demise, Led Zeppelin's music is as popular today as it was when they reigned supreme as the world's greatest rock attraction. This book is a celebration of their music; music that has entertained and inspired their fans for nearly a quarter of a century.

In the pages that follow, I have attempted to amass a host of reference material that will help enthusiasts old and new in their appreciation of Led Zeppelin and its individual members. It includes a complete chronicle of every track the band recorded, a rare insight into their studio work, the legacy of the live Zeppelin concert experience, full details of the post-1980 activities of Jimmy Page, Robert Plant and John Paul Jones, plus a reference section that includes a log of every known Zeppelin concert, an extensive discography with pre and post Zepp information, plus a full chronology that brings the story up to date with the Led Zeppelin 'Remasters' project.

The end result is an absorbing reference work that I hope stands as a lasting companion to the musical legacy of Led Zeppelin.

They remain Tight But Loose . . .

Enjoy this celebration.

The enigmatic guitar hero, 1975.

THE MASTER AND HIS ART

Jimmy Page

Long before he ever conceived the idea of Led Zeppelin, Jimmy Page was carving a name for himself as one of Britain's most gifted guitar players. It seems inconceivable in the here today/gone tomorrow atmosphere of nineties rock and pop that an instrumentalist should spend as long as three years as a studio musician *before* seeking his fortune as a recording artist and performer in his own right, but that is exactly what James Patrick Page did during the early sixties.

This was partly to do with Jimmy's poor health – it was marginally healthier in the studio than on the road – and partly because he was quick to realise that an in-demand session guitarist was better rewarded for his efforts than most musicians in chart bands, even if they did occasionally appear on the cover of *Melody Maker*.

Thus did Jimmy Page equip himself with a formidable array of differing guitar techniques that the session player might be called upon to demonstrate. For every day would present a different problem that required a different solution: from The Who to Val Doonican, from Tom Jones to Joe Cocker, from Petula Clark to The Kinks, and who knows how many film soundtracks or sound-alike albums in between. Jimmy certainly doesn't remember or even care how many sessions he played on and since the documentation for most of them is lost forever, no-one will ever know. But some of this work has been catalogued, especially those sessions where his contribution was of greater creative significance than simply playing what he was told to play.

It is Jimmy Page's guitar that can be heard on number one hits like Chris Farlowe's 'Out Of Time' and Joe Cocker's 'With A Little Help From My Friends' though no-one knew it at the time. In 1979 an album of dubious legitimacy called 'James Patrick Page: Session Man' was released which went some way to demonstrating the extraordinary diversity required of a session man. During this period of British pop there were actually two guitarists who dominated the session scene: 'Big' Jim Sullivan and 'Little' Jimmy Page. Sullivan later went on to become Tom Jones' guitarist and musical arranger while Jimmy went on to join The Yardbirds and, of course, launch Led Zeppelin.

For over a quarter of a century then – even if you didn't know it – the guitar playing of Jimmy Page has thrilled and inspired audiences everywhere, not just hard rock fans.

Throughout this entire period Page's playing, both electric and acoustic, has constantly expanded the barriers of guitar virtuosity. His formula of merging a variety of styles, be it raw rock 'n' roll inspired by Scotty Moore or James Burton, pure blues inspired by Robert Johnson or folk inspired by Bert Jansch and John Renbourn, to create a compelling soundscape of rock guitar, has constantly produced stunning results.

To demonstrate the achievements of Jimmy Page as a guitar player there follow 25 examples of his work spanning every stage of his career, from the early session days right up to the solo 'Outrider' project. Seek out these performances and you will discover an aural history of a guitar master and his art . . .

Jimmy Page, session man, circa 1965.

1 'YOUR MOMMA'S OUT OF TOWN'
Carter Lewis and The Southerners (1963); taken from the album 'James Patrick Page: 'Session Man' (Slipped Disc Records, HOFF 1098).

The story commences in November 1963 with the release of this UK single on the Oriole label. It was actually Page's second session, the first being for ex-Shadows Jet Harris and Tony Meehan's chart topper 'Diamonds'.

The group was fronted by session singers John Carter and Ken Lewis who went on to form The Ivy League and chalk up a couple of Top 10 hits in 1965 with songs that emphasised their strong but somewhat gimmicky falsetto harmonies. On this typically charming beat-boom period piece, young Jimmy can be heard subtly undercutting the innocent pop beat of the day with some clever acoustic picking.

Though not a hit, 'Your Momma's Out Of Town' was well received at the time and led to the group recording some BBC radio sessions on which Page joined them. There exists a promo photo of Page with the Carter Lewis line-up looking for all the world like a fully paid-up member. But for the young Page this was just another date in his increasingly packed session diary.

2 'MONEY HONEY'
Mickie Most (1963); taken from the album 'James Patrick Page: Session Man'.

And here's another. Prior to embarking on an extremely successful career as a record producer, Mickie Most released a series of flop singles on Columbia. Jimmy was employed for the bulk of them and 'Money Honey' – previously recorded by both Elvis Presley and Little Richard – was the B-side to Most's cover version of Frankie Ford's 'Sea Cruise' (which didn't feature Page).

This is an early and aggressive flexing of the Gibson Les Paul custom guitar Page used during his session days which he bought on hire purchase for £185 in 1962. The tempo builds up to a raucous solo – helped along by a rollicking piano – which Page delivers in a twangy, fluent style

1

reminiscent of the American rock 'n' roll pioneers in the fifties that he loved so much. It is an early example of a solo style which Page would constantly revive throughout his career – check out 'Candy Store Rock' on 'Presence'. Short sharp and effective.

3 'I JUST CAN'T GO TO SLEEP'
The Sneekers (1964); taken from the album 'James Patrick Page: Session Man'.

Though this is a rather nondescript and obscure B-side, it is an interesting example of Page's early deployment of guitar effects. Fuzz, distortion and wah-wah can be heard throughout the song and the latter sounds very similar to fellow session man 'Big' Jim Sullivan's weeping wah-wah style featured on Dave Berry's 1964 hit 'The Crying Game'.

'I Just Can't Go To Sleep' was the flip to The Sneekers version of 'Bald Headed Woman', the same song that appeared on the B-side of The Who's first hit 'I Can't Explain'. Here again Page was called in to help (as were his friends Carter and Lewis), and though he only contributed to the rhythm track on 'Explain' his use of a fuzz distortion device on 'Bald Headed Woman' impressed Who guitarist Pete Townshend so much that Pete acquired his own almost immediately.

4 'ONCE IN A WHILE'
The Brooks (1964); taken from the album 'James Patrick Page: Session Man'.

Definitely one of the stand-out singles of the session era. The Brooks were a male duo touted as Britain's answer to The Everly Brothers, but sadly the hits had dried up for them by the time this criminally ignored single surfaced in 1964.

Alongside the boys' uplifting close harmony vocal, Jimmy injects a series of sizzling runs culminating with a brief but quite brilliant solo that is years ahead of its time. As a reference point, it can be compared to the fluttering fade out solo that graces 'Good Times Bad Times' on Led Zeppelin's first album.

This is clearly the work of a supremely proficient 19-year-old musician. One perhaps ready for solo stardom . . .?

5 'SHE JUST SATISFIES'
Jimmy Page (1965); taken from the album 'James Patrick Page: Session Man'.

Or maybe not . . .
No Page career glossary would be complete without this now ultra rare one-off early solo recording. Released on February 4, 1965, on Fontana, it sold only a few

Jimmy Page, psychedelic Yardbird, circa 1967.

copies and today commands one of the highest prices of any UK British single on the collectors' market.

With its stabbing repeated riffs, 'She Just Satisfies' bears a striking resemblance to The Kinks early singles which is not surprising since Page had recently completed sessions for The Kinks' first album (much to the band's distaste) and one of their songs, 'Revenge', is almost a backing track demo of this single.

Aside from being a bizarre curio in the Page catalogue, 'She Just Satisfies' is an early example of Page's ability to manipulate a simple guitar riff and stretch it over the framework of an entire song. Years later he was to nod affectionately back in the direction of this era by employing a similar arrangement on

'Custard Pie' on Zeppelin's 'Physical Graffiti'.

He plays all instruments on this single except drums which are provided by Bobby Graham. And if you're wondering what happened to the follow-up, well . . . Page's idea to cover The Beatles' 'Every Little Thing' with an orchestra didn't quite meet with Fontana's approval. (Four years later Yes covered the same Beatles song in a complex arrangement on their début album.)

6 'HAPPENINGS 10 YEARS TIME AGO'
The Yardbirds (1966); (Columbia single, DB 8024).

We move swiftly into The Yardbirds era with this classic slice of British psychedelic pop.

Page joined The Yardbirds, at the third

time of asking, in June 1966. Initially he replaced the outgoing Paul Samwell-Smith on bass, but rhythm guitarist Chris Dreja soon took on that role, leaving Page to link horns with another inspiring guitar player of the era, Jeff Beck. It was to be a short-lived collaboration and by the end of the year the headstrong Beck had upped and quit, leaving Jimmy to shoulder the full burden of guitar chores.

'Happenings 10 Years Time Ago' is therefore one of the few recorded examples of their association and easily the best. Page recalls that due to Beck's late arrival at the session, he was largely responsible for the song's arrangement and takes credit for the jerky rhythmic chording and the eerie police siren effects that pave the way for a completely astonishing and quite manic Beck solo.

The whole acid-drenched hallucinatory feeling of the track is further enhanced by the strange cockney exchange that occurs in the midst of the solo and exclaims, ''Pop group are yer! Why you all got long hair!''

Not surprisingly this follow-up to the Top 20 hit 'Over Under Sideways Down' went right over the heads of the Tom Jones/Engelbert single buying market of the time and it peaked at a lowly number 43.

As a yardstick for some of the adventurous and unorthodox guitar arrangements that were to follow, 'Happenings 10 Years Time Ago' is another important stepping stone in Jimmy's development as a guitarist as well as a truly great 45 rpm single.

The bass player on the session that produced this single just happened to be one John Baldwin, a.k.a. John Paul Jones.

7 'LITTLE GAMES'
The Yardbirds (1967); Columbia Single DB8165.

The same John Paul Jones had quite a hand in the construction of the next Yardbirds' release. Issued in April 1967, 'Little Games' was the first fruit of the group's production link with Mickie Most. Jones was brought in to arrange the cellos that echo around Page's guitar motif.

Listening today, it clearly represents the subtle beginnings of the Page/Jones guitar/string section interplay that would manifest itself years later and to much greater effect on their composition 'Kashmir'. On the fade-out Page, by now using a Fender Telecaster, plays a beautifully sustained note that echoes above the strings. 'Little Games' is another fine period piece, redolent of the parties in

Chelsea, Regency bucks, swinging London atmospherics captured in the vocals of Keith Relf. It holds up well against anything The Kinks, Stones or Small Faces produced that year and was also released in the US.

However, one successful outcome of The Yardbirds' brief relationship with Mickie Most was that he recommended a new manager to handle their affairs, a man of imposing stature with whom he shared an office. His name was Peter Grant.

8 'TINKER TAILOR SOLDIER SAILOR'
The Yardbirds (1967); taken from The Yardbirds' album 'Little Games' (US: Epic BN 26313).

Forget Keith Relf's rather banal lyrics on this 'Little Games' album track and instead concentrate on the slashing shimmering guitar chordings that drive the song along. It's a very similar style to the layered effect on Zeppelin's own 'The Song Remains The Same'.

This is a precursor to another important Page trademark – the violin bow. As the song slows down Jimmy uses a bow to scrape the guitar strings and produce the atmospheric, almost majestic, sound that was to become a highlight of almost every live Zeppelin concert during 'Dazed And Confused'.

It is difficult to pinpoint the exact origins of the guitar played with bow technique, but Jimmy recalls that it was first sug-

Beck and Page with The Yardbirds, 1966.

gested to him by a session violinist whose son was the actor David McCallum. He subsequently used the technique on several sessions but again he can't remember which. With The Yardbirds, it can be heard on 'Tinker Tailor' and one other 'Little Games' album track, 'Glimpses'.

9 'WHITE SUMMER'
The Yardbirds (1967); taken from The Yardbirds' album 'Little Games'.

Another landmark composition. 'White Summer' was the first flowering of Jimmy's flirtation with a finger-picked acoustic guitar. He had long since admired the acoustic styles of folk players such as Davy Graham, Bert Jansch and John Renbourne and the classical master Segovia whose 'Rodrigo's Guitar Concerto' had been a particular favourite.

In producing 'White Summer', Jimmy combined these acoustic influences with a growing interest in Indian and Moroccan tunings. He had dabbled with the sitar a year or two earlier, but he was anxious not to join the Indian music pop bandwagon of the time and never used it on record.

Instead, 'White Summer' has Tabla drums and a very Eastern flavoured electric guitar melody, layered over a complex acoustic arrangement.

It still sounds most impressive and is the first master-stroke in a trilogy of Page studio performances that would continue with 'Black Mountain Side' and climax with 'Kashmir'.

10 'THINK ABOUT IT'
The Yardbirds (1968); B-side of The Yardbirds' single 'Goodnight Sweet Josephine' (Columbia DB 8368).

Alongside the live rendition of 'I'm Confused', 'Think About It' can clearly be viewed as a stepping-off point from which Jimmy Page was able to transfer his musical identity and relocate it within the framework that was to become Led Zeppelin's first album.

Recorded in December 1967, this track was the flipside of The Yardbirds' last single issued in the UK in March 1968. It's an excellent vehicle for Page's expanding guitar technology. Over a strident mid-tempo rhythm, Keith Relf eulogises philosophically before Jimmy wades in with a solo that is very similar in construction to the one he recorded a few months later on 'Dazed And Confused'. A fast but coherent fusion of notes paves the way for a new beginning and the track's strange closing backward tape effects signify the end of this particular era . . .

11 'DAZED AND CONFUSED'
Led Zeppelin (1969); taken from the album 'Led Zeppelin'
(Atlantic K40031).

And the start of a new one. Spurred on
by the youthful enthusiasm of Messrs
Plant and Bonham and the seasoned pro-
fessionalism of John Paul Jones, Page was
free to express himself in the studio more
fully than ever before. From its sonic sig-
nalling intro, right through to its
mesmerising climax, 'Dazed And Confused' remains one of his most complete
performances.

12 'WHOLE LOTTA LOVE'
Led Zeppelin (1969); taken from the album 'Led Zeppelin II'
(Atlantic K40037).

Opening 'Led Zeppelin II', this early
anthem is an illuminating example of
Jimmy's prowess as a producer.
Every inch of drama is compressed into
the arrangement and there's just so much
to enjoy: the slightly understated opening
riff, the slide guitar effect on the descending chord passages, the backwards echo
sound waves that assist Plant towards his
climax, the biting solo that follows it and
the final flurry of echoed riffing at the
close. A pioneering five minutes and 33
seconds.
'Whole Lotta Love' was issued as a single
in the US where it reached number four in
the charts. It thus became the staple climax to Led Zeppelin's concerts, segueing
into rockabilly and free-form sonic booms,
and it is widely regarded as the blueprint
for what has since become known as
heavy metal music.

13 'SINCE I'VE BEEN LOVING YOU'
Led Zeppelin (1970); taken from the album 'Led Zeppelin
III' (Atlantic K50002).

· Throughout his career, the blues have
been of paramount importance to Jimmy
Page as a guitar player. The influence of
original blues masters such as B.B. King
and Elmore James has often coloured his
own playing and the arrival of a fellow
blues enthusiast into Led Zeppelin stepped up his commitment to merge rock
and blues styles to maximum effect.
After covering a pair of Willie Dixon
tunes on the first Zeppelin album, Page
and Plant felt confident enough to produce their own custom-made blues
compositions and 'Since I've Been Loving
You' remains the most successful.
Against John Bonham's superbly spaced
drum shots, Jimmy leads into the track
with consummate ease. He had by now
switched from the Telecaster back to a
Gibson Les Paul guitar and the choice of

Low slung Gibson Les Paul, 1973.

instrument brings a sustained fluency to his playing, particularly during the tortured solo, that is quite breathtaking.

14 'TANGERINE'
Led Zeppelin (1970); taken from the album 'Led Zeppelin III'.

A Page composition left over from The Yardbirds era, 'Tangerine' is a three-pronged demonstration of his guitar craft.
Here, Page strums an acoustic guitar for the melody before moving to electric for a smooth woman-tone solo. Finally he overdubs a pleasingly wah-wah-ed pedal steel guitar solo for the four-part harmony ending. A perfect illustration of the light and shade of his expansive style.

15 'NO QUARTER'
(live version) Led Zeppelin (1973); taken from the soundtrack album 'The Song Remains The Same' (Swan Song SSK 89402).

One of the most adventurous of all Zeppelin's studio recordings, this track took on an extra dimension when played live as it became an extended vehicle for John Paul Jones and Jimmy Page not only to flex their respective talents but to play off each other by weaving melodies together.
This version, taken from a 1973 Madison Square Garden concert, has Jimmy emerging from the dry ice to follow Jones with a solo that twists and turns in all the right places, before entering into a jazz-like improvisation against Bonzo's shuffling beat and J.P's electric piano. Then it's a step on the wah-wah pedal and a head for home with Robert back at the helm.

16 'IN MY TIME OF DYING'
Led Zeppelin (1975); taken from the album 'Physical Graffiti' (Swan Song SSK 89400).

'In My Time Of Dying' is an 11-minute showcase for Page's bottleneck banshee wailings. There are just so many peaks on this track and the intensity provided by all four musicians is both invigorating and unnerving.
The whole thing reaches an artistic zenith when Plant, after sustaining yet another Page flurry, cries out from the vocal booth "Feels pretty good up here . . .!" A devastating Page performance from a devastating Led Zeppelin album.

17 'KASHMIR'
Led Zeppelin (1975); taken from the album 'Physical Graffiti'.

Here we have a clear example of the potency of the Led Zeppelin chemistry – and a vivid reminder of just how effectively Jimmy Page played off John Bonham.

Led Zeppelin, 1969.

The basic time signature to 'Kashmir' has Bonham pacing the hypnotic tempo superbly, leaving just the right amount of space between the snare and bass drum for Jimmy to filter in those riveting riffs which in turn merge with Jones' Arabian string symphony. Bring in Robert Plant at his most expressive and what you have left is 'Kashmir' . . . so let them take you there.
Plant has often been quoted as saying that 'Kashmir' is his all-time favourite Zeppelin track, and the oddly complex time signatures, the unusual chord structure and Eastern feel all combine to sustain his judgement.

18 'ACHILLES LAST STAND'
Led Zeppelin (1976); taken from the album 'Presence' (Swan Song SSK 59402).

The 'Presence' album came together almost as therapy for the injured Robert Plant and recording under such forced circumstances brought a new level of urgency and intensity to their playing.
The whole atmosphere of this period of inner group survival is best preserved on 'Achilles Last Stand', the epic opening track. It fully illustrates how working under the pressure of a studio deadline urged Jimmy on to a peak of creativity, as he produces a stream of structured overdubs that formulate a quite stunning display of guitar orchestration.
Even John Paul Jones had his doubts about Page's ability to interlock the various sections successfully, but it works beautifully and provides the perfect soundtrack to a bizarre and electrifying Plant narrative.
'Achilles Last Stand' just might be Jimmy Page's finest achievement.

Page in full flight, 1973 US tour.

19 'WHO'S TO BLAME (MAIN TITLE)'/
'CAROLE'S THEME'
*Jimmy Page (1982); taken from the Japanese issued single
(Swan Song [Japan] P1673).*

Jimmy's first post-Zeppelin recording
certainly contains parallels to previous
performances. Like the 'Presence' sessions, the *Death Wish 2* soundtrack
required working to a deadline and this
discipline seemed to ignite his imagina-
tion. Also like 'Achilles', the 'Who's To
Blame' instrumental is an amalgamation
of cleverly overdubbed guitar parts,
linked with a multi-layered riff straight
out of the Zeppelin copybook. All this is
undercut by a new addition to the Page
armoury – the use of a Roland synthesiser
guitar, a curious device with a rod linking
the body and fretboard, which adds yet
more colour to the canvas.
'Carole's Theme' is a poignant instrumental over which Jimmy stretches and
slides a guitar solo of immense purity.
Strangely enough, these particular *Death
Wish* excerpts are absent from the actual
soundtrack album and exist only on an
obscure single issued only in Japan. An
item well worth seeking out.

20 'STAIRWAY TO HEAVEN'
*Jimmy Page (1984); taken from the video soundtrack of the
ARMS concert (Vestron Video VFV17 1984).*

Page's return to live performance
occurred in the autumn of 1983 when he
joined Eric Clapton, Jeff Beck, Steve Winwood and a host of other sixties
contemporaries for two shows at
London's Royal Albert Hall in aid of the
Ronnie Lane ARMS appeal.
Invited to perform a 20-minute set,
Jimmy began with some *Death Wish 2*
soundtrack material then strapped on the
Gibson double-neck from which only one
composition could emerge.
This was a genuinely moving occasion.
Gracefully omitting any vocals, Jimmy,
showing obvious signs of nerves, takes it
tentatively during the opening section
and Jeff Beck's non-appearance – he'd
been scheduled to assist with the melody
lines – does little to aid his confidence, but
by the time Simon Phillips adds his percussive edge to proceedings, Page gains
the momentum to produce a solo that displays much of the style and fluency asso-
ciated with his previous work.
The image of one quarter of Led Zeppelin
alone in the spotlight for the first time,
paying homage to their most famous
song, is one that will stay etched on the
minds of all who witnessed his return that
autumn evening.

Encore: Page during the ARMS tour, 1983.

21 'SEA OF LOVE'
*The Honeydrippers (1984); taken from the album 'The Hon-
eydrippers Volume One' (Es Paranza 790220–1).*

For his 1984 alter ego Honeydrippers set,
Robert asked Jimmy to contribute solos to
two of the numbers cut with Ahmet
Ertegun over a wild weekend following
the 'Principle Of Moments' tour.
The solo which graces this fifties do-wop
cover, is a lovely string-bending affair that
fits the mood of the song perfectly. That it
works so well says much for the affinity
Page and Plant still have with each other
as musicians, and of their affection for the
rhythm and blues music of a bygone era.

22 'MIDNIGHT MOONLIGHT'
*The Firm (1985); taken from the album 'The Firm' (Atlantic
781239–1).*

When the ARMS tour moved to America,
Jimmy linked up with Paul Rodgers for
his segment of the show, a collaboration
that was to evolve into The Firm a matter
of months later.
'Midnight Moonlight' is one of the few
highlights of their patchy début album. A

lengthy acoustic/electric workout, it was
originally conceived on the ARMS tour
when it was known as 'Bird On A Wing'.
Page's acoustic playing here is highly
reminiscent of the early live versions of
'White Summer'. Hampered somewhat
by a rather lame production, it is never-
theless an ambitious arrangement that
harks back to the adventurous spirit of his
previous quartet.

23 'RADIO-ACTIVE'
The Firm (1985); taken from the album 'The Firm'.

An infectious offering from the début Firm
album, this was an obvious choice as a single and came complete with a performance
video to match which featured Page attired
in jack boots and double-neck.
The attraction of this performance is a
totally off-the-wall descending chord
sequence that swivels across the speakers
with delightful regularity. Pure James
Patrick . . .

24 'EMERALD EYES'
*Jimmy Page (1988); taken from the album 'Outrider'
(Geffen WX155).*

The 'Outrider' project gave Page the
opportunity to mirror the differing
approaches and textures of his playing
once again, and this in turn signalled a
return to the guitar diversity of the Zeppelin era.
'Emerald Eyes' is therefore a fine example of Jimmy's cinematic style, a lilting
instrumental that redeploys the acoustic-
electric minor chord pattern evident on
the 'Physical Graffiti' epic '10 Years
Gone'. Commencing with some heavily
strummed acoustic parts, it builds into a
multi-layered exercise in guitar expression
and ranks as one of his finest compositions of the eighties.

25 'BLUES ANTHEM (IF I CANNOT
HAVE YOUR LOVE . . .)'
Jimmy Page (1988); taken from the album 'Outrider'.

And finally to 'Blues Anthem'. A reassuring example of the emotional quality
Jimmy Page can still attain in terms of
both performance and composition.
This semi-blues ballad, with vocals by
Chris Farlowe, finds Page not only supplying the regular guitar part but also at
the helm of a string symphony accompaniment delivered from a synthesised
guitar.
His solo is one of those gorgeous twangy
affairs in the grand tradition of 'Tangerine' or 'All My Love'. A final fitting
testament to 25 years of inventive and
often astonishing guitar technique.

Jimmy Page: the solo musician, 1986.

A long way from Stourbridge: Earls Court Arena, London, May 1975.

EARLY PLANTATIONS

Robert Plant

I left home at 16 and started my real education musically – moving from group to group, furthering my knowledge of the blues and other music which had weight and was worth listening to. I decided that if I didn't get anywhere by the time I was 20, I would pack it all in.''

While Jimmy Page was establishing himself as a session player and guitarist of some repute, the young Robert Anthony Plant could be found cutting his own musical teeth in the backwoods of the Black Country, that area of the British Midlands centred around Wolverhampton, Worcester and Warwick.

It was around the tender age of 15 that the Stourbridge schoolboy discovered a passion for the blues, and developed a desire to sing that style of music on stage. At that time the Midlands scene was bursting with activity, and when young Plant left school in 1964, it took him just three weeks to decide that life as a trainee chartered accountant was unlikely to prove compatible with his addiction to recreating the blues-wailing of such masters as Robert Johnson, Tommy McClelland and Otis Clay.

To the chagrin of his parents (Plant was the only member of Led Zeppelin whose family discouraged a musical career), Robert went through the ranks of a variety of local bands with colourful names such as The New Memphis Blues-breakers, The Black Snake Moan, The Delta Blues Band and The Crawling King Snakes, the last of which included John 'Bonzo' Bonham, a young drummer whose powerful physique had been honed by working alongside his father on local building sites. Such was Bonham's strength that bands – and audiences – often complained that he hit the drums too hard for comfort.

Robert's distinctive vocal range was soon much in demand on the Midlands circuit and the first settled line-up he joined was called Listen. Formerly The Tennessee Teens, the group included Plant with Lee John Crutchley, Geoff Thompson and

The CBS recording artist, 1966.

Roger Beamer.

The year was 1966 and major record company moguls were increasingly turning their attention beyond Liverpool and London for fresh unsigned beat talent. In the Midlands The Spencer Davis Group featuring Steve Winwood led the Brummie assault on the charts and others such as The Move and Moody Blues would soon follow suit.

It was during this period that Robert Plant received his first break. Performing a broad-based blues and soul style (the influence of Wilson Pickett and Otis Redding and the great Stax Records session musicians was then taking effect), Listen attracted the attention of CBS Records. They were particularly impressed with Plant's vocal range and a deal was struck for them to record a single.

This duly appeared in November of 1966 and coupled a version of The Young Rascals' US smash 'You Better Run' with a group composition 'Everybody's Gonna Say'. Though credited to Listen, the actual record featured Plant backed by session musicians. The A-side was a big production, complete with brass and female backing singers.

Listening to this début Plant vinyl offering years on, it's clear that his voice had yet to acquire that expandable tilt that would later characterise his every syllable. He had power for sure, but sugary American cover versions were a long way

removed from his blues leanings. The flip-side, a group composition, was a typical beaty mid-sixties work-out that again displayed little of the singer's real potential.

A rival cover version of 'You Better Run' by another Midlands group The N'Betweens (whose singer Noddy Holder was an occasional roadie for Listen and who would later achieve great success when they changed their name to Slade), did nothing to assist sales, and it flopped ignominiously. Holder, incidentally, had at one time vaguely considered offering Robert Plant a job in his N'Betweens but when he and their bass player Jim Lea went to watch him on stage they came away with the impression that he was more of a dancer than a singer! Even at this stage in his career, at a time when it was considered uncool for singers to move further than a few feet away from their microphone stands, Robert's on-stage agility aroused local comment.

The CBS contract required two further singles for which Robert would assume solo status and the story goes that given the opportunity to make a single in his own name, Robert insisted he record a version of 'Incense' by The Anglos. CBS saw it differently, however, and lined up an Italian ballad with an English lyric for his next release. By then, as Plant once put it, ''I already had a cigar in my back,'' and March 1967 saw the release of 'Our Song'.

For all its shortcomings this track yielded a much improved Plant studio performance. There were definite pointers to the future in the way he phrased certain lines, in particular his bending of the word 'love'. 'Our Song' may not have been the ideal vehicle for this teenager, but it contained early rumblings of the way Robert Plant's vocal style would develop. The B-side, 'Laughin', Cryin', Laughin'', another mid-sixties romp, also had a certain quaintness about it.

The third single in this curious trilogy followed in September 1967. 'Long Time Coming', a lush big ballad production, provided the young Plant with the plat-

The pot smoking protester, 1967.

The Band of Joy, 1967: left to right – John Bonham, Chris Brown, Carlisle Egypt (Kevyn Gammond), Robert Plant, Paul Locky.

form to add a bluesy edge to the proceedings. The way he stretched his vocal cords over lines like 'You changed my tears to happiness' was not that dissimilar to how he would express himself at Olympic studios a little under two years hence. However, the appallingly banal flipside 'I've Got A Secret', also betrayed a complete lack of understanding or sympathy in the selection of material on CBS' part.

While the CBS contract ran its course, Robert continued to gig around the Midlands area. His next long-term outfit was The Band Of Joy who went through various line-up changes and musical styles including blue beat and ska. By late 1967 Robert was fronting the group's most stable line-up which included John Bonham on drums, Kevyn Gammond on guitar, Chris Brown on keyboards and Paul Locky on bass.

It was around this period that Robert began listening to – and became influenced by – emerging West Coast acts such as Moby Grape, Love and Buffalo Springfield. This influence was twofold – musical and philosophical – and both would play their part in Robert's work and personality over the coming decade. In the meantime, The Band Of Joy adopted the loose blues structures and free-form experiments favoured by the Californian bands, a style with which Robert was very comfortable.

By early 1968, the group was enjoying regular residencies at London's Middle Earth and Marquee clubs. Though they never secured a record deal, The Band Of Joy recorded some demos at Regent Sound studios and in recent years some of these vintage tapes have surfaced on acetates. In 1989 Robert donated a rare Band Of Joy track from the Regent Sound ace-

tates to a community project at Kidderminster College administered by former Band Of Joy guitarist Kevyn Gammond.

'Adriatic Sea View' by Robert Plant and The Band Of Joy, took pride of place on the college's fund raising cassette compilation. This spacey slow blues is a superb pre-Zeppelin remnant which demonstrates how Robert's vocal range was beginning to blossom into that coarse holler destined to inspire a host of imitators. Not that far removed from the similar styled 'I Can't Quit You Baby', right down to a Plant moan during the break, its pleading lyrical theme – 'Gotta find my baby' – was one to which he would return many times on future recordings. In fact one of the final verses on this Band Of Joy outing includes the line 'I've had nothing but hard luck and trouble.' If that sounds familiar, check out track one side one of

Madison Square Garden, June 1977.

Bath Festival 1969.

Early group publicity shot, 1968.

'In Through The Out Door' for a variation on the same theme.

Two other examples of Robert Plant's work with The Band Of Joy have come to light, and both are cover versions. Their interpretation of Buffalo Springfield's 'For What It's Worth' stays fairly faithful to the original and finds Plant well at home. The way he bends and stretches the lyrics to employ that primal scream is further evidence of his, as yet, unrecognised potential.

'Hey Joe', the traditional song that provided Jimi Hendrix with his début hit in the UK in 1967, and which every garage outfit the length and breadth of the UK included in its repertoire as a result, is equally impressive. The Band Of Joy's version features some inspired drumming from John Bonham who attacks the kit in a manner that would soon become a trademark of the Led Zeppelin sound.

Kevyn Gammond's guitar echoes around Plant who wraps the whole thing up with a cry of ''Stop!''

This track, although over-familiar and therefore unacceptable by Jimmy Page's standards, would not have been entirely out of place on the first Zeppelin album; it offers an illustration of the musical identity both Robert and Bonzo were able to bring with them into the soon-to-be-renamed New Yardbirds.

Despite the promise of their acetate, The Band Of Joy failed to secure a record deal, a sad comment on the perspicacity of A&R men of the period, and by the spring of 1968 they had gone their separate ways: Bonham to tour with Tim Rose, Plant to spread his wings by seeking further employment in London. The Band Of Joy demo eventually found its way to Tony Secunda, then the manager of The Move, and a more imaginative impresario

On stage, 1973.

than the record company A&R men who had already rejected it.

Suitably impressed, Secunda asked Robert to record an audition tape at London's Marquee studios. The idea was that this would lead to a solo deal with The Move's label, Regal Zonophone. Secunda played the tape to producer and label boss Denny Cordell but he turned down the opportunity to sign Plant because he was too busy producing Joe Cocker who was then on the brink of a major breakthrough.

Instead Robert linked up with British blues legend Alexis Korner, the Paris-born guitarist and singer who encouraged Brian Jones and whose Blues Incorporated had at one time included both Mick Jagger and Charlie Watts. Robert first met Korner at London's Speakeasy club, and the pair made some loose plans for future gigs together. Plans were also afoot to record an album, and one of the tracks 'Operator' turned up some years later on an anthology of Korner's work known as 'Bootleg Him'.

'Operator' was recorded under the name Duo and featured Robert on vocals and harmonica, Alexis on guitar and an English piano player called Steve Millar. It was a sparse blues performance, a return to Robert's initial influences.

Earls Court 1975.

The next chapter in Robert's story is now part of rock folklore. In between working with Alexis Korner, Robert gigged around the Birmingham area with a group called Hobbstweedle, another outlet for his blues/West Coast leanings. At the same time Jimmy Page, abandoned by his colleagues in the final version of The Yardbirds, was in the process of putting together a new group with that name to fulfil some dates in Scandinavia. Page initially offered the role of vocalist to former Peter Jay And The Jay Walkers singer Terry Reid. To what must have been his eternal regret, Reid had to turn down the opportunity as he had just signed a solo deal with Mickie Most.

Reid recommended Page check out Robert Plant whom he remembered from The Band Of Joy. So along with Peter Grant, latterly the manager of The Yardbirds, Jimmy went to see Robert performing with Hobbstweedle at a teacher training college gig just outside Birmingham. Page and Grant could hardly believe their good fortune: Plant was their ideal choice.

After seeing Robert that night and listening to The Band Of Joy's Regent Sound demo, Jimmy Page invited him down to his house in Pangbourne to discuss the New Yardbirds project in detail. It was here that Robert Plant's four-year search for a true musical identity was to end. He and Page got on extremely well, and when Page invited Robert to select some albums from his extensive collection it was discovered they shared much common ground in musical tastes.

Robert accepted Jimmy's offer to join The New Yardbirds and in turn recommended his old sparring partner John Bonham for the vacant drum stool. It took some persuasion – in the form of several telegrams from Grant's office – before Bonzo agreed to join the bandwagon. By then he was enjoying a steady well paid gig with Tim Rose, and had offers coming in from Chris Farlowe and Joe Cocker. Luckily he did eventually heed Plant's advice, principally because Page was offering an opportunity to tour the US.

The New Yardbirds line-up was completed with the addition of John Paul Jones (a.k.a. John Baldwin) on bass and

keyboards. A much sought after session player and musical arranger who had often worked with Page in the past, he made himself immediately available when he heard of Jimmy's intentions to create a new group.

In September 1968, the four held their first rehearsal in a room in London's Gerard Street. It was the first time that Plant and Bonham had met Jones and, having heard from Jimmy that the bass player was "a good session man," they had conjured up an image of him as an elderly chap dressed in a cardigan who smoked a pipe!

Among the numbers they experimented on were Page's 'I'm Confused' (later to be retitled 'Dazed And Confused'), the old Yardbirds' stage favourite 'Train Kept A Rollin'', Band Of Joy chestnuts such as Garnett Mimms' 'As Long As I Have You', and blues work-outs like 'I Can't Quit You Baby'.

The chemistry was instant.

A tour of Scandinavia billed as The New Yardbirds quickly followed and by October they were recording their first album in Olympic studios. By this time they had

Bearded portrait circa 1970.

On stage, 1973.

changed their name to Led Zeppelin, a phrase Page remembered Keith Moon using in jest on a session many months earlier. 'Led' was spelled the way it was to avoid mispronunciation.

Robert Plant turned 20 on August 20, thus reaching his original deadline for fame. His musical journey had taken him from Stourbridge to the brink of world success. Along the way there had been a host of trials and tribulations, and many influences had been assimilated. From the early R&B of Muddy Waters, Howlin' Wolf and Sonny Boy Williamson, through the Mod Stax and ska periods to the American West Coast divide of the late sixties . . . Robert Plant took from them all.

His solo singles on CBS may not have set the world alight, and The Band Of Joy may never have enjoyed the acceptance they deserved, but the groundwork of the past three years was about to be rewarded. Toiling around the club circuits of the Midlands, and latterly London's underground scene, would soon be a thing of the past.

The apprenticeship had been served. Led Zeppelin was about to fly . . .

The ambient studio producer, 1969.

LED ZEPPELIN
IN THE STUDIO

"Shall We Roll It Jimmy?"

I can remember Bonzo, Plant, Page and Jones out on the lawn listening to playbacks of 'D'yer Mak'er' and 'Dancing Days' all walking like Groucho Marx in sync, with back steps and forward steps in time to the music like kids.

"The thing I want to emphasise more than anything else, is that we had so much fun making those records. I rejoice in the memories of those Led Zeppelin days."
Eddie Kramer – Led Zeppelin recording engineer, 1969 – 1976.

The creative process of recording the 10 Led Zeppelin albums began with a mere 30 hours in Olympic studios close to the River Thames in Barnes in West London during October 1968.

In the hi-tech atmosphere of the nineties, an era when groups of far less distinction or pedigree than the fledgling Led Zeppelin will happily spend well over a year (and £100,000) making an album, it seems incongruous that this was all the time it took Jimmy Page and engineer Glyn Johns to produce 'Led Zeppelin I'. But Led Zeppelin (or at least two of them and Peter Grant, their manager) were already seasoned studio professionals and since the group didn't have a record contract at the time Jimmy Page and Grant were obliged to pay for the studio time. Unlike so many of today's profligate 'stars', there was no record company money to waste on excessive studio time; Zeppelin, acting according to an unofficial credo that in time would change the face of the rock industry, were self-sufficient every step of the way.

The songs that the group recorded in a period of just nine days at a reputed cost of £1,782 had been well rehearsed and arranged on the Scandinavian tour the four undertook as The New Yardbirds, and 'old' studio hands with the experience of Page and John Paul Jones could be relied upon to get maximum value from every hour (and pound) spent at Olympic. With the possible exception of the 12 hours that The Beatles took to record their first album, rarely has studio time been used more economically: Led Zeppelin's début album went on to gross more than £3.5 million.

Glyn Johns recalls the immediacy of this first album session. "They had rehearsed themselves very healthily before they got into the studio, and it was a very exciting record to cut," he says. "I had never heard arrangements of that ilk and certainly never heard a band play in that way before. It was just unbelievable, and when you're in a studio with something as creative as that you can't help but feed off it."

Glyn Johns' experience certainly proved invaluable to Jimmy in his early role as producer. Johns does, however, tell a tale of how a naïvely enthusiastic Page took the tapes to New York where he added all manner of unnecessary equalisation to the original mixes. Overall though, Jimmy's years of hanging around in studios during his session days had provided him with a good grounding in production techniques.

As he was to comment later, "I was into ambiance right from the first album. I wanted to hear drums sound like drums and realised that if you close miked them, they tended to sound like cardboard boxes. My studio maxim was 'distance makes depth' and I've applied that to a lot of our recordings over the years."

Little time was lost between the recording of their début and the sessions that would result in the follow-up. 'Led Zeppelin II' was the group's first introduction to Eddie Kramer whose work with Jimi Hendrix had already impressed Page, but studio time had to be grabbed between months of persistent touring, principally in the US.

Consequently all manner of primitive studios were tried. Jimmy recalls one eight-track set up in Vancouver that didn't even boast proper headphone facilities. That the album turned out to be such a triumph, in particular for its production quality that still sounds fresh today, was in no small way due to the successful alliance of Page and Kramer in supervising the end result.

One of the more successful studios Zeppelin entered for the second album was Mystic in Hollywood. Page had previously recorded there for the 'Lord Sutch And Heavy Friends' album, and he returned with his new group to lay down tracks such as 'The Lemon Song' completely live in Mystic's 16x16 room, with Chris Huston on the controls.

"It had wooden walls and lots of ambiance," recalled Page. "It was a small room. Richie Valens and Bobby Fuller had once recorded there, and when you listen to those fifties records you can tell it's a small room but the energy of it comes through."

A further round of recording at Olympic and Morgan studios in London, with Kramer and assistants Andy Johns and George Chkiantz, completed the basic tracks which were then mixed over one weekend by Page and Kramer in New York. As Kramer observed, "When we did something together, for instance the famous 'Whole Lotta Love' mix where everything is panning and going bananas, it's a combination of Jimmy and myself just flying around on a small console twiddling every knob known to man!"

Listening to playback of 'Led Zeppelin II', 1969.

Bron-Y-Aur, the inspiration for the ethereal Page and Plant, 1970.

After the often absurd studio conditions endured for the second album, the group made a conscious effort to alter the pace of future recording. Fortunately their strategy of self-sufficiency had paid off in spades, and it was most unlikely that there would ever be a repeat of the pressures that caused them to record as hurriedly as they did in 1969. Fate, as we shall see, would change all that down the line but in the meantime their third album could be approached at a considerably more leisurely pace.

Page and Plant set the ball rolling with their much-documented trip to Bron-Y-Aur, a cottage on the side of Snowdonia where they would play and compose into the night, working by candlelight and the soft glow of a wood fire. Such surroundings – and the lack of electric power – not unnaturally signalled a slight change of direction with an emphasis on acoustic arrangements.

After preparing the material that would emerge on 'Led Zeppelin III', they rehearsed the songs at a run-down mansion in Hampshire. This proved to be a significant move. With its relaxed atmosphere and rural surroundings, Headley Grange provided a favoured alternative to the discipline of a conventional studio.

heir third album was recorded in a series of May/June sessions at Headley Grange and Olympic with Andy Johns engineering. Some additional work was put in at the newly opened Island studios in July. It was all wrapped up with a mixdown at Ardent studios in Memphis during Zeppelin's sixth American tour in August 1970. The whole album proved to be a watershed release, not only in content and construction, but also composition. After Page's domination of the first two albums, 'Led Zeppelin III' was a more democratic affair, and given increased rehearsal time, all four group members were able to offer up their own compositions and ideas. It was a pattern that would continue in future sessions.

When Led Zeppelin returned to Headley Grange for the fourth album sessions in early 1971, they took along The Rolling Stones' mobile studio to record the whole process. "We needed the sort of facilities where we could have a cup of tea and wander round the garden and then go in and do what we had to do," said Page.

By moving into Headley Grange for the whole period of recording, many of the tracks were made up almost on the spot and committed to tape there and then. "A recording studio is an immediate imposi-

tion as compared to sitting around a fire strumming," said Robert Plant at the time. "With Headley Grange we can put something down and hear the results immediately."

Initial sessions for the fourth album had begun at the new Island studios in December 1970, but the real work fell into place at Headley Grange early in 1971. Once inside the great hall of the mansion the ideas flowed freely. It was here that Page stumbled on that monster snare and bass drum sound by spaciously miking Bonzo's newly acquired drum kit.

With the basic tracks recorded, many of them live, they added overdubs at Island and on the recommendation of engineer Andrew Johns took the completed master tapes to be mixed at Los Angeles Sunset Sound studios. This mix proved to be a great disappointment, causing a delay in the release of the album. They had hoped to have it out in time for their late summer American tour, but further mixing back in London resulted in the album eventually surfacing in November 1971. Such delays did not prevent 'Led Zeppelin IV' – or 'Four Symbols' as it is often referred to – from becoming the best selling LP in the entire Zeppelin canon.

Overall though, the location recording process employed for the fourth album

Receiving gold and platinum records from the Parliamentary Secretary, Christmas 1969.

had been successful and when the group set about laying down ideas for their next project in the spring of 1972, it was a formula they were keen to repeat.

Just prior to commencing the fifth album, Page and Plant stopped off in Bombay on their way back from a tour of Australasia. Here they made experimental recordings of two tracks – 'Friends' from the third album and 'Four Sticks' from 'Led Zeppelin IV' – with various local musicians including members of the Bombay Symphony Orchestra. They remain unreleased, though they must still be in their archives somewhere.

Eddie Kramer returned to the controls for the sessions that would emerge as 'Houses Of The Holy'. This time they took the mobile studio to Mick Jagger's country estate Stargroves. That spring of 1972 found Led Zeppelin eager to commit to tape the material that had slowly been taking shape during their travels around the world.

Both Jimmy and John Paul Jones had by now installed home studios of their own, enabling them to demo their own songs. Thus, Jimmy was able to present to the group at Stargroves complete arrangements of 'The Rain Song' with its strange tunings and *chiaroscuro* arrangements, and another guitar extravaganza then

known as 'Over The Hills'. Jones, meanwhile, had honed 'No Quarter', a track first tried out a year earlier at Headley Grange, into a brooding, quivering, synth-enhanced mantra. Once installed in Stargroves other songs came from rehearsing together. These sessions on location, together with a further bout of recording at Olympic studios in May, proved so productive that some numbers didn't even make the final 'Houses Of The Holy' line-up. 'Black Country Woman', 'Walters Walk', 'The Rover', and even the intended title track would all appear on later Led Zeppelin albums. However, one song known as 'Slush' remains in the vaults.

Following the overdubbing sessions at Olympic, Zeppelin commenced another extensive American tour. Along the way Eddie Kramer booked more studio time at Electric Lady studios in New York's Greenwich Village where Jimi Hendrix had once held court. It's rumoured that during this session the group committed to tape a series of rock 'n' roll classics, including most of the tracks on 'Elvis' Gold Records Volume One' which they liked to play at soundchecks before concerts.

It's been noted that Jimmy was not as happy with the overall sound from Star-

groves compared to that at Headley Grange. This I find surprising. There's a confidence and maturity about the 'Houses' album that accounted for a notable progression in their playing. It backs up Eddie Kramer's vision of happy times within the Zeppelin camp, and tracks such as 'Dancing Days' still vividly illustrate the 'good to be alive' feel of the period. One final observation of the 'Houses Of The Holy' sessions: the crispness and clarity of Robert Plant's vocal performances are among the finest recorded of all the Zeppelin albums.

The tape machines next officially rolled for Led Zeppelin when they decided to film the last few dates of their 1973 American tour. Joe Massot's film crew captured footage of shows at the Baltimore Civic Theatre, the Three Rivers Stadium in Pittsburgh and three nights at Madison Square Garden in New York. Only the New York dates were taped with Eddie Kramer on the soundboard. It was the Madison Square Garden shows that were to form the concert footage for their *The Song Remains The Same* movie, but it would be another two years before Kramer was called in to mix the tapes for release.

After the hugely successful 1973 American tour, Led Zeppelin unwound, did some home movie work for their film, and took their time approaching their next recording sessions. This time they returned to Headley Grange, hiring Ronnie Lane's mobile studio for a location recording. The sixth album sessions kicked off with a few ideas laid down in November 1973. These sessions came to a halt fairly quickly however, and the studio time was handed over to Bad Company to record their début album.

At the time the reason given for the break-up of this initial session was that John Paul Jones was ill. Years later Peter Grant revealed that what had actually happened was that Jones came to see him to tender his resignation from the group. Fed up with the rigours of touring, he felt he needed a change. Grant told him to think it over and by the New Year the group were back at Headley Grange, Jones refreshed from the Christmas holiday and all notions of quitting behind him. It was a period that signalled another creative high for the group.

Reunited at Headley Grange, it was a case of "What has anybody got?" as Page put it. And mostly what they had was, as Robert described them, 'the belters'. "We got eight tracks off,'' he explained in the early spring of 1974. ''And a lot of them are really raunchy. We did some real belters with live vocals, off-the-wall stuff that turned out really nice.''

Similar to sessions for the previous two albums, the location recording technique gave them ample time to develop material along the way. Plant again: ''Some of the tracks we assembled in our own fashioned way of running through a track and realising before we knew it that we had stumbled on something completely different.''

Those eight tracks, engineered by Ron Nevison, extended beyond the length of a conventional album and this prompted them to construct a double set. This was achieved by reassessing the material recorded for earlier albums, from which seven tracks were added. The whole package was mixed down by the late Keith Harwood at Olympic, and released as 'Physical Graffiti' in early 1975. A massive outpouring of Zeppelin music that proved to be the definitive summary of their studio abilities.

Led Zeppelin were never again to approach an album in the relaxed location manner of the era 1971 to 1974. Various unexpected and unfortunate circumstances would dictate the pace of all future studio projects, commencing with the aftermath of the events of Monday August 4, 1975.

This was the day that Robert Plant suffered multiple injuries when the car in which he was travelling left a narrow road on a hillside on the Greek island paradise of Rhodes. The accident and its aftermath caused the immediate cancellation of a projected world tour due to start later that month in California, along with plans to shoot more live footage for their film on location in South America and Asia Minor during the tour, and Page's unresolved plans for a live chronological album set. Instead the quartet threw all their energies into recording a new studio album from scratch.

With Plant recovering from his injuries in a wheelchair, Zeppelin began writing and rehearsing over a three-week period in their adopted home of Los Angeles. It was assumed that this would lead to their first all-American recorded album, but tax problems meant they had to move to Europe. So in November 1975, the four of them assembled in Munich's Musicland studios and came out a mere 18 days later with 'Presence', engineered again by Keith Harwood.

The immediate and unexpected circumstances in which they found themselves had a profound effect on the music that came out of Munich. As Jimmy commented: ''I think it was just a reflection of the total anxiety and emotion of the period. There's a hell of a lot of spontaneity about that album. We went in with virtually nothing and everything just came pouring out.''

With his partner at less than full fitness, Page took on total responsibility for the album's completion. Because of this, 'Presence' is definitely one of his foremost achievements. His playing and production dominates the album's seven tracks. In stark contrast to the relaxed atmosphere of previous studio affairs, this album came together through intense 18-hour-day sessions. In fact the studio time booked actually overran, forcing Page to borrow two days from the incoming Rolling Stones, during which time he completed all the album's overdubs. (When Page graciously requested the extra time from Mick Jagger, the venerable Stones' singer was reportedly amazed that Zeppelin had put their album together so quickly and that Jimmy required only *two* extra days for overdubs. Rolling Stones albums, it seems, often took many months to complete.)

It was the state-of-the-art multi-dubbing facility of the Musicland studio console that accounted for 'Achilles Last Stand' – a major Zeppelin opus, and the track that excited Plant so much on playback that he fell over and nearly reopened his wounds. It may have lacked the diversity of 'Physical Graffiti' but 'Presence' presented Led Zeppelin at their most spontaneous, and has in retrospect emerged as a vital part of their catalogue.

It was to take Plant another year to regain full fitness, though the band were able to remain in the spotlight with the release of their much delayed movie *The Song Remains The Same*. Jimmy Page had begun dubbing the soundtrack in the summer of 1975, and he returned to the project with Eddie Kramer on hand, over the holiday period of 1975/6 at Electric Lady studios in New York. The album was wrapped up with more mixing at London's Trident studios the following August. Much preparation went into securing a quality cinema sound for the film itself, with Kramer spending more time on a sub-mix at Todd A.O. studios in California. Originally prepared in four-track and quaint sound, the final mix for cinema use was eventually reduced to two-track, as few cinemas had the right facilities to present Dolby four-track sound.

During the autumn of 1976 rumours emerged that John Bonham was in the process of recording a solo album. These reports were greatly exaggerated; in fact Bonham and Page were working in Montreux's Mountain studios on an electronically treated percussion track for inclusion on a future Zeppelin album.

It was to be a full two years before all four re-entered a recording studio together. Following the aborted 1977 US tour, a lengthy period of silence was interrupted only by news of a rehearsal session that took place at Clearwell Castle in the spring of 1978. By the end of the year though, Led Zeppelin regrouped in London to begin writing and rehearsing material for a new studio album. In November the group flew over to Stockholm to commence a month's recording at Abba's Polar Music studio.

The relief at being able to record new music together again brought a wave of optimism to the sessions, and the material was swiftly laid down.

Unlike the urgency of Munich in 1975, the Swedish expedition was a much more relaxed affair. Most of the new songs had been well rehearsed in London and there was little requirement for the studio composing method of earlier recording sessions. They knew what they had to do, and made full use of the studio facilities with Leif Masses and Lennart Ostlund on hand to engineer it all.

The most significant musical contribution to this album, astutely titled 'In Through The Out Door', was that of Mr John Paul Jones. With tongue firmly planted in cheek, he said at the time that his considerable influence on proceedings was due to his arriving at the studio earlier than his colleagues on most days. With lead composing credits on all but one of the seven tracks selected for the album, his contribution was immense.

Rollicking piano on 'South Bound Suarez', an Argentinian soccer burst midway through 'Fool In The Rain', a *Gone With The Wind* string-synth intro for 'I'm Gonna Crawl', and a cluster of classical notes on 'All My Love' – all this was the work of the often underrated man from Royal Orleans.

With initial recording finished by December 1978, Jimmy worked on producing the tapes at his Plumpton studio over Christmas, and the whole project was finalised at a mixing session back in Sweden early in 1979. As with previous releases, Led Zeppelin came out of Polar with more than enough material for one album. It had been planned to issue two of the tracks, 'Wearing And Tearing' and 'Darlene', as a special commemorative single to be made available at the Knebworth shows. Unfortunately time ran out on that plan, but those tracks plus 'Ozone Baby' from the same sessions did eventually surface on the 'Coda' album.

'Darlene' epitomised the sense of fun that prevailed throughout the recording of 'In Through The Out Door' while the manic 'Wearing And Tearing' had been considered for inclusion as a live number for the 1980 US tour, and would have been a rehearsal contender but for the tragic death of John Bonham on September 25, 1980. A decade later, Plant and Page would revive this number at the Knebworth Silver Clef reunion show.

After their retirement there was one final album. Released to complete the five-album deal they had signed with Atlantic in 1974, 'Coda' surfaced in November 1982. Compiled and mixed by Jimmy Page early in that year at his Sol recording complex with Stuart Epps engineering, it gathered together (in a similar style to 'Physical Graffiti') nine unreleased performances to form a closing summary of their studio development from 1969 to 1978. At least two of the tracks ('We're Gonna Groove' and 'Ozone Baby') were overdubbed by Jimmy and Robert at Sol in early 1982. The songs selected for 'Coda' included the three Polar out-takes (possibly one more titled 'The Hook' remains in the can), Ben E. King's 'We're Gonna Groove' from mid 1969, 'Poor Tom', a leftover from 'Led Zeppelin III', a 1970 Albert Hall run through of 'I Can't

Quit You Baby', 'Walter's Walk', a superb Stargroves/Eddie Kramer remnant, and the often touted Bonham/Page total percussion number from Montreux. Although short in duration, the whole set lasting a mere 33 minutes, 'Coda' was an enjoyable and affectionate vinyl finale.

Although countless unofficial live recordings have continued to surface over the years, comparatively few studio tapes have been discovered. What little there is does offer an illuminating and enlightening insight into how the group formulated and honed their songs to studio perfection.

What follows is a transcript of some of the rehearsal sessions that have come to light. From 1970 there's an acoustic strum-through from the 'Led Zeppelin III' era. From the following year a rehearsal session for the fourth album made on location at Headley Grange. The epic 'Physical Graffiti' album is represented by an intensive session at the Grange in early 1974. Finally it's to Stockholm for 'In Through The Outakes', a series of alternate mixes culled from late 1978.

So with the studio light showing red, this is an opportunity to share in an intimate and revealing recording experience. This is Led Zeppelin in the studio, responding to that much requested plea from the console . . .

"Shall we roll it, Jimmy?"

The Transcript

REEL ONE
Location: Headley Grange, May 1970.

F resh from the trip to Snowdonia, this tape finds Jimmy Page and Robert Plant recalling those nights spent by the fireside as they work out together on a pair of acoustic guitars. Within a lengthy period of strumming, several fragments of songs emerge that were to develop on future Zeppelin albums.

The first is 'The Rover'. Page runs through a very basic instrumental chord structure of a song later to be electrified for the Stargroves sessions in 1972. A pretty acoustic instrumental follows, with some minor chord changes not unlike those later employed on 'Stairway To Heaven'.

Plant comes back in to scat sing a primitive version of 'Poor Tom'. This track was discarded for 'Led Zeppelin III' but it eventually emerged on 'Coda'. Here it's performed in a bluesy jugband arrangement and skips along at a faster pace than

the official Olympic studio take. "That's about it," exclaims Plant at the finish.

There follows another gentle instrumental with Page overlaying some subtle electric guitar, after which Plant can be heard commenting, "That's not necessarily anything like a vocal is it." Page and Plant then run through five takes of 'That's The Way'. Take one is similar in feel to 'Poor Tom' with ad-libbed unfinished lyrics. Take two is an incomplete extract, this time with more familiar lyrical content.

Take three commences with the fade out refrain guitar coda used on the finished version. To add to the location atmosphere, a dog can be clearly heard barking in the background. Could it be the same mutt that hung around during the recording of track one, side one of the fourth album? For take five, Jimmy's refrain guitar coda is now slotted between each verse. This arrangement is taken at a faster tempo and Robert sings the choruses slightly differently.

Listening to these embryonic versions of one of the most successful cuts on the third album perfectly illustrates the transitional process that many of Led Zeppelin's songs underwent during rehearsal.

Reel one from Headley Grange in 1970 continues with a brief extract of 'Friends'. This appears to be a group recording and features John Bonham on bongos and backing vocals from possibly Jones or Page. Finally, there's a rough run through of Page's solo acoustic piece 'Bron-Y-Aur', which, by the time it came to be performed live on their American tour later in the year, had come a long way from this skeleton framework.

A second take has Bonzo on bongos and Robert scat-singing against Page's acoustic playing. In the background a child

Bonham in the studio, an inspirational sound.

(Carmen?) can be heard giggling throughout the song. Another attempt at 'Poor Tom', with Bonzo tapping out that shuffling intro on bongos, has Robert again guiding his way through on improvised vocals. 'Hey Hey What Can I Do', that celebrated 'Zeppelin III' leftover, is tried next, an all-acoustic arrangement with chorus only structures. Backing vocals supplement Plant's warm, countryish singing.

Finally the Marshall amps are back on for a run through of 'Immigrant Song'. Plant again mainly ad-libs the lyrics but that primal scream is well in evidence. The riff, even in this primitive state, sounds truly wonderful. Page also attempts a solo not unlike the live arrangement. A second attempt at 'Immigrant Song' segues into a verseless 'Out On The Tiles'. Bonzo's forceful drumming is ample evidence of the major part he played in this song's construction.

REEL TWO
Location: Headley Grange, January/February 1971.

A year on, this tape captures Page and Plant again in acoustic harmony, this time trading ideas and rehearsing material for the fourth album. An unreleased song in progress, 'I'm Gonna Be Her Man', in which Plant sings the aforementioned lyric in a vaguely Neil Young fashion, opens proceedings. "Sounds like the martian hop," comments Plant.

Page then goes into an acoustic chord pattern. "Nice that, perhaps it needs four chords," suggests Plant. Jimmy acknowledges that by creating the melody of 'Down By The Seaside'. A lengthy period of acoustic jamming follows, with Page pulling out a few 'Hats Off To Harper' slide runs, and picking in the best Bert Jansch tradition.

"How's it begin?" Robert asks Jimmy, and the guitarist duly obliges by returning to the melody of 'Down By The Seaside'. This lilting song of nature was originally conceived at Bron-Y-Aur, and then recorded at Island studios for the fourth album. It eventually surfaced on 'Physical Graffiti'. This 1971 rehearsal try out finds Plant singing a slightly amended set of lyrics ('The people turn and go'), and making two attempts to return to the main verses after the speeded up middle section. It all adds up to another fascinating glimpse of a future Zeppelin standard undergoing transition.

Following Robert's final crying vocal line on 'Down By The Seaside', Jimmy sows

"D to G?" JP works a riff, circa 1971.

the seed of another future Zeppelin creation. During a spontaneous acoustic ramble, he can be clearly heard running through the jerky chord sequence of 'The Crunge', a full year before its proper studio recording.

To hear the genesis of their most famous song is a truly enlightening listening experience. The first version of 'Stairway To Heaven' is a gorgeous acoustic instrumental with Jimmy repeatedly returning to the opening minor chord pattern. There's a subtle organ accompaniment from Jones, and as Page speeds it up slightly, Plant claps along enthusiastically.

Take two is a similar instrumental which commences halfway through the song's eventual arrangement. Here we find Jones and Page trying to take the song from the bridge part into the solo finale. It breaks down when Page owns up to a miscue. "I should have gone down a bit," he admits.

Take three attempts the same section more successfully, and moves into a meandering acoustic solo which then goes off on a tangent of its own. Take four is a further run through, with electric piano and the first proper ending. This features the same crying chords as the later live versions.

Robert comes in for take five, an early stab at a complete version with guide vocals. The fact that he only manages to sing a couple of verses (and mostly with different words), backs up Jimmy's claim that most of the lyrics were composed at the session. His vocal delivery is in a lower key and benefits from an echo effect at the beginning. To keep the song flowing, Plant repeats the first verse again

halfway through, but before Bonzo can add his weight to the proceedings this take grinds to a halt.

Take six is a near finished version. "Right," shouts Plant, as he ushers in that familiar opening line, which on this occasion includes the later amended line: 'If the stores are all closed she can call in and see a movie.' Robert has the correct vocal phrasing for this version which is delicately sung. Four verses are delivered ('If there's a bustle in your hedgerow . . .' doesn't appear at all), after which Bonzo joins in with some subtle rimshots. He then beefs it up on the snare as Robert ad libs 'But I really wanna know how it hurts me so,' and then la-la's the 'Your head is humming' verse. For the finale, Jimmy switches to electric guitar for a rousing solo, and Jonesy keeps the rhythm steady on bass.

"Let's have a listen to that . . . did yer mark the bloody thing!" Bonzo can be heard requesting in his thick Midlands accent. "That's alright, isn't it?" Plant asks Page. "Yes, it's going to be very nice," he replies.

Indeed it was.

An obscure country-flavoured instrumental, with a 'Gallows Pole' tempo completes the acoustic segment, and then it's back to the Marshall amps for an intensive rehearsal of 'Black Dog'.

This is a very early work-in-progress version, with Jones explaining to the rest of the band an impossible part of the riff. "D to G?" asks Robert. "Oh, I see," says Page. The lyrics are all ad libbed, and sung in a jazzy jump-blues manner.

Throughout this session, John Bonham plays magnificently. As the various takes break down, he is often left on his own, which provides an ample opportunity to marvel at his bass and snare drum co-ordination. 'Black Dog' is followed by a brief work-out on a riff which may have led on to something more substantial at a later stage.

When 'No Quarter' was introduced on stage at the LA Forum on the 1973 tour, Robert informed the audience that it was a song . . . "That we've had kicking around for quite a while." This fourth album session is ample proof of that statement, as they run through a very different arrangement of the song.

This particular version of 'No Quarter' is taken at a much faster tempo than its later incarnation. It opens with a timpani display from Bonzo before Jones' electric piano reverberates to that familiar riff. Its primitive construction is further emphasised by Plant's scat singing of the verses. At this point, it had no real lyrics or title.

Page comes in to add a punch to the chorus, and then layers on a jazzy solo. 'No Quarter' 1971-style is a fascinating preview of a track that they would revamp further a year later at Olympic.

Finally from this era, though it's difficult to pinpoint quite when, there's an all too short Page/Plant rendition of 'The Rover'. "Do it once with vocals," says Plant following Jimmy's finely picked intro. The lyrics are almost word for word as they were to appear on the electric version and are superbly sung. The whole atmosphere is similar to Plant's solo blues retread 'Liar's Dance', which would appear many years later on 'Manic Nirvana'.

REEL THREE
Location: Headley Grange, January/February 1974.

Having had time to recuperate from their recent American tour and play at home movies a bit, Led Zeppelin returned to Headley Grange brimming with enthusiasm. Eight brand new recordings would emerge from these early 1974 sessions to form the basis of their sixth album 'Physical Graffiti'. This transcript is another revealing insight into how some of those songs were honed from skeleton ideas to become full-blown epics.

One such epic was 'In The Light'. The officially released version remains a personal Page favourite, with its periodical drone effect, optimistic lyrical content and melodic guitar phasing. Aural evidence from this session reveals that it started life as a track called 'In The Morning'. The structure was adapted to fit between the drone effects of the released version of 'In The Light'.

The origin of the song is beautifully illustrated on this Headley Grange rehearsal. The tape picks up the pre-take atmosphere with Bonzo coughing in familiar 'In My Time Of Dying' finale manner, Plant whistling the tune, Page picking out a couple of chords and Jones informing the assembled company that it's time for take four.

The song commences with a simple piano/guitar melody reminiscent of 'Babe I'm Gonna Leave You'. Plant sings an entirely different set of lyrics opening with 'Sing a song in the morning – come on the one I love.' Jones, Page and Bonzo then add some dynamic interjections at all the right moments. This all leads towards Jonesy's electric piano part (as in the official version), over which Plant repeatedly

screams 'In the morning, in the morning, in the morning . . .' until near the end of Page's cascading guitar melody, he adds 'In the light, in the light, in the light.' A pointer as to where the song was heading.

The second version of 'In The Morning/In The Light', has a more complete lyrical theme. This was certainly no ad libbed affair, as Plant reels off some idealistic couplets. 'Sing a song in the morning, sing a song of the ocean, hear it every day, it's a song of salvation.' He adds some quite stunning soaring vocal screams as the whole thing reaches a climax. Instead of the 'In the morning/In the light' vocal refrain though, the chorus out of Jones piano solo is a repeated plea to 'Take me ho-o-o-me, take me ho-o-o-me, take me ho-o-o-me . . .' Stirring stuff indeed.

'In The Morning/In The Light' would certainly have made a great track in its own right. As it was, it was put to good use when it was merged into the drone/chant structure of the revamped and subsequently issued 'In The Light'.

A fairly straight run through of 'Sick Again' follows. "Rock it!" says Plant. That's the signal for Page to pull out the chords of 'The Rover', which like the later live versions of the song, is employed to kick start the track into life. Jimmy would later add his own intro for the released version. The main rhythm track of this rehearsal take seems to have been well thought out in advance. Plant's lyrics though, which are sung in a higher register than the released version, are mostly unfinished and nondescript. When the whole thing grinds to a halt, Bonzo plays on for a few bars, displaying another example of his craft.

Two takes of 'The Wanton Song' follow. Like 'Sick Again', the structure of the song is already well formulated. Robert's contribution is minimal, throwing in a couple of guide vocal verses. Take two commences halfway through the track and is an opportunity for Jones, Page and Bonham to perfect the machete Zep riff, in between which Bonzo inserts some hi-hat shuffles.

The next track appears to be a stab at 'Custard Pie', though you would have to be told that. It's virtually unrecognisable in this format, being a jerkily riffed and speeded up rocker. Plant's vocal contribution consists of him 'Talkin' 'bout my sweet girl, oh my sweet girl.' The intention to capture a light-hearted Eel-Pie bent is certainly in evidence, and after the first

take breaks down, Page and Jones trade licks, to resume the track a second time. At this point Page plays a pleasing Gibson run in a melodic 'Over The Hills/Wanton' vein. It's hard to judge whether this composition was entirely discarded or perhaps used as the basis for what was to become track one, side one on the sixth Led Zeppelin album.

The seeds of another future Zeppelin recording are sown when the boys jam through a swingish instrumental improvisation. This is clearly the same basic rhythmical shift that was later to be applied to the 'Presence' track 'Hots On For Nowhere'. It's a perfect vehicle for the three to flex their talents, and it's Bonzo who leads the way with some inventive patterns. Halfway through Page steps on his wah-wah pedal to trade in some very tasteful guitar. When it all comes to an abrupt end John Bonham celebrates with an expletive deleted.

Talking about 'Trampled Underfoot' in 1975 John Bonham said "When we first ran through it, John Paul and Jimmy started off the riff and then we thought it was a bit souly for us. Then we changed it around a bit." Indeed they did as nine takes of the track reveal here.

Take one fades in with Jonesy's clavinet pulling the track together. Robert sings the lyrics in a fairly nondescript manner and they then attempt to fall back in line from Jones' bridge section with limited success. Take two is a similar affair that breaks down when Plant sings 'Talking 'bout love.' A few words of studio banter precede take three. This has a Bonzo intro, which employs the cymbal crashing style of 'Rock And Roll' and the use of the hi-hat count-in that can also be heard on 'Night Flight'. The arrangement now contains a slight twist in the riff making it sound even more funky. There's a nice point where they all come back in from the keyboard break, with comparative ease.

"Now, one, two, three, four," shouts Bonzo, and take four gets under way. This is taken at a slightly slower pace and finds Plant singing the lines in a low-key Elvis manner. Jimmy experiments with the riff, before it all stops abruptly. Take five kicks off via the Jones clavinet. "I stopped singing 'cause that's when I thought you did your thing," says Plant, and they get back to work on take six which is a laid-back jam.

A seventh attempt is dominated by Jones working out on bass. "No no don't record it," requests Page as he practises chang-

Bonzo pictured shortly after the sessions for the sixth album, 1974.

ing the riff. Bonzo then comments, "That's what I'm on about, the way you've got the riff makes it completely different, doesn't it?" "Alright we'll start then," pronounces Page, and after a 'Crunge'-type drum shuffle and Plant hand clapping in the background, they attempt a more complete run through. At last we can now hear Page twisting the riff into more familiar territory. Plant ditches the laid-back approach and gets back into some proper phrasing. Take nine attempts to perfect this arrangement, and then it all fades out.

Being something of a departure, 'Trampled Underfoot' was a contentious recording session for the group, and as these illuminating takes reveal, took some manner of rehearsal time before it came together in the five-minute, 35-second duration that we now know.

Another track that underwent some intensive discussion was 'In My Time Of Dying'. A traditional blues tune once delivered by a protest singer by the name of Bob Dylan, the group came up with their own complex creation which clocked in at an exhaustive 11 minutes. Again it owed much of its inspiration to the percussive vision of John Bonham. The stop-start intervals built around Plant's frenzied vocals provided them with a few problems as a six-take transcript from Headley Grange illustrates.

The main area of difficulty centred on coming out of the line 'Doncha make it my dying bed,' before Page comes in with that flurry of strident riffs. Take one promptly pulls up as they reach that stage. A further run through still finds them a little out of sync. "It starts it off if you remember, after the whole blues guitar," Jimmy explains.

Take three is an attempt at the song from start to finish. Page fits in some shimmering lines here, not too far removed from the official version which would suggest that he had the arrangement well worked out beforehand. After eight minutes the tape cuts out, which is followed by John Paul Jones who can be heard saying "The way you come out of it." "Back to the verse then," adds Page. A snippet of a fourth effort, leads into take five. Here a messy break from the vocal prompts Bonzo to take a hold of proceedings and there follows a studio dialogue between him and Plant.

Bonzo: "We have to have a count."

Robert: "Where are you counting from now?"

Bonzo: "Well we can't count from where you stopped because your vocals might be different. Your voice might go on half a beat and we're gonna be fucked."

Robert: "Yeah, but if you do that it will be like 'Black Dog', and then it gives me room to move."

Bonzo: "But the reason we did it in 'Black Dog' was we counted it and you did it afterwards."

Page: "Alright."

Bonzo: "It's the only way we can do this."

Having ironed out that point, they try take six, which does show an element of tightness leading out of Plant's moanings. So ends another peep inside the studio walls. These 'Physical Graffiti' rehearsals demonstrate the painstaking process that was often applied by the four during the construction of their songs. This session also reveals the influence John Bonham often had on the arranging of the material, and how deserving his lead songwriting credit was on 'In My Time Of Dying'.

REEL FOUR
Location: Polar Music Studios, November 1978.

When Led Zeppelin reached Abba's Polar Music complex in Stockholm to record 'In Through The Out Door', they were fresh from six weeks' rehearsal. Subsequently plenty of their new songs were at the ready to record stage, and within a month they had laid down more than enough tracks to fill an album.

Compared to previous reels, these Polar studio out-takes exist in almost mixed and completed form. There are however, a number of differences to report as they mix down the new material enthusiastically.

'Darlene' opens with a "one, two, three, four" count-in from John Bonham. Very similar to the take that eventually surfaced on 'Coda', it pummels along in friendly, live in the studio, style. This is clearly an alternate Plant vocal mix as can be detected after the 'Pink carnation and a pick up truck' line. From that point he accompanies Jimmy's delightful solo adding, 'I don't care what they say, I love you anyway, I'll drive you wild.' Like most of these Polar mixes, instead of fading out the track grinds to a halt with a tinkling of Jones' electric piano.

Two versions of 'Fool In The Rain', show this composition nearing its completed mix. Some of the studio banter retained from Polar demonstrates the fun atmosphere that the four were working in. The beginning of 'Fool In The Rain', version one is an example, as after Page counts in "two, three" Plant wades in with a "quatro!" This mix has the basic piano and guitar backing track but is devoid of the overdubbed Jones/Bonham Argentinian middle section. Robert's vocal delivery also displays differences from the official version. 'Oh baby, oh darlin',' he pronounces in the intro, while for the song's finale he stretches the line 'Just a fool waiting on the wrong block' into a familiar warble, not that far removed from that famous war cry of 'Immigrant Song' on 'Led Zeppelin III'. This take also has an alternate ending leaving just Robert to wind down the final 'Light of the love that I've found' chorus unaccompanied.

The second mix of 'Fool In The Rain', commences with a count-in from Bonzo. Early on Jonesy's piano is lacking from this mix, but appears for the middle section, which this time does feature the blowing of whistles and the calypso percussion from Bonzo. The latter performance was almost certainly retained for the released mix. Jimmy meanwhile, had yet to overdub that inventive guitar solo and merely guides the boys back into the verses.

That vibrant, good to be back together atmosphere of the Polar sessions is well in evidence on an early punchy mix of 'Hot Dog', the humorous if somewhat expendable Page/Plant 'Out Door' rockabilly hoedown. Jimmy's guitar intro has a different texture to the official version, and Robert's vocal is an alternate performance. It includes a couple of delightful off-the-cuff lines thrown in during the solo break. ''Ah that's my kind of music'' he shouts across the studio and then further taunts Pagey with ''Come on Mr Phillips, you can do it again'' – an oblique reference to the famous producer of the legendary Sun studios in Memphis.

This mix also reveals a slight alteration in the closing seconds of the song as Bonzo follows Jones' final piano chord with a snare and bass drum flurry, later to be edited off the released version.

A straight run down of 'South Bound Suarez' follows. This take is missing Jimmy's guitar solo overdub, and features a heavily harmonised Plant vocal particularly on the 'Sha-la-la-la Sha-la-la-la' outro. Overall this is a fairly undistinguished mix of a fairly undistinguished song, one of a batch of simplistic rockers they took with them to Polar ('Darlene' and 'Ozone Baby' come under this description) and the only one to make it on to the intended album.

Much more impressive is 'In The Evening'. This is a full-blown Zepic prepared for 'In Through The Out Door' that even in this primitive mixdown condition reveals plenty of majestic qualities. Fol-

lowing the eerie drone intro, Bonzo kicks them into action via a couple of taps on the sticks. This particular mix brings Jones' bass much more to the fore and demonstrates just what a fluent technician of the instrument he really is. During the slowed-up passage, he plays some achingly beautiful notes against Page's stretching solo that are not nearly as evident on the issued mix. As the song heads for a climax, Plant is all over the place on the pleading 'Gotta have all your love' phrasing, before it all comes to a shuddering halt. Listening to the playback of this track must have been a moment of true reformation for the four, as it crystallises everything that was positive about the 1979 Led Zeppelin.

Another track that certainly displayed a major sense of ambition was 'Carouselambra'. A rather muddy vocal mix somewhat dulled the effect of the released version, and here an eight-minute alternate take reveals again what a potentially lethal track this was. The arrangement and the vocal is very similar to the finished article, though differences include a Plant giggle during the intro, a less echoed effect on the vocal during the slowed-up section, and a curious wah-wah bass sound in evidence during the fade. The track cuts off abruptly before the intended crescendo is realised.

An instrumental alternative version of 'Carouselambra', virtually mixed except for a few overdubs, is a further indication of the potency of this song. It's driven along by John Paul Jones' relentless keyboard effects, behind which Bonzo's drumming is quite exemplary. The middle section finds Page interweaving some delicate guitar from which JP reverberates the synth into the finale. Instead of the

usual fade out, this version is extinguished by a machine gun snare attack from Bonham.

Finally to 'Wearing And Tearing'. Left off 'In Through The Out Door', nearly the A-side of a commemorative single for Knebworth, finally released on 'Coda', this was the breakneck speed-rocker they reckoned would show the punk clientèle that this particular dinosaur was far from extinct.

Page stabs the Gibson and Bonzo counts in for a studio run through of a track that should have received a public airing long before it did. ''Yeah yeah,'' enthuses Plant. There are some noticeable vocal changes towards the song's finish when Robert screams, 'Can you feel it, can you feel it, oh I found out!'

There were rumours that 'Wearing And Tearing' was under consideration for inclusion in the set of their projected autumn tour of the USA in 1980. Given the opportunity, it would have been a proverbial barnstormer live.

Sadly, John Bonham's untimely death in September 1980 brought the Led Zeppelin era to a close. Never again would they make new music together in a studio. Which is a great shame because the Polar sessions showed they were still hungry to explore new territory.

However, their original studio legacy still remains in the albums that came together during a decade of recording from 1968 to 1978. A decade that, as these rare studio transcripts demonstrate, found Page, Plant, Jones and Bonham constantly in pursuit of fresh ideas and angles from which to exploit their collective musical talent. Upholding that unspoken Led Zeppelin ethic of progressing *ever onward . . .*

At LBC Radio, 1979.

1. *Early photo session at the Chateau Marmont Hotel, Hollywood, during the summer of 1969.*
2. *Jimmy relaxing at his Pangbourne boathouse, February 1970.*
3. *Robert strumming acoustic guitar, 1970.*
4. *Led Zeppelin live, mid 1969.*

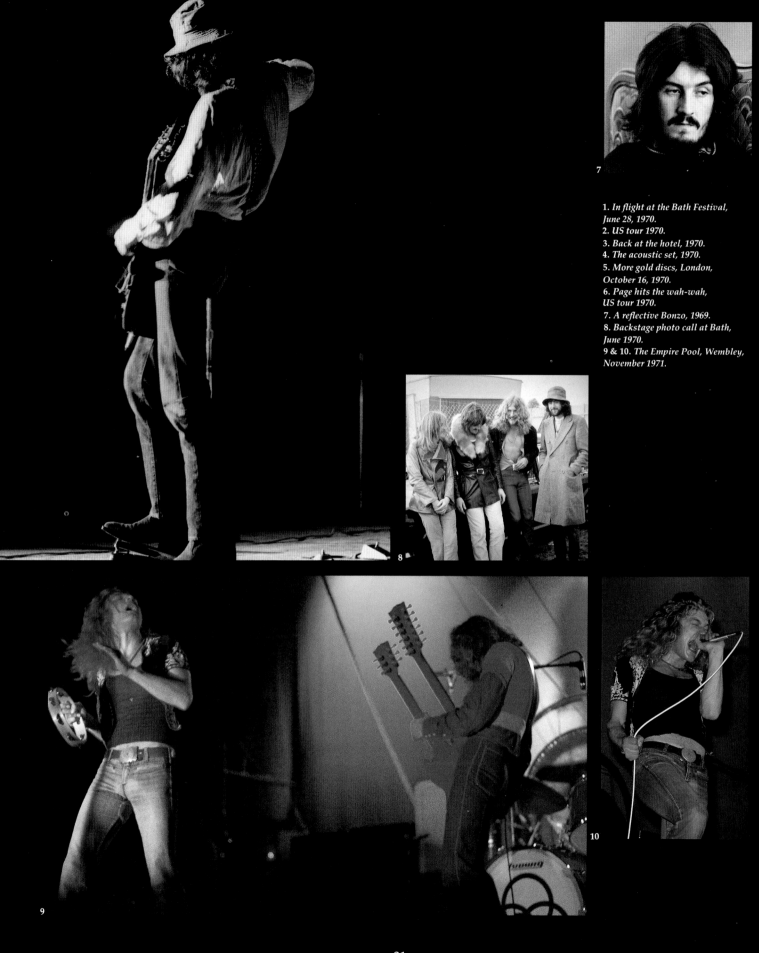

1. *In flight at the Bath Festival,
June 28, 1970.*
2. *US tour 1970.*
3. *Back at the hotel, 1970.*
4. *The acoustic set, 1970.*
5. *More gold discs, London,
October 16, 1970.*
6. *Page hits the wah-wah,
US tour 1970.*
7. *A reflective Bonzo, 1969.*
8. *Backstage photo call at Bath,
June 1970.*
9 & 10. *The Empire Pool, Wembley,
November 1971.*

2

3

1. *Madison Square Garden, July 1973.*
2. *Atlantic Records press reception at the close of the 1973 US tour.*
3. *Between flights: Jones, Page and Peter Grant in Europe, October 1972.*
4. *Plant sits it out, 1973.*
5. *JP at the keyboards.*
6. *Bonzo with perspex Ludwig kit, US tour 1973.*
7. *Page during the 1972 UK tour.*
8. *Flying out for the second leg of the US tour, July 1973.*

1, 2, 3 & 4. *Earls Court, London,*
May 1975.
5. *Plant at Madison Square Garden,*
New York, 1975.
6. *Jimmy at Earls Court, 1975.*
7. *A clockwork drummer, Detroit,*
January 31, 1975.

1. *Madison Square Garden, June 1977.*
2. *John Paul Jones with the Andy Mason custom built triple neck guitar, US tour 1977.*
3. *Robert playing soccer in Central Park, New York, June 1977.*
4. *The Battle of Evermore; a return to the acoustic set, US tour 1977.*
5. *John Bonham with his metallic Ludwig kit, US tour 1977.*
6. *Achilles' Last Stand in the UK: Knebworth, August 1979.*
7. *Peter Grant, Robert and JP backstage at Knebworth.*
8. *The 1979 Led Zeppelin pictured by the Knebworth site.*
9. *Jimmy at the Swansong office, July 1979.*

2

4

5

6

7

1. & 2. Led Zeppelin live in Europe, 1980.
3. Robert during his Principle Of Moments tour, circa 1983.
4. Page with his Dan Electro guitar during the ARMS tour, 1983.
5. Non Stop Go: Robert Plant, circa 1988.
6. The double-neck remains the same: the Atlantic Records reunion concert, May 1988.
7. Led Zeppelin after Led Zeppelin: backstage at Knebworth, June 30, 1990.
8. Still wearing, still tearing: Plant and Page, June 30, 1990.

8

Madison Square Garden, June 1977.

LED ZEPPELIN LIVE!

What Is And What Might Have Been . . .

"We have so much good live stuff. We've got six live concerts on tape which were good nights. We've got some ancient stuff live at the Royal Albert Hall in 1970. It's very interesting to listen to. You can compare different versions of tunes as they span the years. So a chronological live compilation is a thing I've always been keen on, but the soundtrack came out so it's been shelved for a while."
Jimmy Page, 1976.

"It's an honest soundtrack live album, but a chronological live album is something I've always fancied. There's great stuff there and it takes us right up to this year. There's a winning version of 'No Quarter' from Earls Court and from the Albert Hall 'I Can't Quit You Baby'. The 'How Many More Times' is also pretty good. It's great hearing those numbers that we'll probably never do again. We've also got numbers from Southampton University and some small clubs."
Jimmy Page, 1977.

"It's all in the tape vaults still but it would take a long time to do it. It would be a monumental task at this point in time."
Jimmy Page, 1988.

Much of the reputation Led Zeppelin attained during their 12-year reign was achieved through their ever-evolving live show. Right from their first tour of the US in early 1969, through to the huge stadium gigs of the late seventies, Jimmy, Robert, John Paul and Bonzo employed the concert platform to develop an on-stage intensity that few of their peers could rival.

Never just a mere show, Led Zeppelin live was a demonstration of musical telepathy. Given their undoubted ability to improvise and expand on any given musical structure, live performances of their album tracks often took on new dimensions. Free of the constraints of the studio, when interpreted in a concert setting, numbers such as 'No Quarter', 'Dazed And Confused', 'Over The Hills And Far Away' and 'Kashmir', grew in stature. Never quite the same on any given night, and often enhanced by Plant's ad-libs, Jonesy's innovations, Bonzo dropping and stitching the beat and Page meandering into unexplored guitar territory, these performances turned the Led Zeppelin concert trip into a kaleidoscope of spontaneous on-stage excitement.

It's therefore unfortunate that the only official record of the live Led Zeppelin experience is the soundtrack to *The Song Remains The Same*, a decidedly average performance even by their own admission.

Over the years Jimmy Page often expressed a desire to compile a definitive Led Zeppelin live album, taking in every step of their progression along the way. That idea remains at present unfulfilled, and it's left to the legion of Zeppelin fans the world over to speculate on how such a concept might have taken shape. To satisfy my own curiosity, what follows is an imaginary line-up of Led Zeppelin music that I consider would (and still could), do justice to displaying the legacy of the live aspect of Led Zeppelin's career – spanning the years 1969 to 1980.

The contents of this speculative set are taken from two sources: performances known to be lining their archives and performances that exist from the countless unofficial tapes that have flooded the market. Where possible I've avoided repeating songs that appeared on the soundtrack album and, overall, selected material that best monitors their chronological development as the biggest live attraction in the world.

Tailored to fit on a double CD set or a triple album, these 23 tracks represent one version of how a definitive record of Led Zeppelin playing live should sound.

TRACK LISTING:

Side One:
'Train Kept A Rollin'' (1969) 'You Shook Me' (1969)
'Communication Breakdown' (1970)
'Immigrant Song' (1970)
'Heartbreaker' (1970)
Side Two:
'What Is And What Should Never Be' (1971) 'Dancing Days' (1972)
'The Ocean' (1973)
'Since I've Been Loving You' (1973)
Side Three:
'Over The Hills And Far Away' (1975)
'Trampled Underfoot' (1975)
'Kashmir' (1975)
Side Four:
'Tangerine' (1975) 'That's The Way' (1975)
'Woodstock' (1975)
'Sick Again' (1977)
Side Five:
'Ten Years Gone' (1977) 'In The Evening' (1979)
'Whole Lotta Love' (1979)
Side Six:
'Train Kept A Rollin'' (version 2 – 1980)
'Nobody's Fault But Mine' (1980)
'All My Love' (1980)
'Heartbreaker' (version 2 – 1980)

COMMENTARY:

For side one we travel back to 1969 – and an April night on an early Led Zeppelin tour stop-off at The Winterland ballroom in San Francisco. The voice of legendary promoter Bill Graham bawls out "This is Led Zeppelin," as Bonzo and Jimmy kick start the group into a beefed-up version of an old Yardbirds stage favourite 'Train Kept A Rollin''. Robert comes in with some 'Mama Mama' ad libs and later adds harmonica around a confident solo from Page.

This switches to 'You Shook Me'. A slow meandering rendition from the same source. Highlights here include plenty of guitar-vocal interplay and a sonically structured Telecaster run from Jimmy. It all adds up to an authentic reminder of Led Zeppelin's original blues-rooted live set.

From there we plot their progress a year on to January 1970. Riding on the back of the phenomenal success of 'Led Zeppelin II', the band took off on a tour of the UK which included a prestigious show at London's Royal Albert Hall. This gig is known to be in the Atlantic vaults both on tape and film (pirate copies of which are now surfacing). Page used this source to garner the 'I Can't Quit You Baby' take for 'Coda'.

From this show, the selection is a breathless version of 'Communication Breakdown'. For the 1970 tour, this early anthem was elevated to an encore showcase and is spurred on by a great Page wah-wah riff. 'I don't want no Communication Breakdown' squeals Plant, and that night in London he certainly didn't fail to communicate.

To the summer of 1970 for one of the milestone Zepp gigs – their bill-topping appearance at the Bath Festival. This was definitely one of the first peaks of popularity for the group, and from that epic June early evening show, there's the British première of 'Immigrant Song'.

Soon to be the opening track on 'Led Zeppelin III', this particular incarnation was so new to them that Plant half screams most of the lyrics, and coupled with that awesome Viking scream, the overall effect is quite shattering. 'Immigrant Song' switches into 'Heartbreaker', a familiar favourite greeted with much audience cheering.

Page runs through his echo-plexed solo complete with Bach influence, and the whole thing speeds back in, with Plant echoing the final lines across the Somerset countryside. These two Bath extracts were to form the basis for Led Zeppelin's opening on-stage salvo for the next two years.

For track one, side two, we move on to November 20, 1971, the date of Zeppelin's first 'Electric Magic' show at the Wembley Empire Pool. Another reaffirmation of their status, this gig coincided with the release of the fourth album.

From this show, I've chosen 'What Is And What Should Never Be'. A good example of the relaxed and confident air the band displayed that night, this vintage stage fave has a passionate Page solo and a wonderfully sweet guitar coda from the same Gibson. "Good Evening!" says

Plant reassuringly. "This is one from the overdue thing . . ." and it's 'Black Dog'. Given the relief they all felt about the release of the fourth album, this Wembley version has a freshness and vitality fuelled by their enthusiasm. The right performance captured at the right time. "Well it's an amazing sound isn't it," observes the singer after the song. Cut to the enduring riff of 'Dancing Days', taken from a show in Osaka, Japan in October 1972.

Much of the 'Houses Of The Holy' material was broken in on their live set during 1972, some months before the album's release, and this track echoes the good vibes evident within the Zeppelin camp during this era. That good feeling is extended a few months on, into a ramshackle encore version of 'The Ocean', recorded at the LA Forum on their triumphant US jaunt of 1973.

"This is for Wolverhampton Wanderers – a soccer team in England and it's about you." Cue for Page's boys to launch, via Bonzo's shouted intro, into an encore speciality complete with lovely do-wop ending ('It's so good!') and a nod to daughter Carmen's coming of age ('She is only four-years-old') from R. Plant. "LA, thank you very much."

Side two closes with 'Since I've Been Loving You', its inclusion making up for a glaring omission on the official soundtrack album. The 1973 model segues from 'Misty Mountain Hop' via a Page blast, and remains the best version of this durable live work out. There's plenty of pleasing Plant ad-libs and electric piano from John Paul Jones. All as recorded at the Three Rivers Stadium, Pittsburgh on July 24, 1973, just around the time the film crew flew over to capture the last days of the tour.

Record two moves into 1975, for many the peak year of Led Zeppelin's creativity both on record and on-stage. Their three-hour-plus set of that era was a virtual history of their life and times, as Robert explained from the stage of the Dallas Memorial Auditorium on the evening of March 5, 1975. "We intend to try and cut across the spectrum of music that has kept us creatively agile over the past six-and-a-half years. This is a song that relates to . . . well I don't know, it's a song that just relates to life." The song is 'Over The Hills And Far Away', another perfect example of how they improvised and extended the structure of their songs in a live setting. After the revolving intro and initial chorus, Page goes out on a limb

Led Zeppelin's prime, 1975.

to take the song off into another tangent altogether. Aided by Bonzo's jigging hi-hat and snare, he unleashes a cluster of differing solo passages, before allowing it all to slot back into the original framework.

From the same gig a new track, as Robert explains: "To lay evidence upon you that John Paul Jones still exists on the planet, we'd like to feature one of the new tracks off 'Physical Graffiti'. It's a track about a journey to the East, any journey to the East is worth noting down so this is one journey – it's called 'Kashmir' . . ."

With its mesmerising riffs and visual lyrics, 'Kashmir' was a natural for the stage, and whilst never straying too far from the song's studio structure, the four still found enough space so expand on its foundation. Examples include Robert switching the verses around, and later inserting that wonderful 'woman talkin' to ya!' ad-lib before Page and Bonzo lead the way back into the theme. An essential ingredient of any live Zepp show from 1975 onwards.

To open side four it's back to the LA Forum for the last night of the 1975 US tour and 'Trampled Underfoot'. Again the sheer enthusiasm and eagerness to perform this 'Graffiti' track live ensures a staggering performance. Page extracts every conceivable noise from the Gibson during the solo, and the spontaneity of Plant throwing in some lines from 'Gallows Pole' prompts him to acknowledge

the track as 'Trampled Under Gallows' at the close. "And if anybody can hear us in England, well, we're coming back baby!"

And back they came to whip the eerie wastes of Earls Court into a frenzy. "This song is really for our families and friends and the people who've been with us through the lot. It's a song of love in its most innocent stages and it's called 'Tangerine'." With its delicate four-part harmony and electric arrangement, 'Tangerine' was an emotional highlight of these shows and the last time it was ever played live. Page is on double-neck here, and Plant is captured in beautiful voice.

From the same London showcase and representing the acoustic side of the Zepp set, comes 'That's The Way'. The acoustic interlude was a periodical feature of Zeppelin's live show from 1970 through to 1977. 'That's The Way' still stands as one of Robert's foremost compositions and his performance here is full of soaring lyrical phrasing.

To complete a trio of Earls Court extracts, there's the only non-original of the set – the Zepp interpretation of Joni Mitchell's 'Woodstock', which was slotted into the framework of 'Dazed And Confused' just prior to the violin bow episode.

A dreamy psychedelic rendering, with some cascading Page lines, the point where Plant comes back to echo the final 'back to the garden' is a moment of true drama.

Two years later having recovered from

the setback of Plant's injury, the band sound on excellent form caught midway through the 1977 US tour on their old hunting ground of California.

From the LA Forum, June 21 show, 'Sick Again' sounds full of the usual swagger and arrogance. With its tales of the road taunts, it never failed to warm up any audience it encountered.

On to the final album and from the same tour, but taken from a Madison Square Garden show earlier in the month, comes an ambitious arrangement of 'Ten Years Gone'. "A song about a love that could have been good but fell by the wayside," as Plant remarks at the beginning.

Here we find Jonesy on a triple-necked guitar, supplementing Page's subtly bended guitar parts, while Robert makes full use of the vocal harmonizer towards the song's finish. A fine sense of on-stage dynamics at play.

It's fast forward by two years for the next track, taken from the first week's performance at Knebworth. One of the most reassuring aspects of the whole set that day was 'In The Evening'. A new 24-carat prime knockout rocker, full of seductive Page riffing and hyper-frantic Plant pleading, not to mention a perfect showcase for Jones who undercuts the frenzy with a string symphony that mellows out for a pleasing keyboard interval. Live, the whole thing packs considerably more punch than its studio rival.

Also from Knebworth I've picked the 'Whole Lotta Love' revamp. Employed as an encore, it includes a rousing series of newly evolved riffs, perfectly allied to Bonzo's timely hammerings. It was this arrangement that the group returned to when they reunited for the Atlantic Anni-

Bonzo, US tour, 1977.

versary bash in 1988.

The final side of music for this imaginary chronological showpiece is taken from Led Zeppelin's 'Over Europe' performance in Zurich on June 29, 1980 – the final tour. To illustrate how the story had travelled full circle there's a return to 'Train Kept A Rollin'', the first Zepp set opener 10 years previously, now resurrected for the rejuvenation the four were enjoying. With an overload of wah-wah distortion, Page cuts a series of tearing guitar statements, while a breathless Plant is engulfed by the sheer energy of it all. A 'two, three, four' from Bonzo pitches 'Train' straight into 'Nobody's Fault But Mine', the classic 'Presence' bluesy powerhouse. Another latter era stage fave with Plant wailing on harmonica, and introducing yet another sterling solo with the familiar cry of 'Oh Jimmy – Oh Jimmy!'

One of the surprise inclusions of the 1980 tour and one of the best received numbers was 'All My Love', the delicate latter era Plant love song. Another Jones showcase, he gets the classical solo together with ease, out of which Jimmy plays some emotional guitar passages. This track is also a superb vehicle for Plant, who brings sincerity and soul to some heartfelt lyrics.

Finally, to bring the balance right back, another version of one of their most durable stage numbers. By 1980, 'Heartbreaker' had taken on new life as a raging encore. Reason enough for Page to pull out a marathon nine-minute performance for the Zurich show. His playing blazes with an almost inhuman energy and yet never loses control. 'Tight but loose' is an apt description for a virtuoso guitar solo that takes in every trick he had brought to the piece over the previous 11 years. The Bach run, the power chording, even the '59th Street Bridge Song'. It's all here.

"Thanks for being great," exclaims the master of ceremonies at the finish. "See you again some day – thanks from Jimmy, Jonesy, Bonzo and myself – ta."

And that was Led Zeppelin live! 'Heartbreaker' concludes this 11-year journey in the development of Led Zeppelin as a live stage act. From the small ballrooms of America, to the biggest arenas in the world, this is the music that established Led Zeppelin as the top concert attraction of the era.

As a hypothetical chronological live collection, this is what is . . . and what might have been.

Beside the Starship at Pittsburgh Airport, July 1973.

THE TEN ALBUM LEGACY

*A Track By Track Analysis
Of The Official Led Zeppelin Catalogue.*

etween 1969 and 1982 Led Zeppelin released a total of 10 albums. Since their demise in 1980, sales of those albums have continued to build up, ensuring the group's position as the holders of one of the most buoyant back catalogues in the history of recorded sound.

Over the next few pages, these 10 albums are dissected and analysed track by track. Each song's origin, its place in their live repertoire, and its overall standing in the Zeppelin catalogue is reassessed.

The result is an intensive study of the music that can be found within their 10 album legacy.

From 'Good Times Bad Times' to 'Wearing And Tearing', this is the definitive study of Led Zeppelin on record.

'LED ZEPPELIN'
Atlantic Records – Original issue 588 171, re-issue K40031

he début Led Zeppelin album is the recorded statement of their first few weeks together. It's also a fair representation of their initial blues-rock stage act that had been tested on Scandinavian audiences just prior to entering Olympic studios to lay down their first studio tracks.

The material selected for the album had been well rehearsed and pre-arranged by the four, one of the primary reasons it took only 30 studio hours to complete.

When it came to securing a new deal for the group, Peter Grant negotiated a massive five-album £200,000 package with Jerry Wexler and Ahmet Ertegun of Atlantic Records in New York. This ended speculation that they would extend The Yardbirds' previous association with Epic in America and EMI in the UK. Part of the Atlantic deal allowed Grant and Zeppelin to retain virtual complete control on artistic matters. They also formed their own company, Superhype, to handle all publishing rights. It was also agreed that all Led Zeppelin records would appear on the famous red Atlantic label, as opposed to its less distinguished Atco subsidiary which had been used for Atlantic's non soul or R&B acts in the past. This gave them the distinction of being the first white UK act on the prestigious Atlantic label.

The artistic control of their output would extend to their sleeve designs and on the first album, Jimmy chose a simple black on white illustration of the Hindenburg airship going down, as Keith Moon had put it, like a Lead Zeppelin. It was later claimed by The Who's John Entwistle that this sleeve design had been earmarked for the group he, Moon and Page had talked about forming a couple of years earlier. The back cover photo was taken by former Yardbird Chris Dreja, who quit to take up a career in photography during the evolution of The New Yardbirds. During the first few weeks of release in the UK, the sleeve was printed with the name and Atlantic logo in turquoise. This was switched to the common orange print later in the year, creating a much sought after sleeve rarity. The whole design was co-ordinated by George Hardie, with whom they would later work on future sleeves.

The Led Zeppelin album was initially released in America on January 17, 1969, to capitalise on their first US visit. Before that, Atlantic distributed a few hundred advance white label copies to key radio stations and reviewers. A positive reaction to its contents, coupled with a good reaction to their opening gigs, resulted in the album generating 50,000 advance orders. It entered the *Billboard* chart at number 99. From there it rose to number 40, then 28, reaching the Top 20 and rising as high as number 10. In all it enjoyed 73 weeks on the chart, returning for further spells in 1975 and 1979.

In the UK it was issued on March 28. Originally it appeared as Atlantic 588 171 via Polydor's distribution. It was one of a new breed of stereo only releases, as up until 1969 most albums were available as stereo or mono versions. When the Warner group took over the Atlantic catalogue in 1972, the number switched to K40031. On April 12, 1969, the Led Zeppelin début album began a 79-week run on the British chart, peaking at number six. The album was advertised in selected music papers under the slogan 'Led Zeppelin – the only way to fly.'

And fly it certainly did. Time has done nothing to diminish the quality of one of the finest début albums ever recorded. There's an urgency and enthusiasm about their performance that retains timeless charm. The nine cuts offer a *tour de force* of powerful yet often subtle dynamics.

There are just so many highlights: the spacey blues feel of 'I Can't Quit Baby', the clever light and shade approach on 'Babe I'm Gonna Leave You', Page bowing manically on 'Dazed And Confused' and 'How Many More Times', and throughout it all the young Robert Plant lays down a piercing vocal style set to become the group's trademark. And let's not forget the fact that with this album, Page virtually invents the guitar riff as a key songwriting component.

It was one helluva trip then, and it's still one helluva trip now.

'GOOD TIMES BAD TIMES'
Page, Jones and Bonham
Studio: Olympic Studios, London.

At two minutes, 43 seconds, this is a perfectly compact overture to set the scene. Bonham and Jones hold down a powerful and inventive rhythm section, and when the time comes, Jimmy flexes the Telecaster (played through a Leslie speaker to create that soaring effect) in a late Yardbirds-era fashion.

From the onset though, it's the Plant vocal that strikes home instantly. He executes all manner of vocal somersaults with the lyric but never loses control. Aided by a catchy chorus, 'Good Times Bad Times' is one of their most commercial offerings, and was at one time considered for release as their début single.

Live performances: Never an integral part of their set, 'Good Times Bad Times' was featured on their début tour of Scandinavia, and resurfaced on their late 1969 set as an opening instrumental riff link for 'Communication Breakdown'. On the sixth US tour in the late summer of 1970, it returned as a vocal version inserted in the 'Communication Breakdown' medley.

'BABE I'M GONNA LEAVE YOU'
Traditional – arranged by Page (Remasters credits Anne Bredon/Page)
Studio: Olympic.

This was a number Page played to Plant from a Joan Baez album during their initial meeting at Jimmy's riverside home at Pangbourne in August 1968. It was then that he first suggested covering the song with his new-found singing partner.

When it came to recording, Jimmy re-arranged this traditional folk tune to fit both acoustic and electric moulds. Thus, it emerges as an early example of their musical diversity, combining the energy of a forceful Plant vocal, and a strident crash-cymbal driven chorus, with some superbly picked Spanish guitar. It was one of the few tracks on the first album to use overdubs, and is also an early flowering of Robert's much repeated 'Baby, baby, baby' vocal mannerism.

Live performances: Used on the initial 1968/69 tours and then discarded after the second US tour. A particularly vibrant version exists from their Danish TV special filmed in March 1969.

'YOU SHOOK ME'
Willie Dixon
Studio: Olympic.

It's often forgotten just how heavily the early Led Zeppelin relied on the blues for inspiration. Their launch coincided with the British blues boom of 1968, and as can be seen from this showcase, they felt very at home in the company of standards like 'You Shook Me'. Robert in particular revelled in the song, extending the style he had perfected in The Band Of Joy to great effect.

Instrumentally, the track certainly packs some punch. From Jones' swirling organ, through Plant's harmonica wailings to the point where Jimmy's solo cascades around Bonzo's stereo panned tom tom attack, this is prime vintage Zeppelin. And the final incessant by-play between Page and Plant that leads out of the track is a masterful production technique, and one that would be further emphasised on stage.

'You Shook Me' also appeared on The Jeff Beck Group's album 'Truth'. Released a few months before the début Led Zeppelin album, Beck has gone on record as stating that Jimmy copied their arrangement for his own devices and was well upset when the Zeppelin album stormed the charts.

Live performances: Featured on all the early 1968/69 tours, and was then deleted for the late 1969 US tour. Revived for the US, Japan, UK and Australian dates in 1971/72, when it was part of the 'Whole Lotta Love' medley. A brief reprise of the song was tagged on to the end of 'In My Time Of Dying' at Earls Court, and on the 1977 US tour.

'DAZED AND CONFUSED'
Page
Studio: Olympic.

Originates from the mid-sixties, when it was known as an acoustic folk tune sung by Jake Holmes. In The Yardbirds, Jimmy arranged it as 'I'm Confused' and it was played live on stage and on radio sessions. For the début album, Page added new lyrics, and spiced up the arrangement to extend the guitar played with violin bow episode. It still retains an air of menace and drama, and crystallises the electricity developing between the four at that time. It also beautifully illustrates Jones' walking bass style that lights up the track from start to finish.

Live performances: A cornerstone of every Led Zeppelin live show until 1975. It became a vehicle for intensive improvisation, often encompassing snippets of other songs. These included Plant vocal ad libs of 'Woodstock', The Eagles' 'Take It Easy', and Scott Mackenzie's 'San Francisco', plus Page riffing out on 'The Crunge', 'Walter's Walk', and 'West Side Story'. It also often stretched to 30 minutes in length. On the 1975 US tour, the number had to be dropped for the first two weeks, when Jimmy injured his finger just before the tour. It made its reappearance during a stunning show at Madison Square Garden in New York on February 3. For the 1977 tour dates and

Copenhagen/Knebworth in 1979, the violin bow section was extracted from 'Dazed And Confused' to form the visual centrepiece of the set. This section was also used with The Firm and on Page's solo 'Outrider' tour.

'YOUR TIME IS GONNA COME'
Page, Jones
Studio: Olympic.

Opening with a grand church organ display from Jones, this track builds into a hypnotic fade-out chorus, sung by all four members. Plant's phrasing throughout is superb – 'You been bad to me woman, but it's comin' back home to you' – and Jimmy overlays some tasteful pedal steel guitar. It all evaporates beautifully into the next cut.

Live performances: Played on the first tour but then dropped. Made a one-off appearance in a medley of 'How Many More Times' on the Japan tour of 1971.

'BLACK MOUNTAIN SIDE'
Page
Studio: Olympic.

The melody of this Page virtuoso acoustic guitar instrumental owes more than a passing nod to an old folk song recorded by both Bert Jansch and John Renbourn, known as 'Black Waterside'. Accompanied by the tabla playing of Viram Jasnai, Jimmy wades through a pleasing interlude that acts as light relief before the energy level clocks back up. Incidentally, Jimmy plays a borrowed Gibson J 200 acoustic.

Live performances: Incorporated into the Page/Yardbirds solo number 'White Summer' on all their gigs up to the fifth US jaunt in 1970. Restored to the set for the 1977 US tour, Copenhagen and Knebworth in 1979 and the 'Over Europe' tour in 1980. Part of this number was revived by Page on his 'Outrider' tour in 1988.

'COMMUNICATION BREAKDOWN'
Page, Jones, Bonham
Studio: Olympic.

An early Zeppelin anthem, this track grew out of their Scandinavian set when it dovetailed into the similar tempoed show opener 'Train Kept A Rollin''. A brilliant example of Page's ability to create a whole song around a repeated guitar riff, 'Communication Breakdown' is a storming rocker that peaks just around the point Plant screams 'Suck it!' and Page cuts a screeching guitar path across the speakers. It has survived the test of time to become one of the true all time greats of the Zeppelin catalogue.

Live performances: Developing during their first tour in September 1968, it went on to be a lasting part of their show. It was used on all dates in 1969, becoming the set opener after the second US tour. In 1970 it was elevated to encore status. On the sixth US tour it was used as an encore medley. It subsequently appeared as an encore on each successive tour, including the last night at Earls Court, and the second Knebworth date. It was again an encore special for Europe 1980, and was part of Plant's 1988 and 1990 solo set. This was also the number they played on their only live UK TV appearance in March 1969.

'I CAN'T QUIT YOU BABY'
Willie Dixon
Studio: Olympic.

Another slow Willie Dixon blues, this is notable for its ambient production quality that brings to the fore John Bonham's wonderfully laid-back drumming, and Jimmy's deceptively mellow guitar sparring. There's a great 'just having a blow' atmosphere about this track that makes for a very relaxed outing.

Live performances: Included in their set from 1968 up to the fifth US tour in 1970. Revived as part of the 'Whole Lotta Love' medley on the Japan, UK and Europe tours 1972/3. This track was also rehearsed for the Atlantic 40th Anniversary reunion in May 1988, but was not included on the night. Page and Plant performed a short version of this song at the Hammersmith show a month earlier.

'HOW MANY MORE TIMES'
Page, Jones, Bonham
Studio: Olympic.

The closing number of their early stage act and appropriately enough the parting shot of their début album, 'How Many More Times' is a lengthy, high energy exit. Along the way all sorts of playful things occur. From the suitably dramatic intro, complete with stinging Page wah-wah, the track develops into a medley of its own. Apparently the appearance of 'Rosie' and 'The Hunter' came spontaneously on the night of the session itself. Plant is quite fantastic here. He comes on as a supremely confident carnal gourmet boasting of much excess, but with a smile never too far from his lips. Note also Page's bowing technique. Alongside 'Dazed And Confused', this track has its origins in the old Yardbirds repertoire.

Live performances: 'How Many More Times' held down the closing slot in the Zeppelin set up to and including their 1970 Bath Festival appearance. It reappeared briefly on the Japan 1971 dates,

and at a date at Southampton University in January 1973. It came back into the set for the 1975 US tour, when it replaced 'Dazed And Confused' for the first two weeks due to Jimmy's injured finger.

UNISSUED MATERIAL:

Additional material rehearsed and prepared around this period, included a version of Garnett Mimms 'As Long As I Have You', Elmer Gentry's 'Flames', The Band's 'Chest Fever', Spirit's 'Fresh Garbage', and The Yardbirds' treatment of 'Train Kept A Rollin''. Some of these numbers formed the basis of the early live set, and may have been under consideration for recording when the time came to enter Olympic studios in October 1968.

'LED ZEPPELIN II'
Atlantic – original issue 588 198, reissue K40037

L ed Zeppelin II' was released on October 31, 1969. In America it had advance orders for half a million copies. It entered the *Billboard* chart at 15, and by the end of the year it had dislodged The Beatles' 'Abbey Road' to take the top spot, where it remained for seven weeks. By April 1970 it had registered three million American sales. It was a similar success story at home. On November 8, 1969, it began a 138-week residency on the LP chart, climbing to the top spot in February 1970. The sleeve design was based on a David Juniper poster, and the advertising campaign was built around the slogan 'Led Zeppelin II – Now Flying!'

Recorded in various locations, it was a dynamic hybrid of rock styles. In between the harder-edged material however, there were some examples of the ever widening scope of the group's intentions. This album also marked the emergence of

Robert Plant as a serious songwriter. His name had been notably absent from the début album credits due to previous contractual commitments that resulted from his association with CBS Records. Now, his influence on tracks such as 'What Is And What Should Never Be' and 'Ramble On' were definite pointers to the musical future of Led Zeppelin.

'Led Zeppelin II' marks a very creative period for the group, and it remains a nostalgic reflection of the sheer exuberance inspired by the intensive tour schedule aimed (successfully) at conquering America.

'WHOLE LOTTA LOVE'
Page, Bonham, Plant, Jones Studio: Olympic; Sunset Sound, Los Angeles; A and R, New York.

The catalyst. A masterful Page/Kramer production. From Plant's off-mike cough through to the 'Keepa coolin' baby' squeals, this is five minutes and 33 seconds of aural and sexual delight. The song originally took shape around Page's killer three-note riff, and a descending chord structure which employed backwards echo effects first used by Jimmy on a Mickie Most session. Devoid of any lyrics of their own, Plant took from Willie Dixon's 'You Need Love'. In failing to credit Dixon, the group were subsequently sued and they settled out of court.

But the most impressive part of 'Whole Lotta Love' had nothing whatsoever to do with Willie Dixon. This was the apocalyptic central section in which Page mixed all manner of crazy sound effects – full tilt whoops, screams, sirens and demolition noises interspersed with what sounded remarkably like Robert squealing in orgasmic bliss from the depths of a coal mine – into a truly mind-blowing sequence which careered wildly from speaker to speaker and suggested total mayhem.

This section was missing – inevitably – when 'Whole Lotta Love' was edited down to become a Top Five hit single in America. It also reached number one in Belgium and Germany. In the UK, Atlantic had expected to issue the edited version themselves, and pressed initial copies for release on December 5, 1969. However, Peter Grant halted the release, stating that to issue singles off albums was not Led Zeppelin's policy. An official statement added that they had written a special number which they intended to be their first British single. This never materialised, and despite much record company pressure, they declined to issue official singles in the UK throughout their career.

In many respects 'Whole Lotta Love' would become a millstone around Led Zeppelin's collective neck. An instrumental version of the song (by CCS, a large rock band put together by Alexis Korner) became the signature tune for the UK weekly TV show *Top Of The Pops*, thus ensuring that it would seep into the consciousness of every pop fan in the land, whether or not they were fans of Led Zeppelin.

It also came to be regarded as the definitive expression of heavy metal, a term of reference yet to come into common usage when 'Led Zeppelin II' was released, and as a result Led Zeppelin would eventually become known as the definitive heavy metal band. It was a pejorative description they would come to abhor, which they would never be able to shake off, and which they certainly didn't deserve. They were not to know how many thousands of future bands would rip off the concept of 'Whole Lotta Love' – the directness of a repeated riff awash in echo – in the years to come or how many bands would take their style and look, simplify it back to basics and refer to it and themselves as heavy metal. Musical eclecticism was Led Zeppelin's *real* hallmark, and that eclecticism incorporated much more than the simple yet explosive noise that was 'Whole Lotta Love'.

Live performances: 'Whole Lotta Love' made its live début on the second US tour in April 1969 as part of a medley with 'As Long As I Have You'. In June 1969 they previewed it on a BBC session. It was then part of each subsequent set list. For the early 1970 dates it was an encore number. From the sixth US tour in 1970 up to the 1973 US tour, it was the closing finale of every Zeppelin performance, extending in length to include a rock 'n' roll medley. On their 1975 dates it was an encore medley with 'Black Dog'. In 1977 a medley encore with 'Rock And Roll'. It was given a new arrangement for the 1979 Copenhagen/Knebworth encores (the same version was revived for the Atlantic 40th Anniversary reunion in May 1988), and returned to the 'Let That Boy Boogie' medley workout for the 1980 Europe dates. It holds the distinction of being the last track Led Zeppelin performed live, when it received a 17-minute work-out at the final gig in Berlin on July 7, 1980. It was also played at the *Live Aid* get together on July 13, 1985.

'WHAT IS AND WHAT SHOULD NEVER BE'
Page, Plant
Studio: Olympic; Groove, New York; A and R.

The genesis of Robert Plant's career as a songwriter, this dreamy affair is a marked departure from the dizzy atmosphere of 'Whole Lotta Love'. It's also another superb Page production with its flanging vocal effects and powerful stereo separation on the fade out. Jimmy had now switched to the Gibson Les Paul for recording, and the sustained solo here is really quite beautiful.

Live performances: Previewed in June 1969 on a BBC radio session, then inserted on the late 1969 US tour and played at every gig through 1970/71 up to the US tour in June 1972. Discarded thereafter.

'THE LEMON SONG'
Chester Burnett
Studio: Mystic, Los Angeles; A and R.

This track was originally credited to Page, Plant, Jones and Bonham but claims from publishers Jewel Music that the song was heavily based on Chester Burnett's 'Killing Floor' led to another settlement and a change of sleeve credit. In fact some cassette copies of the album do list the track as 'Killing Floor'. This arrangement also takes from Albert King's 'Cross-Cut Saw', a staple of the gigs Plant would perform with The Honeydrippers in 1981. Recorded virtually live in New York's Mystic studios, the track combined 'Killing Floor', which they had been performing at their early gigs, with the Robert Johnson inspired 'Squeeze my lemon' sequence with its intense erotic overtones.

Live performances: 'Killing Floor' was used on the début American tour, and was to evolve into 'The Lemon Song' for the second and third tours. Dropped in late 1969, though the 'Squeeze my lemon' sequence was often inserted into the 'Whole Lotta Love' medley and ad-libbed elsewhere.

'THANK YOU'
Page, Plant
Studio: Morgan, London; A and R.

This emotional love song to his wife brings out the best in Robert Plant, as he commits to tape one of his finest vocal performances. Elsewhere in the arrangement John Paul Jones excels on Hammond organ, and Jimmy complements it all with some delicate Rickenbacker 12-string picking.

Live performances: Made its début in the set on the November 1969 US tour. Stayed in the show throughout 1970/71 acting as a spotlight for Jonesy's keyboard solo.

Used as a marathon encore on the 1972/3 tours and then deleted from the act.

'HEARTBREAKER'
Page, Plant, Jones, Bonham
Studio: A and R.

'Heartbreaker' is another integral part of the recorded Zeppelin canon and a platform for Page to express his guitar virtuosity. On this studio cut, he offers up a breathtaking exercise in string-bending guitar technique, while on the road he extended the track to include snippets of Bach's Lute Suite No.1 and Simon and Garfunkel's '59th Street Bridge Song'.

Live performances: A long-standing live fave, it joined the set at the Lyceum in October 1969. From the Bath Festival onwards and throughout the rest of their dates in 1970/71, it provided a dual thrust set opener with 'Immigrant Song'. For the US, Japan, UK and Europe tours of 1972/73, it became part of the encore. It was back in the main set as a medley with 'Whole Lotta Love' for the 1973 US dates (see *Song Remains The Same* movie), and then an encore again on the 1975 US tour, the last night at Earls Court, the 1977 US tour, Knebworth 1, and the Europe 1980 tour. It was also performed at the Atlantic 40th Anniversary reunion in 1988.

'LIVIN' LOVIN' MAID (SHE'S JUST A WOMAN)'
Page, Plant
Studio: Morgan, London; A and R, New York.

Jimmy returned to the Telecaster to knock out what the band always considered to be something of a production line filler. However, this tight, hook-laden ditty, found much favour on the radio, and when 'Whole Lotta Love' finished its chart run in America, 'Livin' Lovin' Maid' was flipped over to become an A-side in its own right. It then climbed to Number 65 on the *Billboard* chart. The song is rumoured to be about one of their early, persistent West Coast groupies.

Live performance: Such was their distaste for this track, it never received a public airing. The nearest it came to it was when Plant sang the opening line in jest at Earls Court on May 24, 1975. Explaining the intention of the show he said, "We don't just mean we're gonna groove around on anything that could be groovy like 'With the purple umbrella and the 50 cent hat' – no none of that!'' In a surprise move Plant brought the song into his 'Manic Nirvana' US solo tour set in 1990.

'RAMBLE ON'
Page, Plant
Studio: Juggy Sound; A and R.

Enter the ethereal Page and Plant.

'Ramble On', with its Tolkien-inspired lyrical content was for Plant in particular the highlight of 'Led Zeppelin II'. It remains a splendid illustration of the light and shade dynamism that would characterise so much of their future work. It slips effortlessly from quiet mournful passages into an uplifting chorus, and Page's overdubbed interweaving Gibson run is an early attempt at the guitar army assault.

Live performances: Surprisingly, 'Ramble On' was never performed live in a full version. On the Spring 1970 US tour Plant did throw in lines from the song during 'Communication Breakdown' (see 'Mudslide' bootleg) and 'Whole Lotta Love'.

'MOBY DICK'
Bonham, Jones, Page
Studio: Mirror Sound, L.A.; May Fair, New York; A and R.

John Bonham's percussive showcase took shape on the second US tour when it was known as 'Pat's Delight' (a reference to his wife). Built between a killer Page riff, which was used as the theme to BBC 2's *Disco 2* rock show, Bonzo does his thing with sticks and bare hands.

Live performances: Came in on the 1969 November US tour and stayed in the set on every tour up to 1977. It developed into an excessive 20-minute showcase which provided the others with a break in the show. By 1975 Bonzo was incorporating a 'Whole Lotta Love' riff segment played on electronically treated kettle drums. On the 1977 US tour, the track was aptly renamed 'Over The Top', and employed the riff of 'Out On The Tiles' instead of the 'Moby Dick' theme.

'BRING IT ON HOME'
Page, Plant
Studio: Mystic, Los Angeles; Vancouver; A and R.

Opens with a straight lift from Sonny Boy Williamson's 'Bring It On Home' it soon snaps into electric action, but it's a rather hackneyed blues rocker that always worked better live.

Live performances: Used on stage from the November 1969 US tour and retained for their 1970 itinerary. Live, it developed into a lengthy piece with a great Page/ Bonham guitar-drum battle. Revived briefly for the 1972 US tour as an encore, 'Bring It On Home' was also played at the reunion staged at Jason Bonham's wedding reception in May 1990.

UNRELEASED MATERIAL
Very little information has emerged on the possibility of out-takes remaining

from the 'Led Zeppelin II' era. 'We're Gonna Groove', a 1970 set opener cut at Morgan in mid 1969, did surface on 'Coda'. It's possible they had one or two other left-overs from this period, including a studio run through of 'Train Kept A Rollin''.

'LED ZEPPELIN III'
Atlantic – original issue 2401 002, reissued as K50002.

L ed Zeppelin III' was the most eagerly awaited album of 1970. After what was to become a traditional Led Zeppelin delay (this time two months), it finally surfaced in October of that year. Advance orders in America were close to the million mark, and it spent four weeks at the top of the *Billboard* chart. It entered the British chart at number one and remained there for three weeks. It returned to the top for a further week on December 12.

The elaborate gatefold sleeve, which held up release, was designed by Richard Drew, a lecturer in fine arts at Leeds Polytechnic college. Its rotating inner wheel, an idea of Page's, was based on crop rotation charts but the end result was not quite how Jimmy had originally conceived it. Its release was trailered by a full page ad taken out in the *Melody Maker* at the end of September. In reference to their runaway success in that year's *Melody Maker* readers' poll, the ad simply said, 'Thank you for making us the world's number one band.'

The diverse content of the album, with its accent on more acoustically based arrangements, confused both critics and the public alike. Hindsight was to prove that this change in direction was a natural progression for the group. At no point would they restrict themselves to one musical genre.

'Led Zeppelin III' is another triumph for Jimmy Page as a producer. He brings out the best qualities of each song here, from the dramatic intro of 'Since I've Been Loving You' through to the delicacy of 'That's The Way'. It all adds up to one of their most absorbing and intimate listening experiences.

'IMMIGRANT SONG'
Page, Plant
Studio: Headley Grange, Hampshire; Island and Olympic, London; Ardent, Memphis.

Nothing less than a classic. Built around an incessant Page/Jones/Bonham battering riff, this Plant tale of Viking lust is a compulsive attack on the senses as well as a call to arms. In addition to containing some of Plant's most memorable lines, it also boasts a wailing war-cry destined to delight rabid audiences across the world. The lyrics were partly inspired by their trip to Iceland in June 1970. The count in at the start, by the way, is coupled with echo tape feedback – hence the hiss.

In America 'Immigrant Song' was lifted as a single and after a 13-week chart run peaked at 16.

Live performance: 'Immigrant Song' was premièred to UK audiences at the opening of Led Zeppelin's 1970 Bath Festival appearance. This version features varying verses to the later studio issue. The live arrangement included an extended guitar solo. It was the set opener of every show played from Bath 1970 up to the 1972 US tour. For the Japan, UK and Europe 1972/73 dates it emerged as part of the encore. It was then deleted from the set. Robert Plant was to revive the song in an amended arrangement on his solo tours of 1988/1990.

'FRIENDS'
Page, Plant
Studio: Olympic; Ardent

A few seconds of studio chat precedes this hypnotic swirling mass of sound. It's surprising that John Paul Jones has no composing credit here, as he is wholly responsible for the track's compelling string arrangement. There's a Moog synthesiser added on the outro which provides a link to the next track. With its repeated acoustic guitar motifs and bongo percussion, this bizarre outing was unlike anything else they attempted.

Live performances: The only documented live performance of 'Friends' is a version played in Osaka on the 1971 Japanese tour. This was also, along with 'Four Sticks', one of the experimental songs Jimmy and Robert recorded with the Bombay Orchestra in March 1972.

'CELEBRATION DAY'
Page, Plant, Jones
Studio: Headley Grange; Island; Olympic; Ardent.

A track that nearly didn't appear at all. Due to a studio oversight, the intro of this track was crinkled on the master tape, making it impossible to thread, but by seguing the swirling link from 'Friends' into the guitar riff and Plant's opening lyrics, the song was salvaged. A good thing too, as it's an excellent vehicle for a succession of Page's guitar effects, and Plant's happy tour of New York.

Live performances: Came in to the set on the late summer tour of America in 1971, and stayed for the Japanese, UK and Australian tours of late 1971 early 1972. Revived for the 1973 US dates and then again for the Copenhagen and Knebworth gigs in 1979.

'SINCE I'VE BEEN LOVING YOU'
Page, Plant
Studio: Island; Olympic; Ardent.

One of the first songs prepared for 'Zeppelin III', it was previewed as early as the January tour of the UK in 1970. A self-styled and somewhat mannered slow blues, with some lovely organ from J.P., it featured one of Jimmy's most expressive solos prefaced by a dramatic shout of 'Watch out!' from Plant.

Live performances: Entered the set in early 1970 and retained throughout their 1970/71 dates. From the Japan tour in 1972 up to the 1973 American dates, it formed the second half of a medley with 'Misty Mountain Hop'. It came back into the set in its own right for the latter part of the 1975 US tour, and reappeared for the 1977 US tour, Copenhagen/Knebworth 1979, and Europe 1980. On Plant's solo tours part of the track was aired in 'Slow Dancer'. Also performed in a version at Hammersmith in 1988 with Page guesting.

'OUT ON THE TILES'
Page, Plant, Bonham
Studio: Headley Grange; Olympic; Ardent, Memphis.

After Page's domination of the first two albums, the more leisurely paced recording of 'Zeppelin III' allowed for a more democratic pool of ideas. This track came out of a Bonham-inspired riff and is a much underrated part of their output.

With an infectious chorus and enthusiastic Plant vocal, it bubbles along with an unnerving energy. The title relates to a previously written set of lyrics that were revamped for this version. The spacey sound mix evident here is another example of distance miking in the studio by Page.

Live performances: This track was only ever used on the sixth US tour of September 1970. However, the opening riff was later applied to the live arrangement of 'Black Dog'. Then on the 1977 US tour the riff structure of 'Out On The Tiles' replaced 'Moby Dick' as the lead intro to Bonham's drum solo which was retitled by Plant as 'Over The Top'.

'GALLOWS POLE'
Traditional: arranged by Page and Plant
Studio: Headley Grange; Olympic; Ardent.

This traditional folk tune can be traced back to Leadbelly. Jimmy adapted it from a version by Fred Gerlach. Instrumentally, it has Page on banjo, six and 12 acoustic guitar and electric guitar. John Paul Jones is on mandolin and bass. While Plant unfolds a tale of medieval woe, the tension builds beautifully as Bonzo wades in, and Page adds an understated but frenzied Gibson run. One of their most adventurous outings and quite brilliant in its execution – lyrically and musically.

Live performances: Played on some of the April/May UK and European tour dates in 1971. Robert did sometimes throw in some lines of this during 'Trampled Underfoot', remarking on its performance on the last night of the 1975 US tour as being 'Trampled Under Gallows'.

'TANGERINE'
Page
Studio: Headley Grange; Olympic; Ardent.

Jimmy provides an eight-second count-in to a mellow solo composition left over from his Yardbirds era. Robert duets with himself on the double-tracked vocal, and Pagey layers on some tasteful pedal steel guitar.

Live performances: Joined the acoustic set on the UK and European tour in the spring of 1971. Remained in the set on all tours up to the US dates in the summer of 1972. Revived as a four-part harmony rendition for the Earls Court season in 1975, for which Jimmy pulled out the Gibson double-neck.

'THAT'S THE WAY'
Page, Plant
Studio: Headley Grange; Olympic; Ardent.

One of their very best performances and definitely Robert's best ever lyric, 'That's The Way' carried the working title of 'The Boy Next Door'. It was written at the cottage in Bron-Y-Aur, and centres around the dissolution of a pair of star crossed lovers. The lyrics were influenced in part by the unrest Robert witnessed on their Spring 1970 US travels. The tale unfolds against a rush of acoustic guitars, and a

moving horn-like electric solo from Jimmy.

Live performances: Premièred at Bath, and a standard feature of the acoustic set during 1970/71 and up to the American tour in 1972. Recalled for the Earls Court season in 1975.

'BRON-Y-AUR STOMP'
Page, Plant, Jones
Studio: Headley Grange; Olympic; Ardent.

Some light relief. A playful folksy singalong, written at the cottage about Plant's dog Strider. Page gets in some fine picking, Bonzo adds spoons and castanets, and Jones plays an acoustic bass. The tune itself was tried in an electric rockier arrangement at the commencement of the third album sessions late in 1969, when it was known as 'Jennings Farm Blues'.

Live performances: Used in the acoustic set from the UK dates in Spring 1971 through to the American tour in 1972. A revamped arrangement with Jonesy on stand-up bass was used for the Japan/UK/Europe 1972/73 dates. Recalled in this format for Earls Court in 1975, and then as a medley with 'Black Country Woman' on the 1977 US tour.

'HATS OFF TO (ROY) HARPER'
Traditional; arranged by Charles Obscure
Studio: Headley Grange; Olympic; Ardent.

Nothing more than a Page/Plant jam, loosely based on Bukka White's old blues tune 'Shake 'Em On Down'. Page does get in some fairly authentic bottleneck guitar but it's hardly essential listening. The title is a bold acknowledgement of their admiration for the eccentric Mr H. A six-minute, similar styled blues medley was also recorded during this session.

Live performances: None.

UNRELEASED MATERIAL
Jimmy Page revealed at the time of the third album's release that they had 17 tracks recorded for 'Zeppelin III'. Of the outstanding seven out-takes, four are fairly easy to identify:

'Hey Hey What Can I Do' is an excellent group composition, officially issued as the B-side to 'Immigrant Song' in the US and Europe, and in the UK on a sampler album titled 'The New Age Of Atlantic' in 1972. A warm friendly semi-acoustic groove, recorded at Island Studios in July, 1970.

'Poor Tom' was recorded on June 5, 1970. Later to surface on 'Coda'.

'Down By The Seaside' was written at Bron-Y-Aur. An acoustic version was prepared for the 'Zeppelin III' sessions. It was later recorded for the fourth album and eventually released on 'Physical Graffiti'.

'Bron-Y-Aur' was an acoustic instrumental written at the cottage and recorded at Island studios in August 1970. It was aired live on the US tour the following month and eventually issued in 1975 as part of 'Physical Graffiti'.

Of the remaining out-takes, Page talked about an all-piano piece by John Paul Jones being left over. This may have been an early version of 'No Quarter'. A backing track known as 'Jennings Farm Blues' was also laid down – the tune of which formed the basis of 'Bron-Y-Aur Stomp' – Jennings Farm being the name of Plant's farmhouse home at the time. Jimmy also revealed that 'Hats Off To Roy Harper' had been taken from . . . "a whole tape of us bashing out different blues things." This was a six-minute performance with a similar backing track to 'Hats Off', and featured snippets of 'Feel So Bad', 'Fixing To Die' and 'That's Alright Mama'. An alternative take of 'Since I've Been Loving You' also exists from the late 1969 sessions.

'LED ZEPPELIN FOURTH ALBUM'

Atlantic – original issue 2401 012 , reissued as K 50008.

After 'Led Zeppelin III' received a mixed reception, the group deliberately played down the release of their fourth album. There had been talk of releasing a double set at one time, and Page also had an idea to issue the fourth album as four EPs. In the end they decided on a single album which after the usual delay was finally issued in November 1971.

When it came to a title, instead of the expected 'Led Zeppelin IV', they decided to set a precedent by selecting four sym-

bols, each representing a member of the band, to form the title. Each member chose their own symbol. John Bonham's came from a book of runes and took the form of three linked circles. Said to represent the man-wife-child trilogy, Plant was heard to remark that it resembled the emblem of Ballantine beer! John Paul Jones' came from the same book and is meant to represent confidence and competence. Plant's feather in a circle design was his own, based on the sign of the ancient Mu civilisation. Jimmy Page's mysterious symbol, which has often been mistaken for a word that could be pronounced 'Zoso', was also his own work. The group could hardly have known at the time what lasting imagery these runes would have on their following.

To further throw the media (and the music industry, their fans and everyone else!), the sleeve design was wordless except for a barely decipherable Oxfam poster hanging amidst the urban decay depicted on the front. This cover print was actually bought from a junk shop in Reading by Plant. A tarot card illustration of the Hermit formed the inner gatefold illustration.

As a result of all this mystery, no-one has ever been quite quite sure what to actually call the album, and it has been variously referred to over the years as 'Led Zeppelin IV', 'Untitled', 'Four Symbols', 'Zoso' and 'The Runes'. And since no-one from the Zeppelin camp has ever actually confirmed a title, the mystery is unlikely ever to be solved. Which is exactly what the increasingly mysterious Led Zeppelin wanted!

In the run up to the album's release a series of teaser adverts depicting each symbol was placed in the music press. It did not take their fans too long to associate these mystical images with the album, and, title or no title, the fourth Zeppelin album was an instant massive seller.

It entered the UK chart at number one and stayed on the chart for 62 weeks. In America it remained on the chart longer than any other Zeppelin album, though it failed to knock Carole King's mega-selling 'Tapestry' off the top. Ultimately the fourth Zeppelin album would be the most durable seller in their catalogue and the most impressive critical and commercial success of their career.

'BLACK DOG'
Page, Plant, Jones
Studio: Headley Grange, Hampshire, with The Rolling Stones' Mobile; Island, London.

If 'Zeppelin III' had thrown up doubts in

some corners as to their ability to still flex the power displayed on the first two albums, here was the perfect antidote. The moment Page warms up the Gibsons, this is one of the most instantly recognisable Zepp tracks.

The impossible part of the riff was a Jones input, while the a cappella vocal arrangement, Page would admit years later, was influenced by Fleetwood Mac's 'Oh Well'. The solo is constructed out of four overdubbed Les Paul fills. 'Black Dog' takes its title from a hound that hung around at the Grange. It is held in great esteem by Plant in particular, who would later add snippets of the song into his solo tracks 'Tall Cool One', and 'Your Ma Said She Cried In Her Sleep Last Night'.

Live performances: Joined the set on the UK tour April 1971. Retained for each subsequent tour up to the 1973 US tour. Used as an encore medley with 'Whole Lotta Love' on the 1975 US tour and Earls Court. Recalled to the set for the 1979 Copenhagen/Knebworth dates and Europe 1980 (complete with rare spoken intro from Jimmy).

'ROCK AND ROLL'
Page, Plant, Jones, Bonham
Studio: Headley Grange, with The Rolling Stones' Mobile; Island.

Another instantly identifiable Zeppelin anthem. This track came out of a jam with The Stones' mentor Ian Stewart on piano. Bonzo played the intro of 'Good Golly Miss Molly'/'Keep A Knockin'', and Page added a riff. Fifteen minutes later the nucleus of 'Rock And Roll' was down on tape – displaying the full benefit of recording on location with the tapes ever running.

Live performances: A lasting part of their history, 'Rock And Roll' came in as an encore on the spring 1971 dates. It was inserted into the main set for the US, Japanese, UK and Australian tour schedule of 1971/2. When they revamped the set in late 1972 for the Japan and UK dates it was elevated to the opening number and its opening line – 'It's been a long time since I rock and rolled' – was highly appropriate. It retained this status on every show up to the Earls Court season in 1975. It became a medley encore with 'Whole Lotta Love' in America in 1977. For Knebworth and Europe it was an encore in its own right. Post-Zeppelin, it has enjoyed airings at *Live Aid*, at Hammersmith with Plant and Page in 1988, at Jason Bonham's wedding bash, and The Knebworth Silver Clef reunion.

It has also been a staple of US band Heart's live set.

'THE BATTLE OF EVERMORE'
Page, Plant
Studio: Headley Grange with The Rolling Stones' Mobile; Olympic, London.

The tune for this was written by Page late one night at the Grange while he experimented on Jones' mandolin. Robert came up with a set of lyrics inspired by a book he was reading on the Scottish wars. Sandy Denny was called in to sing the answer lines to Plant's play-ette. Another impressive arrangement.

Live performances: Only ever played live on the 1977 US tour, with John Paul Jones taking on the dual vocal task.

'STAIRWAY TO HEAVEN'
Page, Plant
Studio: Headley Grange with The Rolling Stones' Mobile; Island.

The big one. 'Stairway' started out as a fairly complete chord progression that Page brought in when they commenced recording at Island studios in December 1970. At Headley Grange the song developed around the log fire with Robert composing a set of lyrics full of hippy mysticism that told the tale of a search for spiritual perfection. The song's arrangement with Jones contributing bass-recorder on the intro and Bonzo entering as the track built to a crescendo, came together very quickly. This left Jimmy to add the solo, for which he returned to the Telecaster, back at Island. For the live version he would invest in a custom-made Gibson SG double-neck guitar.

'Stairway To Heaven' was undoubtedly the stand out track on the fourth album, and was well received when they performed it on the UK and US dates prior to the album's release. When they went back to the States in the summer of 1972, Atlantic were naturally keen to issue the track as a single. Grant refused and was to do the same again the next year. The upshot of that decision was that record buyers began to invest in the fourth album as if it were a single.

'Stairway To Heaven' went on to become the most requested song on American radio, and achieve truly classic status worldwide. Far from being a mere rock song, it has become something of a people's favourite, cover version fodder for symphony orchestras and night club singers alike. So well known has the dreamy opening riff become that guitarists trying out guitars in music shops must pay a fine of £5 if they play 'Stairway' in the shop! Alongside songs like 'A Whiter Shade Of Pale' and 'You've Lost That Loving Feeling', it has a pastoral opening cadence that is classical in feel and which has ensured its immortality.

This air of respectability may be the reason why Robert Plant has turned away from the song, declaring it a great song written at the right time for all the right reasons, but now sanctimonious in the extreme. Free from the burden of having to interpret the lyrics, Jimmy Page remains justly proud of the composition, happy to celebrate its legacy as an instrumental live showpiece.

When they sat around that log fire all those years ago, they certainly could never have envisaged the impact 'Stairway To Heaven' would have on their career, nor that the song would become *the* single most requested track on American FM radio for most of the seventies.

Live performances: Premièred at the Ulster Hall, Belfast, on March 5, 1971. Performed at every gig thereafter. Became the closing finale of the set from Brussels in 1975 to Berlin in 1980. Post-Zeppelin airings include the *Live Aid* and Atlantic reunions, plus instrumental versions by Page on the ARMS shows in 1983 and the 'Outrider' tour in 1988.

'MISTY MOUNTAIN HOP'
Page, Plant, Jones
Studio: Headley Grange with The Rolling Stones' Mobile; Olympic, London.

A happy uptempo outing, written and recorded at the Grange, with Jones on electric piano. This is certainly a vintage Zeppelin song of which Plant has not grown tired. He has been more than happy to roll out its nostalgic hippy ideals during the eighties, both on his solo tours, and at reunions with Page and Jones.

Live performances: Joined the set on the European tour in 1971. Used as a link track for 'Since I've Been Loving You' from the Japan tour in 1972 up to the US tour in 1973. Dropped from the set then, but did reappear at the Copenhagen/Knebworth dates. Post-Zeppelin, it has been played by Plant on his solo tours, with Page at the Atlantic reunion, on a guest spot at Hammersmith in 1988, and at the Knebworth Silver Clef show in 1990.

'FOUR STICKS'
Page, Plant
Studio: Headley Grange, with The Rolling Stones' Mobile; Island, London.

A difficult track to record that required many more takes than usual, and so called because Bonzo employed the use of four drum sticks to create the relentless rhythm track. This was one of the tracks they recut with members of the Bombay Symphony Orchestra in 1972. It also features Jones on Moog synthesiser.

Live performances: Only documented live performance is on the 1971 European tour in Copenhagen.

'GOING TO CALIFORNIA'
Page, Plant
Studio: Headley Grange with The Rolling Stones' Mobile; Olympic, London.

Another acoustic beauty with some memorable Plant lyrics, heavily influenced by Joni Mitchell. This started out life as a song about Californian earthquakes and when Jimmy, Andy Johns and Peter Grant travelled to LA to mix the album, lo and behold the mountains did begin to tremble and shake. Then it was known as 'Guide To California'. It also tells of an unrequited search for the ultimate lady. 'It's infinitely hard,' Plant would often ad lib in the live rendition. Some 20 years later he gave an indication that his own search was ongoing, stating, 'Do you know what – it's still hard . . .' during the Knebworth 1990 show.

Live performances: Introduced on the spring UK tour in 1971. Retained for all shows up to the next year's US tour. Returned to the set for Earls Court, and the 1977 US tour. Performed on Plant's solo tours during 1988/89 and at the Knebworth Silver Clef show in 1990.

'WHEN THE LEVEE BREAKS'
Page, Plant, Jones, Bonham, Minnie.
Studio: Headley Grange Hampshire with The Rolling Stones' Mobile; Sunset Sound, Los Angeles.

On June 18, 1929, in New York, Memphis Minnie and Kansas Joe McCoy recorded a blues tune called 'When The Levee Breaks'. Forty years later in leafy Hampshire, Led Zeppelin reconstructed the song to form the spiralling finale of their fourth album. 'Levee' goes down in the annals of Zeppelin history for Bonzo's crushing drum sound performed, according to Page, on a brand new kit that had only just been delivered from the factory. Recorded in the great hall of Headley Grange with just one solitary mike, that sound has become the most sampled drum effect of the hi-tech, production conscious eighties. Alongside that drum sound, Page contributes a rampant bottleneck guitar, while Plant blows a mean mouth harp that cleverly winds it all up in a barrage of backwards echo.

Live performances: Performed only on the opening dates of the 1975 US tour.

UNRELEASED MATERIAL

As with previous albums, these sessions produced a number of left-over tracks. Three of these, 'Boogie With Stu', 'Night Flight' and 'Down By The Seaside' (which had been tried for the third album as an acoustic number), would surface on 'Physical Graffiti'. They also worked on an early incarnation of 'No Quarter' at Headley Grange during this period. It's possible that these fourth album sessions saw the introduction of an acoustic take of 'The Rover'.

'HOUSES OF THE HOLY'
Atlantic K50014

Houses Of The Holy' ushered in the golden middle period of Zeppelin supremacy. By the time of its release on March 26, 1973, Led Zeppelin were unquestionably the most popular live band in America and probably the world.

With The Rolling Stones and The Who they formed a triumvirate of British rock bands who strode the rock concert industry like a colossus.

After the usual long delay due to sleeve problems, 'Houses' tied in nicely with a tour of Europe that was closely followed with a two-legged assault on America. In fact the week the album ascended to the top of the American chart, Led Zeppelin opened their US tour by playing two mammoth dates. In Atlanta they drew 49,000 on May 4, while the next day a staggering 56,800 packed into the Tampa stadium in Florida. This gave them the distinction of attracting the largest audience ever for a single act performance, beating the previous record held by The Beatles for their Shea Stadium show. It was a record that they themselves would top at the Silverdome

Pontiac four years later.

'Houses Of The Holy' had been recorded almost a year previously, and much of the material had been tested on audiences across the US, Japan, the UK and Europe during 1972/3. It was first touted for release early in January, when it was known as 'Led Zeppelin V'. The delays came with the sleeve. This time they chose a collage print depicting a group of children mysteriously scaling the top of a mountain, which, according to Page, denoted the feeling of expectancy for the music contained within. Trouble with the colouring held up release until March, by which time they had settled on their first real album title.

The cover was again completely wordless, though Atlantic did reach something of a compromise by including a title wraparound band with UK and European copies. Despite receiving some decidedly mixed reviews, the album entered the UK chart at number one, while in America, its 39-week run on the *Billboard* Top 40 was their longest since the first album.

Much of the press criticism was levelled at the tongue in cheek nature of tracks such as 'The Crunge' and 'D'yer Mak'er'. Once again they had not travelled down the expected path, and in pleasing themselves they may have not pleased the critics. But their ever increasing following, as the 1973 US tour testified, were still with them every step of the way.

In retrospect, 'Houses Of The Holy' holds its ground with the middle period releases quite admirably. The barnstorming effect of the early era was now levelling off. Though devoid of the electricity of 'Zeppelin I' and 'II', or the sheer diversity of the third album, and lacking the classic status of some of the fourth album, 'Houses' took stock of their situation. In doing so, it laid several foundations on which they would expand their future collective musical aspirations.

'THE SONG REMAINS THE SAME'
Page, Plant
Studio: Stargroves, Berkshire, with The Rolling Stones' Mobile; Olympic, London.

This shimmering Page extravaganza was originally conceived as an instrumental known as 'The Overture'. When Plant added the lyrics, it took on the working title of 'The Campaign'. The finished article is an uplifting barrage of six-stringed picking and chording, over which Plant's slightly speeded-up vocal track chronicles their travels and observes that the common denominator to it all is that if you give, you get back, in fact 'The Song

Remains The Same'. Another track that Jimmy transferred to the Gibson double-neck to play live, in the studio he over-dubs on Telecaster, and a Rickenbacker 12-string. John Paul Jones also puts in some wonderful bass lines.

Live performances: Premièred on the Japanese tour in October 1972. Retained for every live gig up to Earls Court in 1975. This arrangement always dove-tailed into its studio counterpart 'The Rain Song'. From the US tour in 1977 up to the 1979 Copenhagen and Knebworth shows, the track was employed as a suitably vibrant set opener in its own right. It was then rested for the Europe dates.

'THE RAIN SONG'
Page, Plant
Studio: Stargroves with The Rolling Stones' Mobile; Olympic; Electric Lady.

This was one of the new songs for 'Houses' that benefited from the recent installation of a studio console at Jimmy's Plumpton home. He was able to bring in a completed arrangement of the melody for which Robert matched some sensitive lyrics. This track marks the début of the John Paul Jones' one-man orchestra. He layers on a drifting string symphony created by a mellotron, an early sampling keyboard synth. Page plays his Dan Electro guitar here.

Live performances: Came into the set as a dual performance with 'The Song Remains The Same'. Retained in this format on every subsequent tour up to Earls Court in 1975. When 'The Song' became the set opener, 'The Rain Song' was dropped for the 1977 dates. However, it was revived as a solo piece for the Copenhagen, Knebworth and Europe 1979/80 gigs. Another number which required the Gibson double-neck guitar on stage.

'OVER THE HILLS AND FAR AWAY'
Page, Plant
Studio: Stargroves with The Rolling Stones' Mobile; Electric Lady.

Opens with some superbly interwoven acoustic playing, before shifting gear for an electric chorus that finds the Jones/Bonham rhythm bond steadfast as ever. Plant meanwhile waxes hippily about that open road (and that Acapulco gold). A cut that displays all the colour and light of the group's maturing musical landscape.

Live performances: One of the new songs to be introduced on stage way ahead of the album's release. This track came in on the 1972 US trip. Usually employed in the early part of the set to provide Page with a chance to warm up the Gibson, it stayed with them for each tour up to the Copenhagen/Knebworth shows in 1979. Performed by Jimmy on his solo 'Outrider' tour in 1988.

'THE CRUNGE'
Bonham, Jones, Page, Plant
Studio: Stargroves with The Rolling Stones' Mobile; Olympic; Electric Lady.

'The Crunge' came out of a Bonham-inspired spontaneous jam at Stargroves. Jimmy came in with a funk riff (and a chord sequence he'd had kicking around since 1970), stepping on and off the beat, rendering the whole thing completely undanceable. This spurred Robert to come up with a set of lyrics that parodied the James Brown/'take it to the bridge' school of funk mannerisms. With tongue firmly planted in cheek, they named this non-dance cult 'The Crunge' and even thought about illustrating the 'dance steps' on the cover. Maybe the critics would then have seen the joke. Incidentally, that's Jimmy and engineer George Chkianz you can hear talking, just as Bonzo comes in on the intro.

Live performances: Never performed as a track in its own right, 'The Crunge' was incorporated firstly during 'Dazed And Confused' on the 1972 US tour, and more commonly within 'Whole Lotta Love' up to the 1975 dates. It was mainly put in as an ad libbed instrumental though on occasions did receive a full Plant vocal.

'DANCING DAYS'
Page, Plant
Studio: Stargroves with The Rolling Stones' Mobile; Electric Lady.

Built around another classically incessant Page riff, this is a complete joy from start to finish. Plant captures the intended 'good to be alive' vibe with a smiling vocal, as he sings about those lazy hazy summer nights. It comes as no surprise to hear Eddie Kramer's story of them dancing out on the Stargroves lawn during the playback of this track. It summarises the positive atmosphere of the time perfectly.

Live performances: Introduced on the US tour in 1972. Played on the Japan, UK, and Europe dates of 1972/73 but then discarded. Plant did, however, throw in a few lines of this song during the acoustic set on the 1977 US tour.

'D'YER MAK'ER'
Bonham, Jones, Page, Plant
Studio: Stargroves with The Rolling Stones' Mobile; Electric Lady.

Another number constructed out of rehearsals at Stargroves. Bonzo came up with the song's structure, which set out to capture a fifties do-wop feel (hence the Rosie And The Originals sleeve credit). By leaving in a slight off-beat on the tempo, a very subtle reggae influence emerged, which the critics were quick to jump on. Such was the commercial appeal of this track, Robert Plant was supremely keen to issue it as a single in the UK. Atlantic even went as far as distributing advance promo copies to DJ's, but the others did not share Plant's enthusiasm for its release. 'D'yer Mak'er' remained on the album only, its old English music hall joke title destined to confuse our American cousins, while the music profiled Bonzo at his very best.

Live performances: No live performances ever undertaken.

'NO QUARTER'
Jones, Page, Plant
Studio: Stargroves with The Rolling Stones' Mobile; Olympic; Electric Lady.

This brooding Jones creation had been tried a year earlier at Headley Grange. Now slowed down in tempo, and with added synth, bass and piano effects, it took on a dark mysterious texture. It remains one of their foremost achievements. Plant's vocals are superbly treated, while the instrumental passage, where Jones' grand piano merges with Page and Bonham's understated rhythmic touches, is a sequence of high drama and quite breathtaking in its delivery.

Live performances: Not surprisingly this particular journey became a centrepiece of their live shows. Thus from its introduction to the set on the 1973 US tour, it developed into a marathon Jones showcase, played at every show through to Knebworth in 1979. It was deleted from the set on the scaled down Europe shows of 1980. Plant reintroduced the number to his 'Manic Nirvana' tour in 1990. The arrangement on this occasion, however, did not remain the same.

'THE OCEAN'
Bonham, Jones, Page, Plant
Studio: Stargroves with The Rolling Stones' Mobile; Olympic; Electric Lady.

'We've done four already but now we're steady and then they went . . .' John Bonham's thick Midlands accent rings in this delightful closing rocker. Just as the title of the song had been a Plant metaphor for the sea of heads he faced in the auditoriums they were now filling, 'The Ocean' refers to Zeppelin's ever growing and ever faithful army of fans. 'Has the ocean lost its way, I don't think so,' he reflects, going on to explain his devotion to baby Carmen ('She is only three-years-old').

Page and Co meanwhile strut out another memorable riff that would later inspire a few thousand sales of Beastie Boys albums. The closing do-wop finale is a further joy. 'So good!' shouts Plant and he's so right.

Live performances: This high energy outing came into the set as an encore during the UK tour dates of 1973. It was further employed on the European trek in the spring, and the summer tour of the US. Deleted thereafter. During Plant's solo tours samples of the track and the 'la-la-la-la-la-la' chorus were inserted into 'Tall Cool One'.

UNRELEASED MATERIAL

Four numbers are known to have been left over from the fifth album sessions. The title track itself, as recorded at Olympic, and 'Black Country Woman' from a Stargroves session recorded out in the garden emerged later on 'Physical Graffiti'. 'Walter's Walk', also from Stargroves, eventually surfaced on 'Coda'. That leaves a number known as 'Slush', worked on at Olympic in May 1972, still remaining in the can.

'PHYSICAL GRAFFITI'
Swan Song SSK 89400

For their inaugural Swan Song release, Led Zeppelin finally succumbed to the double album format. A combination of new material recorded early in 1974 at Headley Grange, coupled with a summary of strong material from previous sessions, made up the contents of this blockbuster release.

The sleeve design is one of their most elaborate. The front cover depicts a New

York tenement block (actual location: 96 St. Marks, NYC), through which inter-changing window illustrations reveal such candid shots as the group dressed in drag, and Bonzo in tights for the Roy Harper St. Valentines Day gig.

The title 'Physical Graffiti' was coined by Page to illustrate the whole physical and written energy that had gone into pro-ducing the set. The release date was timed to coincide with their 1975 tour campaign which commenced in America in January. Minor delays kept it from appearing until late February. When it did appear the demand was staggering.

'Physical Graffiti' made what had by now become Led Zeppelin's customary entry at number one on the UK chart, while America just went 'Graffiti' mad. It entered every US chart at number three, a then record for a new entry, before lodg-ing itself at the top for six weeks. Even more remarkable was the fact all five pre-vious Zepp albums returned to the *Billboard* chart. No other rock act had ever been so well represented.

It had been two years since their last album, but the waiting had been worth it. Led Zeppelin had delivered. It still stands as their finest recorded achievement. Given the luxury of the double format, 'Physical Graffiti' mirrors every facet of the Zeppelin repertoire. The end result is a finely balanced embarrassment of riches. Through light and shade, from a whisper to a scream, this one has it all.

'CUSTARD PIE'
Page, Plant
Studio: Headley Grange with Ronnie Lane's Mobile; Olympic.

One of the belters from Headley Grange, 'Custard Pie' is a prime knockabout rocker with a vintage Page riff, finely undercut by J.P. on clavinet. Plant delves back to the Bukka White songbook for the 'Shake 'em on down' refrain, throwing in a bluesy mouth harp to aid the effect. Page filters a piercing solo through an ARP synthesiser, and it all dances off to a pleasing fade. 'Drop down!' squeals Plant and Bonzo duly obliges with a typically robust attack on the bass drum.

Live performances: Although rehearsed for the 1975 set, 'Custard Pie' never received a public Zeppelin airing. Years later, Plant would redress the balance by incorporat-ing a chorus of the song on the end of the live version of 'Tall Cool One'. Page also produced his own live version on the 'Outrider' tour during the same year. It was also performed at the Jason Bonham wedding reunion in 1990.

'THE ROVER'
Page, Plant
Studio: Stargroves, Berkshire, with The Rolling Stones' Mobile; Olympic.

A track that dates back to 1970, 'The Rover' was rehearsed as an acoustic blues piece before being recorded at Stargroves with Eddie Kramer for the fifth album. When it didn't make the final 'Houses Of The Holy' selection, Page returned to it in 1974, overdubbing and re-mixing the basic track with Keith Harwood. The curious 'Guitar lost courtesy Nevison. Sal-vaged by the grace of Harwood' sleeve credit would appear to be a reference to certain mixing difficulties they may have had here – Nevison being engineer Ron Nevison.

'The Rover' possesses a stirring melodic base, from which Plant waxes ide-alistically about the need for solidarity, and Page strings together one of his most perfectly constructed solos.

Live performances: Another track rehearsed for live performance but never performed in its entirety. A snippet of the riff, which testifies to its vintage, did appear within a 'Whole Lotta Love' medley on the Australian tour of 1972, and the opening riff part was employed as a link between 'The Song Remains The Same' and 'Sick Again' on the 1977 US tour.

'IN MY TIME OF DYING'
Bonham, Jones, Page, Plant
Studio: Headley Grange with Ronnie Lane's Mobile, Olympic.

A traditional song that can be found on Bob Dylan's first album, Zeppelin's arrangement came together during the initial sixth album sessions in 1974. As well as containing one of the most power-ful drum sounds ever committed to tape, the point where Page straps in for a peer-less bottleneck frenzy backed by Jonesy and Bonzo at the nerve centre, has to be one of the most scintillating moments in the whole of the Zeppelin catalogue. The intensity is quite frightening. It eventually winds down via a studio cough from Bonzo. ''That's gotta be the one hasn't it?'' inquires the drummer from behind the screens. Indeed it was . . .

Live performances: Brought in to the revamped set for all their 1975 dates and used again on some of the 1977 US tour where it was alternated with 'Over The Hills And Far Away'. It was a number that Plant was unsure of performing after his 1975 car crash, due to its fatalistic lyri-cal theme. Also performed by Page on his solo 'Outrider' tour.

'HOUSES OF THE HOLY'
Page, Plant
Studio: Olympic; Electric Lady.

Another fifth album overspill, this title track was recalled for the double set and required no further re-mixing, having been tied up by Eddie Kramer as far back as the Electric Lady sessions in June 1972. A strident mid-tempo exercise with the same smiling friendliness in its grooves as can be heard on 'Dancing Days'. This sim-ilarity may have accounted for its absence on the 'Houses Of The Holy' album.

Live performances: Never performed live.

'TRAMPLED UNDERFOOT'
Jones, Page, Plant
Studio: Headley Grange with Ronnie Lane's Mobile; Olympic.

Much rehearsal went into perfecting the semi-funk riff that dominates this driving tale of the motor car and its relation with the sexual act. Jones's clavinet and Jimmy's wah-wah and backwards echo make for a formidable partnership. Plant's vocals are a little too back in the mix (a characteristic of most of the Headley Grange tracks) but not enough to dim the overall incessant effect, which remains quite irresistible.

Special UK singles of this track were pressed for promotional purposes in time for the Earls Court shows.

Live performances: Another Zeppelin con-cert showpiece, this track was played on every live show from 1975 through to the last gig in Berlin in 1980. For some of the 1977 US shows it became an encore num-ber. In 1988 it was revived by Plant for his 'Now And Zen' tour, including a memor-able performance with Jimmy at Hammersmith in April.

'KASHMIR'
Bonham, Page, Plant
Studio: Headley Grange with Ronnie Lane's Mobile; Olympic.

This particular epic grew out of a Page/ Bonham demo recorded late in 1973. Robert wrote the lyrics while holidaying in South Morocco immediately after the 1973 US tour. When it came to recording in early 1974, J.P. scored a suitable East-ern string arrangement. Kashmir's real beauty of course, lies in Page's Moorish chord riff that carries the song towards those desert wastelands. There is an eth-ereal, slightly discordant and somewhat eerie quality to this music that hints at the mysteries of the East and seems derived from musical signatures not normally found in the standard Western scale. Page has revealed that outside session musi-cians were brought in to add strings and horns, a rare occurrence on a Zeppelin session.

Unquestionably the most 'startling and impressive track on 'Physical Graffiti', 'Kashmir' went a long way towards establishing Led Zeppelin's credibility with otherwise sceptical rock critics. Many would regard this track as the finest example of the sheer majesty of the Zeppelin chemistry.

Live performances: Made its début in Rotterdam on January 11, 1975. Performed on every subsequent gig right up to the final show in Berlin on July 7, 1980. From the 1977 US dates onwards, 'Kashmir' led out of Jimmy's 'White Summer'/'Black Mountain Side' solo spot, for which he switched to playing a Dan Electro guitar. Post-Zeppelin, it was aired at the Atlantic Records 21st birthday celebrations at Madison Square Garden.

Jimmy also slotted in a few riffs of this epic during the 'Moonlight Midnight' medley on his 'Outrider' tour.

'IN THE LIGHT'
Jones, Page, Plant
Studio: Headley Grange with Ronnie Lane's Mobile; Olympic.

'In The Light' grew out of a similar-styled rehearsal number known as 'In The Morning'. Opening with a drone-like keyboard effect from Jonesy, the track travels down more than one tempo change, as Robert sings with much passion about the need for eternal optimism. The fade out is another wonderful example of the interplay enjoyed by Jimmy and Bonzo, as a mass of overdubbed guitar parts filter round some exemplary percussion. More than enough reason for Jimmy to select this number as his favourite of the whole album.

Live performances: Surprisingly enough this was never attempted live. It was, however, used as an intro link to 'Nobody's Fault But Mine' on some of Plant's 'Now And Zen' American shows in 1988.

'BRON-Y-AUR'
Page
Studio: Island, London; Olympic.

A short winsome acoustic solo, written and tried for 'Zeppelin III'. Later to appear as a background segment in *The Song Remains The Same* movie.

Live performances: Briefly part of the acoustic set on the sixth American tour August/September 1970.

'DOWN BY THE SEASIDE'
Page, Plant
Studio: Island; Olympic.

Another song written at Bron-Y-Aur in the Spring of 1970. Originally conceived as a Neil Young-influenced acoustic strum-along (with Robert playing guitar), this electric arrangement was recorded at the time of the fourth album sessions. It features some lovely electric piano, a sensitive Plant vocal, and an unexpected rise in tempo half way through. The manner in which Page and Bonham turn away from the tranquil landscape of the song to take it all up a gear, and then slip back to the original lilting theme with effortless ease, is a master-stroke of controlled dynamics.

Live performances: Never performed live.

'TEN YEARS GONE'
Page, Plant
Studio: Headley Grange with Ronnie Lane's Mobile; Olympic.

A moving Plant narrative about an age old love affair that still digs deep. The emotional content of this piece is further emphasised by the subtle Page embellishments that colour the song. A series of overdubbed guitar parts, all in perfect harmony, hint at the original intention of this track being an instrumental tour-de-force. As it turned out, it stands as one of their finest arrangements.

Live performances: Brought in for the 1977 US tour, where it required John Paul Jones to play a special three-necked guitar that encompassed bass pedals, mandolin and six and 12-stringed acoustics. Played again at the Copenhagen warm-up shows and the August 4 Knebworth show in 1979. The problems encountered in setting up Jones' multi-faceted instrument, probably accounted for its omission at the following week's concert.

'NIGHT FLIGHT'
Jones, Page, Plant
Studio: Headley Grange with The Rolling Stones' Mobile, Olympic.

A bright rollercoaster rocker from the sessions at Headley Grange for the fourth album. Robert and Bonzo are on dazzling form here. Plant's strident vocals are crystal clear and supported by some turbulent drumming. Page meanwhile, puts in some swirling Leslied guitar, playing off a warm organ sound supplied by J.P.

Live performances: A recording of this number has emerged on a soundcheck tape, but no live performances have been logged.

'THE WANTON SONG'
Page, Plant Studio: Headley Grange with Ronnie Lane's Mobile, Olympic.

'The Wanton Song' is a thrusting Plant tale of carnal delights, ably supported by a devastatingly simple but quite brilliant Page riff that grinds the listener into submission. It must also be noted that Jones and Bonham back up this barrage with equal panache. A reassuringly tough product of the sixth album sessions of early 1974.

Live performances: Played on the opening dates of the 1975 US tour then dropped completely.

'BOOGIE WITH STU'
Bonham, Jones, Page, Plant, Stewart, Mrs Valens
Studio: Headley Grange with The Rolling Stones' Mobile; Olympic.

A loose jam recorded at the same sessions that produced 'Rock And Roll' for the fourth album. This has Ian Stewart, The Rolling Stones' tour manager and resident boogie-woogie specialist, playing barrel-house piano. Heavily based on Richie Valens' fifties hit 'Ooh My Head' (check out the *La Bamba* movie), hence the credit to his widow.

Live performances: Never performed live.

'BLACK COUNTRY WOMAN'
Page, Plant
Studio: The garden at Stargroves with The Rolling Stones' Mobile, Olympic.

Ever on the lookout for off-the-wall recording locations (Plant once tried to record some vocals out in the quadrangle of Headley Grange and had to flee from a gaggle of geese that attacked him!), the boys took to the garden of Stargroves for this session in the spring of 1972. The resulting take was nearly shelved when a plane cruised overhead, but as the opening dialogue reveals, it was all captured for posterity. Prior to release 'Black Country Woman' was sub-titled 'Never Ending Doubting Woman Blues'. This was a reference to a final spoken tag left off the finished version which had Robert proclaiming 'What's the matter with you mama, never ending, nagging, doubting woman blues.'

Live performances: This was performed at one show at least in America in 1972. It was then merged into a medley with 'Bron-Y-Aur Stomp' for the 1977 US dates.

'SICK AGAIN'
Page, Plant
Studio: Headley Grange with Ronnie Lane's Mobile, Olympic.

And finally . . . a mid-tempo rocker based on Plant's still vivid tales of the 1973 US tour and the ladies that surrounded them. It's powered by a series of meandering Page runs and some ferocious Bonham hammering that assist in conjuring up the required images. Juicy and muscular and inevitably tight but loose, 'Sick Again' is a fitting exit. Listen carefully and you can hear Bonzo coughing out loud after Page's suitably sonic finale.

Live performances: Held the distinction of being the second number performed on all the 1975 and 1977 tour dates. On the 1977 tour it was preceded by a link from 'The Rover'. Returned to a spot later in the set for the Copenhagen/Knebworth shows in 1979.

UNRELEASED MATERIAL

With such an outpouring of material, it seems unlikely that much was left in the can from the original sixth album sessions at Headley Grange. From the rehearsal tapes that have surfaced, the genesis of 'In The Light' can be found in a composition called 'In The Morning'. 'Custard Pie' appears in a radically different structure and a riff-worked jam, carries the same chord changes as the later 'Hots On For Nowhere'.

'PRESENCE'
Swan Song SSK 59402

And suddenly there was 'Presence'. Forced by Robert Plant's car smash to cancel a projected world tour due to commence on August 23, 1975, the group wisely used this period of convalescence to write and record a new album.

The seeds of this album began to grow when Page joined Plant recuperating in Malibu (a situation that explains why most of the album consists solely of Page/Plant compositions). Robert had already written some reflective lyrics and coupled with Page's input, these fragments of songs were soon under rehearsal as Jones and Bonham flew over for pre-production sessions at Hollywood's SIR rehearsal studios. After a month of rehearsals, the group were anxious to record. Musicland studios in Munich (a favourite Page haunt) was their next destination. In the

fastest time since the first album, seven tracks were laid down in a period of just three weeks.

The album was completed on November 27, the day before Thanksgiving. In a call to Swan Song the next day, an ecstatic Plant suggested the album be named 'Thanksgiving'. As it turned out, meetings with sleeve designers Hipgnosis dictated otherwise. Telling Page of the incredibly powerful force and presence they felt surrounded the group, he briefed them to come up with a sleeve that displayed this fact. The bizarre result, a series of *Life* magazine prints of everyday events, mostly involving conservative-looking families, interrupted by the 'presence' in the form of a mysterious black obelisk (The Object), confused both media and enthusiasts alike. At one stage the plan was to dub the album 'Obelisk'. Page held out for 'Presence'.

As ever, the sleeve caused delays, and it was eventually released in early April 1976. The promotion for the album centred around The Object, the weird obelisk depicted on the cover. In Britain it attained one of the highest ever advance orders, shipping gold on the day of release. In America it leapt from 24 to number one inside two weeks.

Long term, 'Presence' was not one of Zeppelin's biggest sellers. It was somewhat overshadowed by the late 1976 release of their movie and soundtrack. It has since become a much underrated part of their catalogue. The basic drums-bass-guitars formula may lack the diversity of previous Zeppelin sets, but in terms of sheer energy, 'Presence' packs a considerable punch, and has emerged as one of their most potent performances.

This album is also a triumph for Jimmy Page. His production and dominant guitar style has an urgency and passion that reflects the troubled period that the group were going through at the time. 'Presence' is Led Zeppelin with their backs against the wall. As Page once put it, "We started screaming in rehearsals and never stopped."

'ACHILLES LAST STAND'
Page, Plant
Studio: Musicland, Munich.

'Achilles Last Stand' is a glorious 10-minute opening salvo that finds all the musicians pushing their talents to the limit. John Bonham's drumming is at once both explosive and inventive, driven along by an irresistible chugging Jones bass line. All this acts as a perfect lynchpin for Page to weave his magic. His

playing, constantly overdubbed, is simply magnificent, scaling the song's basic two-pronged structure with amazing dexterity. Robert meanwhile unravels a bizarre tale inspired by his and Page's travels across Africa immediately after the Earls Court shows. With its theme of movement, meeting and positive outlook, his lyrics act as a perfect foil for the relentless pace of the track.

'Achilles Last Stand' is an absolutely crucial performance and one that remains as vital today as it did when it took shape inside Musicland back in 1975. A definitive Led Zeppelin yardstick.

Live performances: The first number to be rehearsed when they regrouped in late 1976 for the 1977 US tour. 'Achilles' held its place in the set through 1977, Copenhagen and Knebworth 1979 and right up to the last night of the 'Over Europe' tour. Strangely it was omitted from what was to be their final show in Berlin. Page expected to use the Gibson double-neck when it came to performing this epic live, but found it worked fine with just the Gibson Les Paul, or as employed at Knebworth 1, the red Telecaster.

'FOR YOUR LIFE'
Page, Plant
Studio: Musicland.

Much to admire here both lyrically and musically. Built on a grinding penetrating riff, it finds Plant in understandably reflective mood. 'In the pits you go no lower, the next stop's underground,' he observes, a phrase that hints at this composition's Malibu period origin. Much of the basic track was created inside Musicland. The cutting solo that Page plays marks the recorded début of a new part of his guitar army – a 1962 Lake Placid blue Fender Stratocaster (supplied by ex-Byrd Gene Parsons) later to be employed on stage during 1979/80 and with The Firm.

Not instantly appealing, 'For Your Life' seeps into the consciousness with repeated hearings.

Live performances: Never performed live.

'ROYAL ORLEANS'
Bonham, Jones, Page, Plant
Studio: Musicland.

Royal Orleans is the name of a hotel in New Orleans often favoured by the group in their touring heyday and the setting of this humorous 'road fever' lament. It tells the tale of 'a man I know' (whose initials were rumoured to be J.P.J.) whose association with the local clientèle provided something of a surprise.

Listen carefully at the end for a great reference to that old soul-swayer Barry White. All this is played out against a short, sharp riff injection, from which Page throws in some funky lines and Bonzo takes to the bongos.

'Royal Orleans'' 'road fever' lyrical content would suggest it was a composition that Plant had written some time previous to this period.

Live performances: Never performed live.

'NOBODY'S FAULT BUT MINE'
Page, Plant
Studio: Musicland.

A full-blooded blues/rock stomper that opens with some suitable sonic embellishments from Jimmy. The upfront preenings of Page and Plant are duly supported on the flanks by some steadfast rhythm work by J.P. and Bonzo, who handle the stop-go interludes with masterful restraint. Plant blows a mean harmonica before yet another stirring Page onslaught. All in all, a great throwback to some earlier blues-inspired performances. The Page/Plant credit here is a little misleading as Blind Willie Johnson may well have been under the impression that he wrote the lyrics back in 1928, a fact Robert acknowledged when introducing the track on stage in Copenhagen in 1979.

Live performances: A welcome addition to the set on the 1977 US tour. It remained a stage favourite through to the Copenhagen, Knebworth and Europe dates in 1979/80. It was also revived by Plant for his solo tours in 1988 and 1990.

'CANDY STORE ROCK'
Page, Plant
Studio: Musicland.

A basic fifties-flavoured rock 'n' roll groove strung along by some Scotty Moore guitar figures from Page. Heavily echoed Plant vocal, upfront bass from J.P. and plenty of timpani in the percussion department add to a pleasant, if rather slight, offering.

Live performances: Never performed live.

'HOTS ON FOR NOWHERE'
Page, Plant
Studio: Musicland.

Light and airy and vaguely swingish, 'Hots On For Nowhere' delights in its off-the-wall quirkiness. Plant unfolds more tales from Malibu, taking a swing at his close friends in the process, throwing in plenty of 'oohs' and 'ahs' for good measure. Page meanwhile makes full use of the tremolo arm on the new blue Strat, as he pulls out a ridiculous twang in the middle of a delightful solo. From the moment Plant shouts, 'Oh, I lost my way home!' Bonzo roars in with some decora-

tive fills, and Page takes it all out on a blistering babble of notes. Friendly.

Live performances: Never performed live.

'TEA FOR ONE'
Page, Plant
Studio: Musicland.

A relaxed blues winds up the proceedings. Lyrically Robert reflects on the post-accident period when he was separated from his wife Maureen. 'Tea For One' definitely tries to recapture the spirit of their earlier, self-penned blues epic 'Since I've Been Loving You'. Unfortunately it never matches that number for excitement. The solo is adequately applied in the expected tradition, but cannot hide the fact that the song itself is a trifle dull. A low key exit.

Live performances: Never performed live.
NB: The lack of live interpretations of the 'Presence' material is quite striking; however, given that it was to be a full year before they returned to the road, perhaps understandable. Had they been able to tour off the back of its release, we may well have enjoyed live takes of 'Candy Store Rock' etc.

UNRELEASED MATERIAL
No details of surplus 'Presence' material being left in the can have emerged. It would be safe to assume that given only three weeks' studio time, little other than what was released was actually recorded.

SOUNDTRACK
FROM THE FILM
THE SONG REMAINS THE SAME
Swan Song 89402

ithin six months there was another Zeppelin album in the shops, the soundtrack album to their much maligned feature film.

There had been previous attempts to produce a Led Zeppelin movie before *The*

Song Remains The Same. Back in 1970, footage from gigs at the Albert Hall, the spring US tour and a trip to Iceland in June were professionally filmed at the request of manager Peter Grant with a view to assembling an hour-long special for TV distribution. Filming in Japan the next year also took place, but the project never materialised.

The story then shifts to May 1973. Film maker Joe Massot approached Jimmy and Peter during the group's mid-tour break with a view to shooting their return leg. The offer was turned down by Grant who told Massot they had plans to make their own film with a famous director.

However, at the tail end of the two-legged, hugely successful American trip, they changed their minds. A call went out from Grant to Joe Massot on July 14. Massot and crew flew over and filmed various backstage shots, screen tested the stage act at gigs in Baltimore and Pittsburgh and then filmed all three of their Madison Square Garden dates on July 27, 28 and 29. These shows were recorded by Eddie Kramer and formed the basis of the resulting soundtrack album. (All the tracks were later mixed down at Electric Lady In New York and Trident Studios in London.)

Coming at the end of a gruelling tour, these particular performances were hardly magic nights. However, as this was the music that matched the footage, it had to be made available.

There had been plans to shoot some more film on the aborted world tour of 1975/76. After Robert's accident, though, with short term plans for live gigs an impossibility, Page used this period of inactivity to tie up the movie and soundtrack, using the footage shot with Joe Massot and employing Peter Clifton to arrange the technical aspects. The movie poster and sleeve design depicted a run down picture house, which was based on Old Street studios, a London rehearsal theatre they used to perfect the 1973 US stage act prior to the tour.

The film was premièred in New York on October 21, with the album hitting the stores the next day. It reached number one in the UK but had to settle for second place in the States. The film went on to be a staple diet of late night movie houses for years to come, and its subsequent issue on video in 1984 has provided a whole new generation of fans with a front row seat on Led Zeppelin.

It has to be said, though, that it's only an adequate representation. Visually and musically their live shows after 1973 were much more spectacular. It is a great shame that there is no official visual record of Earls Court, the US 1977 tour or Knebworth. All these shows were filmed for the group and remain in the archives. Having been privileged enough to have seen these video tapes, I can endorse the fact that they capture the magic of the live Led Zeppelin far better than the official *The Song Remains The Same* movie.

Much the same can be said of the resulting soundtrack album. Keen collectors will know of far better material that has surfaced unofficially. In retrospect, performances such as 'Moby Dick' and 'Dazed And Confused' sound somewhat lack-lustre, and the whole question of the actual track listing still baffles. Why, for instance, does 'Celebration Day' appear on the soundtrack album but is nowhere to be seen (or heard) in the film? How come sizzling filmed performances of 'Since I've Been Loving You' and 'Heartbreaker' were somehow left off the album?

These anomalies all point to the fact that, as Page admitted at the time, *The Song Remains The Same* movie and soundtrack proved to be a rare Led Zeppelin compromise.

Studio: all live material recorded at Madison Square Garden, New York, July 27, 28 and 29, 1973. Mixed at Electric Lady, New York, and Trident, London.

'ROCK AND ROLL'
Bonham, Jones, Page, Plant

A fine opening gambit. For the live version Plant sings in a lower key and Page duck walks into the solo. Vibrant.

'CELEBRATION DAY'
Jones, Page, Plant

In the movie, 'Rock And Roll' is edited into 'Black Dog'. The album, however, has the authentic link into 'Celebration Day'. Strangely edited out of the film, this underrated stage number sounds spot on. Jimmy is particularly impressive weaving a cluster of notes towards the outro. Revives memories of its Knebworth airing.

'THE SONG REMAINS THE SAME'
Page, Plant

An excellent live take with Page switching to the double-neck. In the film, it accompanies Plant's Arthurian fantasy sequence, snippets of which he would later use as a backdrop to 'Immigrant Song' on his 1990 solo tour.

'THE RAIN SONG'
Page, Plant

Dovetails from 'The Song Remains The Same' as was the custom during this era. This version includes some delicate Page strumming and precise Bonham dynamics. At times, though, the mellotron quivers a little unsteadily.

'DAZED AND CONFUSED'
Page

Stripped of the on-stage visuals, this marathon loses its appeal somewhat. There are some high spots, the San Francisco sequence, the bow interlude with its stereo panning and the guitar-vocal interplay. Elsewhere it becomes excessive and lumbering.

'NO QUARTER'
Jones, Page, Plant

The album's standout performance. Everything works perfectly here, from Jones' revolving opening through to a simply divine Page solo. A slightly different version appears in the film.

'STAIRWAY TO HEAVEN'
Page, Plant

'Stairway' had yet to take on truly epic proportions during this era, and it followed 'Dazed And Confused' in the set. Such was the excitement of that number, the audience often drowned out the intro to 'Stairway'. Madison Square Garden was one such venue. Though the album version gives little away, the live outtakes reveal Plant trying to settle the audience down. The intro link retained for the album has Plant saying "This is a song of hope." It edits out his next line "And it's a very quiet song . . . so shurrup!"

'MOBY DICK'
Bonham, Jones, Plant

Another track that loses most of its impact without the visual footage. In the movie it makes a perfect accompaniment to Bonzo's profile. On record it goes on much too long. A far better proposal here would have been to insert the 'Heartbreaker' segment that precedes 'Whole Lotta Love' in the film, run through to the 'Whole Lotta Love' track and then add 'The Ocean' as an encore. Both these tracks were left on the splicing block.

'WHOLE LOTTA LOVE'
Bonham, Jones, Page, Plant

In the film, as in all the shows on the tour, 'Whole Lotta Love' segued in from 'Heartbreaker'. Here it's edited to appear as a track in its own right. Complete with Jimmy on vocals, 'The Crunge' sequence, the theramin attack, and 'Let That Boy

Woogie', it sustains the interest. A live version of the revamped arrangement they played at Knebworth would be most welcome.

UNRELEASED MATERIAL

The following tracks appear in the film but not on record: 'Black Dog', 'Since I've Been Loving You' and 'Heartbreaker'. Jimmy's solo piece from 'Physical Graffiti', 'Bron-Y-Aur', is also heard in the film. Another number, copyrighted as 'Autumn Lake', is played on a hurdy gurdy by Page in an early pre-concert sequence.

Other songs known to have been aired at the Madison Square Garden gigs and likely to have been recorded and filmed are: 'Over The Hills And Far Away', 'Misty Mountain Hop', 'The Ocean', 'Communication Breakdown' and 'Thank You'. 'The Ocean' has surfaced on an outtake film track unofficial tape that also has the 'Heartbreaker'/'Whole Lotta Love' sequence and alternate takes of 'Stairway To Heaven' and 'Moby Dick'.

'IN THROUGH THE OUT DOOR'
Swan Song 59410

After a two-year absence, dictated by the tragic death of Robert Plant's young son Karac from a stomach infection, Led Zeppelin finally became active again. This album was recorded at the tail end of 1978 at Abba's Polar Music studio in Stockholm. The mixing was wrapped up with further sessions in early 1979. There had been talk of a European tour slated for around February. Ultimately they decided to dispense with any conventional gigging (perhaps erroneously), and return to the concert platform in the grandest possible fashion:

two shows in August 1979 at the open air Knebworth festival, estimated capacity 300,000 plus.

The completed album, rumoured in some circles to be titled 'Look', was held back from release to coincide with the Knebworth shows. In a rare lapse of marketing strategy, the album missed the concert deadline, appearing a week after Knebworth on August 20. Not that it made a scrap of difference. The record, eventually titled 'In Through The Out Door' because, as Jimmy put it, "That's the hardest way to get back in," was rapturously received around the world. It made number one in the UK in its first week and number one in America in its second. It also instantly topped the charts in Japan, New Zealand, Australia and Germany. In the first 10 days of release its sales topped two million.

It was in America though, that the real sales phenomena occurred. Its release was heralded as a saviour to the then flagging US record industry. It generated massive store traffic as it held the top spot for seven weeks. Even more remarkable was the renewed demand for previous Zepp albums. Atlantic shifted a staggering one million back catalogue albums during September 1979, a situation that resulted in Led Zeppelin's entire catalogue appearing on the *Billboard* Top 200 during the weeks of October 27 and November 3. This beat the previous record for most albums on the chart set in 1975 held by . . . you guessed it, Led Zeppelin.

What made these figures all the more staggering was that during Led Zeppelin's absence from the music scene during the previous two years punk rock had emerged, and a central philosophy of punk was its contrary stance to – and general loathing of – massively popular 'stadium' bands like Led Zeppelin who, it was claimed, were now redundant in the new era. These claims were taken up by newly appointed, young and somewhat hawkish staff at the various UK music magazines, all of which claimed to be arbiters of taste in rock. Such claims might have been fashionable but they were as preposterous as they were premature: it was Led Zeppelin – not the punks – who sold the most records in the new era, just as they had in the old. (It was also Led Zeppelin who won the annual readers' polls in these magazines, much to the chagrin of the editorial staff who championed punk!)

Then there was the album's sleeve. Easily

their most ambitious to date, the brief to Hipgnosis was simple enough. They all felt the album to be fresh, new and direct. The album sleeve was to indicate just that. Designer Aubrey Powell felt some of the music had a barrel-house, bayou bar, late night blues feel to it. On Page's suggestion, he worked on a bar room scene, travelling to New Orleans to gain some reference. (Some reports indicate the bar as being the Old Absinthe Bar at 400 Bourbon Street, just around the corner from the Royal Orleans hotel.)

On his return, the Hipgnosis team built a New Orleans bar room scene at Shepperton studios, shooting six different scenes. These sepia toned photos formed the six alternate sleeves that were issued, each one depicting the view from the six characters in the scene. To indicate that freshness, or a new lick of paint as Powell described it, an area was wiped clean on each print. This outer stroke led Jimmy to request that the inner bag be prepared in such a way that it would colour when applied with water.

Finally Peter Grant insisted all the sleeves be shrink wrapped into a brown paper bag so that no buyer would know which sleeve he would be receiving, and also to prove that you could stuff a Led Zepp album into a paper bag and it would still sell! And of course it did.

Musically, 'In Through The Out Door' is dominated by John Paul Jones. His influence is stronger than ever before. Disappointingly, the album suffers from a less than crystal clear production, and in hindsight, did posses more than its quota of filler material. Still, what's good is very good indeed, and at the time was indication enough to suggest that Led Zeppelin were ready to enter the new decade with as much enthusiasm as they had entered the seventies.

'IN THE EVENING'
Jones, Page, Plant
Studio: Polar Music, Stockholm; Plumpton, Sussex.

To illustrate the feeling of rebirth, Page pulls out the old violin bow to create a dramatic opening segment (reminiscent of his work on the soundtrack of Kenneth Anger's *Lucifer Rising*). From there on, this is a very satisfying flexing of the muscles.

Plant's arrogant strutting vocal is undercut by a majestic cascading riff that ricochets off every wall. When the whole thing slows up momentarily, some shimmering minor chords and fluid bass take control. Then it's headlong into a powerful fade. A performance that pushed its

chest out as if to say . . . take that! Clearly Led Zeppelin still had . . . it.

Live performances: Premièred at the Copenhagen shows, and in for Knebworth where it stood out as a stunning new creation, entering the set for Page's visual violin bow segment. Also used on the 'Over Europe' 1980 tour. Page played the string-bending blue Strat on this track. Plant then revived the number to great effect on his 'Now And Zen' solo tour in 1988.

'SOUTH BOUND SUAREZ'
Jones, Plant
Studio: Polar Music; Plumpton.

With it's rollicking piano intro, this is a track that conjures up the Louisiana/New Orleans bar room feel of the sleeve. Plant's vocals are somewhat strained and overall the only redeeming feature of a rather lack-lustre outing is a measured Page solo and the do-wop fade out.

Live performances: Never performed live.

'FOOL IN THE RAIN'
Jones, Page, Plant
Studio: Polar Music.

During the summer of 1978, the World Cup was played out in Argentina against a variety of samba-inspired TV soccer themes. Those South American themes were still ringing in the ears of Plant and Jones when Led Zeppelin reconvened to plan this album. Thus the idea emerged to layer on their own samba half way through the hop-skip riff arrangement of this tune. Crazy as it sounds, it works beautifully right through J.P.'s street whistles to Bonzo's delightfully constructed timpani crashes. Back at mid-tempo, Jimmy puts in a quite exquisite solo. A most successful alliance that grew out of Plant's insistence that new territory had to be investigated if they were to sustain his own personal commitment. A point thrashed out at their rehearsal sessions at Clearwell Castle in May of 1978.

'Fool In The Rain' became their sixth US Top 40 hit when it reached number 21 in January 1980.

Live performances: Never performed live.

'HOT DOG'
Page, Plant
Studio: Polar Music.

'Hot Dog' owes much to the state of Texas and to the state of a particular female in Texas. Musically it grew out of their London pre-production rehearsals, where as usual they began by running through old Elvis Presley and Ricky Nelson material from the fifties. A rockabilly country hoe-down, it was obviously great fun to record and did develop into a crowd pleaser on the European tour (though it sounded a little mystifying on its Knebworth première). On record though, time has not been to kind it, and as for that solo . . . are you putting us on J. Page?

Live performances: Brought in for Copenhagen and Knebworth and retained for all the 1980 'Over Europe' dates. An official promo video of this track filmed at Knebworth, was made available by Swan Song to the record industry in America.

'CAROUSELAMBRA'
Jones, Page, Plant
Studio: Polar Music.

The epic. Driven along relentlessly by Jones' keyboard thrusts, 'Carouselambra' is a typically grandiose Zeppelin marathon. This is one of the only tracks cut in the studio that employs the Gibson double-neck guitar, which can be heard to great effect by Page during the slower middle section.

Lyrically, this is a typically mystical affair made even more obscure by a very muddy mix that all but buries Plant's vocal. Allegedly, it harks back to the past to act as a shroud for a contemporary Plant observation of a person who in his words will one day realise it was written about them and proclaim . . . "My God! Was it really like that?"

'Carouselambra' covers a lot of ground during its 10-minute duration, and though the actual recording restricts its majestic quality somewhat, the intentions here remain honourable.

Live performances: Sadly, never played live. They had planned to work on an arrangement of this for 'Led Zeppelin: The Eighties Campaign'. It certainly had the scope to be a compelling live piece.

'ALL MY LOVE'
Jones, Plant
Studio: Polar Music; Plumpton.

As can be observed from the composing credits, this came from an occasion when Plant and Jones arrived at the studio first. A very successful attempt to write a melodic pretty love song, the lyrics are full of sincerity, inspiring Robert to turn in a superb vocal performance. Jones' classical keyboard solo is another revelation, while Jimmy adds some subtle acoustic picking. 'All My Love' mirrors the reflective and mellow mood Plant found himself in during 1978. That he could still transfer those feelings into the group's music proved to them that collectively Led Zeppelin remained very much in the present tense.

N.B. There exists a wonderful, extended alternative version of 'All My Love'. It clocks in at seven minutes and two seconds and has a complete ending, with Plant echoing his 'I get a bit lonely' sentiments in an arrangement that was later employed on the 1980 live version.

Live performances: The only previously untried number inserted into the 'Over Europe' tour in 1980. It became one of the best received performances of the whole tour.

'I'M GONNA CRAWL'
Jones, Page, Plant
Studio: Polar Music; Plumpton.

Enhanced by yet another major Jones contribution, this time a smooth synthesised string arrangement, 'I'm Gonna Crawl' is a relaxed and confident slow blues. Plant saw this as an attempt to capture the laid-back approach of the mid-sixties work of Wilson Pickett, O.V. Wright, and Otis Redding, Pickett's 'It's Too Late' being a particular reference point. Some forceful Bonham sparring with Page brings a typical dynamic quality to the proceedings, while Jimmy's solo is his best slow blues performance since the third album. A pleading Plant vocal brings the track to a satisfying finale.

Live performances: Never performed live.

UNRELEASED MATERIAL

The Polar sessions did prove highly productive, with more than an album's worth of material being committed to tape. It was originally planned to issue two of the Polar out-takes 'Wearing And Tearing' coupled with 'Darlene', as a special single to be made available as a commemorative souvenir at the Knebworth shows. Unfortunately, time ran out on that idea but both tracks, plus another Polar left-over, 'Ozone Baby', later surfaced on the 'Coda' collection released in 1982.

It's rumoured that other unissued tapes (including one reel dated November 17, 1978, and labelled 'The Hook') remain in the can from what was to be Led Zeppelin's final recording trip.

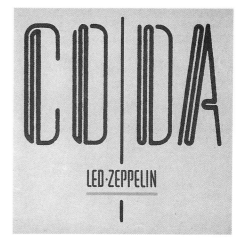

'CODA'
Swan Song A0051.

During 1981 there was much speculation within the inner Swan Song sanctum over whether a final album would be delivered. The original Swan Song contract signed with Atlantic in 1974, called for five albums. With no intention of keeping the group together in any form, contractual and business reasons therefore led Page, Plant and Jones to go ahead with a final album project.

The intention was to profile their 12-year career with a collection of quality left-over tracks. Page began shifting through the tapes at his Sol recording studio in Berkshire during the summer of 1981. After completing the *Death Wish II* soundtrack, he called in Robert and J.P. to mix, and in some cases overdub, the eight selected tracks. The album had a working title of 'Early Days And Latter Days' and was compiled for release early in 1982. Its eventual release was held over until Robert's début solo set 'Pictures At Eleven' hit the shops in the summer.

The sleeve involved collating a selection of off-stage group photos to form a centre spread collage. Ideas thrown around a meeting this author had with Page and Plant to discuss this projected sleeve in March 1982, ranged from using stills from their Knebworth rehearsal video filmed at Bray studios in June 1979, to digging up some celebrated 'road fever' pics from the 1973 US tour. Both of those ideas (in the latter case not surprisingly!) were ultimately vetoed. The final 30 photographs were eventually housed in a grey outer sleeve simply engraved with the words Led Zeppelin and 'Coda', an appropriate revised title, defined in the dictionary as, "An independent passage introduced after the main part of a movement.''

'Coda' was released on November 22, 1982, with little pre-publicity. A low-key advertising campaign employing posters with a symbolic illustration of nine mysterious discs, backed it up. In the UK, only the traditional crop of seasonal TV-advertised titles prevented it reaching the top spot. It entered and stayed at number four. In America 'Coda' reached a credible sixth on the *Billboard* chart.

The release of 'Coda' neatly tied up the loose recorded ends and it remains an enjoyable and affectionate summary of the Led Zeppelin era – chronicling their studio development during the years 1969 to 1978 – with plenty of previously unheard surprises along the way.

'WE'RE GONNA GROOVE'
B.B. King, J. Bethea
Studio: Morgan, London; The Sol, Berkshire.

One of the great 'lost' Zepp performances finally receives an official airing. 'We're Gonna Groove' was recorded during a hectic week in June 1969 when their schedule ran as follows:

Saturday: Gig at Bristol Colston Hall.
Monday: Radio session for John Peel's *Top Gear* in Bond Street, London.
Wednesday: Recording session at Morgan studios London.
Thursday: Gig at Portsmouth Guild Hall.
Friday: Radio concert for the BBC at the Playhouse Theatre London.
Saturday: Live appearance at the Bath Festival Of Blues.
Sunday: 6pm and 9pm appearances at the Royal Albert Hall Pop Proms, London.

Phew! No time for a two-year lay off in those days.

'We're Gonna Groove' was chosen as their set opener on the UK, Europe and US dates in early 1970, and will have already been familiar to keen Zepp collectors as a live bootleg track. This studio version, somehow deemed unusable for 'Led Zeppelin II', is full of slashing Page guitar (with sub-octivider effects added at The Sol in 1982), great Bonham percussion and typically frantic Plant vocal. This *Live performances:* The set opener of the UK, European and US dates January to April 1970, it was then discarded in favour of 'Immigrant Song'.

'POOR TOM'
Page, Plant
Studio: Olympic, London; The Sol.

One of the 'Zeppelin III' leftovers from the June 1970 sessions at Olympic, 'Poor Tom' is another product of the trip to Bron-Y-Aur. A semi-acoustic bluesy jug-band work-out, it's propelled along by an inventive Bonham shuffle that holds up the momentum all the way through. Plant throws in some harmonica blowing for good measure.

Live performances: Never performed live.

'I CAN'T QUIT YOU BABY'
Willie Dixon
Studio: Live sound check recording from the Royal Albert Hall, mixed at The Sol.

Monday, January 9, 1970, is the next dateline revisited. This alleged sound-check rehearsal run-through of a first album blues standard does, in fact, sound very similar to the actual live version performed in the evening (as captured on film by the crew employed to work on the intended Led Zeppelin documentary).

Did the tapes get mislabelled? Well whatever version it is, this a great example of Led Zeppelin, the blues band, having a blow and enjoying every minute of it.

Live performances: Included in the set from 1968 through to the fifth US tour in 1970. Revived as part of the 'Whole Lotta Love' medley for the Japan, UK and Europe dates 1972/3. Also rehearsed at the Atlantic reunion in May 1988.

'WALTER'S WALK'
Page, Plant
Studio: Stargroves, Berkshire, with The Rolling Stones' Mobile; The Sol.

An unexpected gem. Laid down in May 1972 with Eddie Kramer and left off 'Houses Of The Holy', 'Walter's Walk' is a tense, unmelodic rocker spearheaded by a solid Page riff. The overall sound here shares little of the crispness of most of the 'Houses' material. Only the drumming brings to mind that particular era. It obviously didn't fit into the game plan of the time, but emerges as a dense and intoxicating outing.

Live performances: Never performed live in its entirety, the basic structure of 'Walter's Walk' was, however, employed during 'Dazed And Confused' at least once on the 1972 US tour.

'OZONE BABY'
Page, Plant
Studio: Polar Music, Stockholm; The Sol.

It's back to November 1978 for an 'Out Door' left-over. 'Ozone Baby' has affable exuberance spurred on by Plant, who smiles through the whole thing. Uptempo and friendly, its charm is further enhanced by a fluttering Page solo and some harmonised vocal effects.

Live performances: Never performed live.

'DARLENE'
Bonham, Jones, Page, Plant
Studio: Polar Music; The Sol.

Two days later in Stockholm we join the boys for a jiving rock 'n' roll jam. 'Darlene' is just that. Starting out as a jerkily riffed, playful exercise with tinkling Jones piano and off beat drumming, it develops into a rousing fade out with Page pulling out some classic James Burton licks.

Live performances: Never performed live.

'BONZO'S MONTREUX'
Bonham
Studio: Mountain, Montreux; The Sol.

The oft-touted, total percussion number Bonzo cut with Jimmy during their exile in Montreux in September 1976. Bonzo includes all manner of percussive effects here, aided by Jimmy's electronic treatments. A tuneful pattern does emerge from the soloing, primarily a high pitched steel drum sound created by Page's newly acquired harmoniser. An affectionate if unspectacular tribute, though hardly the best representation of John Bonham's vast talent.

Live performances: Never performed live.

'WEARING AND TEARING'
Page, Plant
Studio: Polar Music; The Sol.

A final Tuesday rendezvous with Led Zeppelin in the Abba studios. Recorded on November 21, 1978, 'Wearing And Tearing' is the number Page and Plant had threatened would keep up with the punk rock bands in London. It was also the track nearly made available to the 300,000-plus Knebworth audience.

Thankfully it sees the light of day here. This vibrant Plant plea for the right cure takes off at breakneck speed, side-stepping periodically to let Plant a cappella the lines *à la* 'Black Dog'. It gets more and more frantic with Page playing at a frightening pace, supported by that ever steady Bonham/Jones rhythm section. The intensity accelerates until the song hots up to an abrupt ending.

Live performances: Never performed live in the Zeppelin era, though it was slated to emerge in the 'Led Zeppelin: The Eighties Campaign'. 12 years on it was a live vehicle with which Plant and Page would wow the Knebworth 1990 audience.

The 1990 live delivery of the final track on the tenth Led Zeppelin album proved yet again the sheer potency of their material when in the hands of the original composers. For a few short minutes the song really did remain the same . . .

Inside Caesar's Chariot at the start of the 1977 US tour.

Item 2

Item 3

Item 6

Item 20

Item 22

THE COLLECTABLE
LED ZEPPELIN

Like most major artists, Led Zeppelin's career has thrown up a wealth of collectable memorabilia. Aided considerably by the group's refusal to lend themselves easily to the media, much of this memorabilia adds light to their history and holds a vast attraction for their followers worldwide.

Promo-only UK singles, obscure posters, inflatable airship blimps, juke box EPs, original concert programmes, rare ticket stubs and the like are all much in demand with prices ranging from the ridiculous to the affordable.

To illustrate the type of material that remains a collectable obsession for enthusiasts old and new, the following is a guide (in no specific order) to 100 notable and collectable Led Zeppelin memorabilia items . . . Catch these if you can.

1 Led Zeppelin 'Fourth Album' pressed on lilac coloured vinyl – issued in a limited edition in the UK by WEA/Atlantic in November 1978.

2 Original 'Physical Rocket' poster sold at the Earls Court shows in May 1975.

3 'Led Zeppelin Acoustically' – three-track EP featuring 'Stairway To Heaven', 'That's The Way' and 'Going To California'. Issued in Australia only.

4 Official *The Song Remains The Same* Swan Song invitation card for the première party held at the Covent Garden Floral Hall on November 4, 1976.

5 Original 'Led Zeppelin' first album pressing on UK Atlantic 588 771 with turquoise sleeve lettering. This colouring was changed to the standard orange design soon after release.

6 'Led Zeppelin Over Europe 1980' tour poster – Look-out warden design with full tour itinerary.

7 Rare Argentinian promo seven-inch single, coupling 'All My Love' with 'Hot Dog' released on the Disco-Atlantic label in 1980.

8 May 18, 1975, edition of *The Observer* colour supplement which includes extensive 'Led Zeppelin bigger than The Beatles?' feature by Tony Palmer.

Item 15

9 Official press release issued from the Swan Song US office stating the details of 'Led Zeppelin: The Eighties Part One' campaign dated September 11, 1980. This advises the initial dates planned for their return to America.

10 A concert ticket stub for their last live appearance at the Berlin Sporthalle on Monday July 7, 1980.

11 'The 10 Legendary Singles' seven-inch New Zealand Atlantic/Swan Song box set containing all the Zeppelin New Zealand single releases, in cardboard presentation box.

12 'The Object' three dimensional, upstanding plastic obelisk, issued in a limited edition of 1000 to promote the 'Presence' album in April 1976.

13 Led Zeppelin 'Houses Of The Holy' four-track promotional EP pressed in America for juke box purposes by Little LPs Unlimited.

14 Limited edition UK Swan Song single coupling 'Trampled Underfoot' with 'Black Country Woman'. Issued in a run of 5,000 copies as a promotional item to coincide with the Earls Court shows in May, 1975.

15 Official large format programme produced by Kyodo Tokyo for their 1971 Japanese tour.

16 *Melody Maker* 1979 Poll Awards brochure providing advance embargoed details of Led Zeppelin's success in their annual readers' poll in November 1979.

17 Original white label advance promo pressing of the 'Led Zeppelin' début album issued to key radio stations and reviewers by Atlantic in America in early 1969.

18 Complete set of colour, front of house photo stills, issued by Warner films to UK cinemas for the screening of *The Song Remains The Same*, Autumn 1976.

19 Three dimensional hanging mobile, featuring sleeve reproduction and cardboard 'The Object' obelisk – made available to record stores as a promo item for the 'Presence' album, April 1976.

20 Set of two official posters issued by Atlantic to promote 'Houses Of The Holy', using the slogans 'Does things to people' and 'The effect is shattering' respectively.

21 Rare UK pressing of the withdrawn single 'Whole Lotta Love'/'Living Loving Maid' on red label Atlantic 584 309 pressed up for a projected release on December 5, 1969.

22 'Historia De Led Zeppelin' special Spanish colour magazine published in 1975.

23 Led Zeppelin/Dusty Springfield promo album for in-store promotion issued by Atlantic in America in 1969. The album has four tracks from the first Zeppelin album and one side of songs from the 'Dusty In Memphis' album, introduced by a voice-over link.

24 'Led Zeppelin IV' compact disc packaged in the HMV collectors series as a box set with booklet. Sold through the HMV retail chain in an individually numbered, limited edition of 3,500 in the UK, August 1988.

25 'Stairway To Heaven' Atlantic promo seven-inch single issued to radio stations in America for easy access airplay in a white picture sleeve. Contains stereo seven-minute, 55-second version on both sides.

Item 28

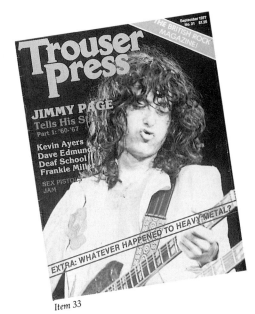
Item 33

Item 42

26 The 'New Age Of Atlantic' sampler album released by Atlantic in the UK in 1972. Includes the non album cut of Led Zeppelin's 'Hey Hey What Can I Do' – a third album left-over only available elsewhere as the B-side to the seven-inch import single of 'Immigrant Song'.

27 P.J. Proby album 'Three Week Hero' released in the UK on Liberty in 1969 – contains all four members of Led Zeppelin on the track 'Jim's Blues'.

28 Official programme for the five Led Zeppelin Earls Court shows in May 1975.

29 'An Evening With Led Zeppelin' official 1977 United States Of America tour programme.

30 'The Led Zeppelin Biography' written by Richie Yorke, published by Methuen in 1976 and long out of print.

31 Advance promotion copy of the UK pressed seven-inch single 'D'yer Mak'er'/'Over The Hills And Far Away' on Atlantic K10296 in orange house bag. Issued to DJs and reviewers but never commercially released.

32 Original green colour poster for Led Zeppelin's appearances at the Winterland Ballroom in San Francisco April 25 and 26, and Fillmore West 24 and 27, 1969. Designed by Tea Lautrec Litho in San Francisco.

33 September, October and November 1977 issues of the US *Trouser Press* magazine, featuring an extensive interview with Jimmy Page spanning the session days to Led Zeppelin's then current activity.

34 Obscure seven-inch US radio-only single, provided for public service on the religious broadcast network in January 1981, including 'An interview with Robert Plant' and some of the group's hit records. Hosted by Bill Huie for *What's It All About*.

35 Complete set of six different sleeves labelled A to F initially pressed for the 'In Through The Out Door' album in the UK, August 1979.

36 Original Knebworth poster for the August 11 show, billing The New Barbarians and The Marshall Tucker Band. (The latter act did not appear.)

37 Promotional Swan Song seven-inch American pressing of 'Trampled Underfoot'. This has stereo and mono versions of the rare three-minute, 48-second edited version of the song.

38 Original prototype sleeve mock-up for the 'Physical Graffiti' sleeve design. Has alternate window illustrations and the title printed in red.

39 1969 hard back, Led Zeppelin LP-sized, tour programme book with rare colour and black and white group photos. Produced by The Visual Thing Inc. of California for their autumn 1969 tour of America.

40 *Guitar World* magazine July 1986, special Jimmy Page issue with extensive interviews and features on Page's entire career.

41 Official front of house poster used by cinemas in the UK to publicise the screening of the Led Zeppelin feature film *The Song Remains The Same* in 1976.

42 Complete set of original Led Zeppelin 'Tight But Loose' fan magazines, issues number one to six.

43 Seven-inch juke box promo single coupling Led Zeppelin's 'The Ocean' with The Eagles' 'Already Gone' on the Atlantic/Asylum label. Issued in Italy only.

44 Original copy of the UK underground magazine *Oz* issue 19. This features the début album reviewed by Felix Dennis and one of the first ever group press advertisement placed by Atlantic proclaiming, 'Led Zeppelin, the only way to fly.'

45 Led Zeppelin fourth album juke box EP featuring 'Rock And Roll', 'Black Dog' and 'Stairway To Heaven'. Pressed in America by Little LPs unlimited. The package includes cut out info cards intended for placing in juke box windows.

46 'Coda' LP sleeve presenter slick, issued by Swan Song in the UK to WEA record company personnel to advise details of the album. Has an alternate front logo design to the grey standard sleeve that was duly issued.

47 *Rolling Stone* magazine dated March 13, 1975, with Page and Plant in colour on the cover and detailed interview inside.

48 UK pressing for promotional purposes only of the single 'Communication Breakdown'/'Good Times Bad Times' on red labelled vinyl, Atlantic 584 269. Never commercially released.

49 Original poster for Led Zeppelin's 'Electric Magic' show at Wembley Empire Pool, November 20, 1971. Sold at this gig and the added second night for 30 pence.

50 Official Led Zeppelin at Knebworth button badge sold at the Knebworth shows.

51 Swan Song advance promotional sleeve mock up slick proclaiming 'Led Zeppelin Seven'. Issued to WEA/UK record company personnel in January 1976 to advise them of the forthcoming Zeppelin album later to be known as 'Presence'.

52 Original large size grey poster issued by Swan Song to promote the 'Coda' album in November 1982.

53 Led Zeppelin at Knebworth 1979, official programme made available at the shows on August 4 and 11.

54 Special promo LP-sized plastic carrier bag depicting the 'Zeppelin At Knebworth' logo design, issued by the HMV retail chain in August 1979.

55 'Summerfeast At The Stadium' button badge advising of 'An Evening With Led Zeppelin' at Buffalo, New York on Saturday August 6, 1977. A show that never took place due to the curtailing of the tour.

56 'The Summit' charity rock compilation album issued in early 1980 in the UK on the K-Tel label. It includes 'Candy Store Rock', an out-take shot of the Knebworth photo call on the cover, and a liner note crediting Led Zeppelin's involvement in the project.

57 'This Is Led Zeppelin' seven-inch EP includes 'Immigrant Song', 'Hey Hey What Can I Do', 'Whole Lotta Love' and 'Good Times Bad Times', packaged in hard cover sleeve. Issued only in Australia.

58 *Rock On The Road* by Mick Gold – long out of print paperback book with major feature on Led Zeppelin at Earls Court plus many photos.

59 Juke box seven-inch single coupling 'Gallows Pole' with 'You Can't Judge A Book By The Cover' by Cactus on the Atlantic label. Pressed in Italy in December 1970.

60 Original advert for Led Zeppelin's four scheduled concerts at the Chicago Stadium on November 10, 12, 13 and 15, 1980 as published in the *Chicago Tribune* on Thursday September 25 – the day John Bonham died.

61 Campaign booklet produced by Warners for UK cinema houses screening *The Song Remains The Same*. Includes various black and white film stills.

62 *New Musical Express* dated May 17, 1975 includes centre spread 'Everything You Ever Wanted To Know About Led Zeppelin' feature with masses of info by Roy Carr and Howard Mylett.

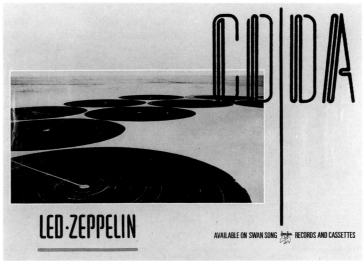

Item 52

Item 57

Item 50

Item 60

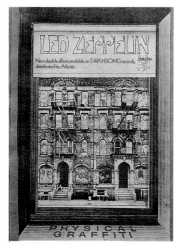

Item 64

Item 83

Item 72

63 'Led Zeppelin II' RCA Record Club issue, pressed in Austria for distribution in Germany. Features totally different sleeve design with live photo on the cover.

64 Promo poster depicting the New York tenement façade of the 'Physical Graffiti' sleeve issued by Swan Song in March 1975.

65 'Led Zeppelin Over Europe 1980' T-shirt with black and yellow Swan Song front and the tour dates on the back. Initially made available for sale during the tour.

66 Official hand out posters printed by Walkerprint for Swan Song after the Knebworth gigs. Two designs available – one live group Knebworth shot and one individual photo montage design.

67 A cardboard Led Zeppelin blimp airship inscribed 'Houses Of The Holy' issued by Atlantic in the UK to promote the album in March 1973.

68 Swan Song US seven-inch promo single with 'Fool In The Rain' long version backed with a special rare three minute, 20 second edited short version. Pressed for radio station use only.

69 Original programme for the 'Bath Festival Of Blues And Progressive Music' which Led Zeppelin headlined on June 28, 1970.

70 Official colour hand out postcard for the Swan Song UK office distributed *circa* 1977 to 1981.

71 Four issues of *Sounds* British rock magazine dated September 16, 23, 30 and October 7, 1978, including pull out 'Complete Led Zeppelin' feature in each issue by Geoff Barton and Dave Lewis.

72 'In Through The Out Door' promo poster with Knebworth photo call colour shot. Issued by UK Swan Song, September 1979.

73 'BBC Rock Hour' promo LP for radio use only, includes 1971 BBC 'Led Zeppelin In Concert' recording, first broadcast on April 4, 1971.

74 Original Polydor distributed Atlantic UK pressing of 'Led Zeppelin II', with light brown gatefold cover. Issued on Atlantic 588 198 in October 1969.

75 Rare Polish post card flexi-disc single coupling 'Friends' with 'Celebration Day'.

76 Japanese 'Viva' photo book *Zeppelin Over Europe* special, packed with colour and black and white photos. Published in 1980.

77 *Rolling Stone*, March 24, 1988 collectors issue with Robert Plant cover and illuminating interview plus 'Tribute To A Rock Legend' Zeppelin feature.

78 'Lord Sutch And Heavy Friends' album issued on Atlantic in 1970. Featuring guest contributions from Jimmy Page and John Bonham.

79 Led Zeppelin *Innerview* radio show music and interview double album on the Sound Communication label, pressed for US radio show use in 1975.

80 Sandie Shaw 'Reviewing The Situation' 1969 album on the Pye label featuring rare cover version of 'Your Time Is Gonna Come'.

81 Rare original pressing of the Japanese single release of 'Immigrant Song' backed with 'Out On The Tiles', on the Atlantic label.

82 'Live Yardbirds With Jimmy Page' – issued on the US Columbia Special Products label in 1971 but withdrawn following an injunction by Page. Recorded in New York, March 30, 1968, on their final US tour. Includes 'White Summer' and 'I'm Confused' – an early version of 'Dazed And Confused'.

83 Led Zeppelin 'Stairway To Heaven' seven-track compilation album issued only in Russia. Released in 1988, five different pressings were made. The pressing plant origin is listed on each sleeve. The rarest are those marked Leningrad or Tashkent.

84 US radio only 'Superstar In Concert' triple album. Includes performances by Yes, Foreigner and Led Zeppelin recorded at Atlantic's 40th Anniversary concert in May 1988.

85 Original poster for Led Zeppelin's appearance at the Fillmore West, San Francisco with Taj Mahal and Country Joe And The Fish in January 1969, during their début American tour. (A copy of this poster used to hang in the main office of the Swan Song London HQ.)

86 'Two Originals Of Led Zeppelin', rare German pressed double album combining the first two Led Zeppelin albums into a double gatefold package. Briefly available on the Atlantic label in Germany during the early seventies.

87 Poster for Led Zeppelin's scheduled 'A Day On The Green' concerts with Joe Walsh And The Pretty Things due to take place at the Oakland Stadium August 23 and 24, 1975. These dates were cancelled due to Plant's car crash.

88 US/Canadian pressing of Led Zeppelin's fourth album on white vinyl issued by Atlantic in a limited edition during 1978.

89 Atlantic promotional seven-inch American pressing of 'Black Dog' – featuring full length version plus rare three-minute, 50-second edited version for radio station play.

90 *Melody Maker* issue dated June 16, 1973. This contains a full back page advert, depicting the record breaking 56,800 audience that came to see Led Zeppelin in Tampa, Florida on May 5, 1973.

91 A set of four unused tickets for Led Zeppelin's planned appearances at the Chicago Stadium on November 10, 12, 13 and 15, 1980.

92 Original copy of UK trade magazine *Record Retailer* dated January 15, 1972. This includes the famous 'Mr Zeppelin Regrets' advert, placed by Peter Grant in reply to the annual Midem music business festival organiser's invitation for 'Mr Zeppelin and his backing group' to appear at one of the gala concerts at the festival.

93 Original inflatable blimp airship model inscribed 'Led Zeppelin II' – issued by Atlantic to promote the second album, November 1969.

94 1972 Led Zeppelin tour of Australia official concert programme.

95 *Melody Maker* dated November 6, 1971. This issue includes 'Zeppelin To Tour' front cover story, a centre spread advertisement for the November 20, Empire Pool Wembley show, plus a series of teaser advertisements illustrating for the first time each member's fourth album symbol.

96 'Led Zeppelin Superstars' Japanese *Music Life* photo book published in 1971.

97 'Chrysalis Presents . . .' poster for Led Zeppelin's January 1970 UK tour dates.

98 Official tour bag for the 'Led Zeppelin: The Eighties Part One' tour campaign. Canvas duffle bag commissioned by Swan Song in the US for use on the scheduled October/November tour dates.

99 *Modern Drummer* magazine dated July 1984. Special John Bonham tribute issue with excellent career retrospective feature and photos.

100 Original UK pressing of 'Led Zeppelin III' on Polydor/Atlantic de luxe 2401 002. Includes 'Do What Thou Wilt' inscription written on the inner groove. Originally issued in October, 1970.

Item 78

Item 67

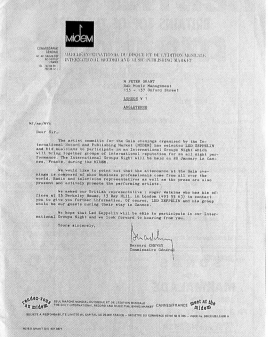

56,800 people came to see Led Zeppelin in Tampa, Florida on May 5th 1973. The largest audience for a single artist performance in history

Item 90

Item 92

MR. ZEPPELIN REGRETS......

Item 96

The last farewell, Europe, 1980.

THE SOLO YEARS

The remodelled solo artist, 1982.

Robert Plant

In November 1980 the remaining members of Led Zeppelin and their management flew to Jersey to discuss at length their future plans following the death of John Bonham. The inevitable decision that came from this meeting was announced to the media on December 4. Without their dear friend and drummer, they could not continue as they were. The Led Zeppelin era was over.

And so began the solo years. For Robert Plant the loss of his lifelong friend was extremely hard to bear. His way of facing up to life without the people and music that had fuelled his ambitions for so long was to retreat to his Midlands roots, with his family and close local associates. Slowly the desire to sing returned, and he forced himself to pick up the pieces of a solo career that he must have thought he had left behind for good back in 1968.

To wipe the slate clean though, Plant went right away from the cloistered superstar trappings of the Zeppelin era. On March 9, 1981 he jumped into a mini-bus with a bunch of local blues players, and travelled to a wine bar in Stourbridge and performed live for the first time since Led Zeppelin's final show some seven months previously. This *ad hoc* pick-up band was dubbed by Plant The Honeydrippers, after an old blues instrumental 'Honeydripper' recorded in 1945 by Joe Liggins, and the old blues pianist Roosevelt Sykes who called himself The Honeydripper. The players included long-term Midlands friends Andy Silvester, Ricky Cool and Robbie Blunt. The music was strictly non-Zeppelin, and a return to the R&B leanings of his formative years. Numbers performed included 'Cross Cut Saw', 'How Many More Years' and 'Queen Of The Hop'. More gigs followed in tiny venues such as the Nottingham Boat Club, Pontypridd Polytechnic and the Retford Porterhouse. For Robert, despite the odd cry of "Where's Jimmy?" and "Play 'Stairway'," the gigs were immense fun and provided a much needed inner rejuvenation.

It was during this tour that Plant began to develop some ideas with guitarist Robbie Blunt, a former member of The Steve Gibbons Band, Savoy Brown and Bronco. Never a permanent set-up, in line-up or intentions, The Honeydrippers went off the road after cancelling a planned date at London's Dingwalls in the summer of 1981. Plant's next step was to demo some new material written with his new partner Robbie Blunt. One of their first collaborations was a song called 'Fat Lip', recorded with a drum machine. Fuelled by the results, the pair booked in some studio time at Monmouth's Rockfield studios. Auditions were held to assist with the project, and from these, Plant recruited Paul Martinez, a seasoned bass player previously with The Adverts and Paice, Ashton And Lord, and Jezz Woodroffe, a keyboard session man and former Black Sabbath back-up member. For the role of drummer, Plant enlisted the help of Phil Collins, and for the initial sessions, Cozy Powell.

Released in June 1982, the début Robert Plant solo set 'Pictures At Eleven' was enthusiastically snapped up by a Zeppelin-starved audience. They were not to be disappointed. The singer had lost none of the characteristics that had coloured his previous recorded work. Particularly outstanding was 'Slow Dancer', an epic outing that Plant had taken to Jimmy Page to earn a nod of approval. Numbers such as 'Moonlight In Samosa' and 'Like I've Never Been Gone' re-emphasised his ability to compose and convey a ballad style with consummate ease.

'Pictures At Eleven' made the Top Five on both sides of the Atlantic, and coming in a period of much transition, remains one of Robert's most impressive achievements. The same month of the album's release, he returned to the London concert stage with an appearance at the Prince's Trust Charity bash at the Dominion Theatre, where he played 'Worse Than Detroit'.

This new-found solo career gave Plant the opportunity to reassess every angle of his persona. Thus the hair became less unruly, the clothes more sophisticated and the media all encompassing. Singles, videos, TV interviews – forbidden territory during the Zepp era – suddenly became the norm.

With the Swan Song label winding down, Plant re-signed to Atlantic and released all future product under his own Es Paranza label. (Legal problems vetoed his original title Es Paradis). A second album cut with the same line-up minus Powell, but with additional percussive help from Jethro Tull's Barriemore Barlow, was issued in the summer of 1983. Titled 'The Principal Of Moments', it combined the traditional elements of the Plant approach with an experimental edge.

Off-the-wall material such as 'Stranger Here . . . Than Over There' shared the spotlight with more conventional numbers like 'Big Log'. This track, a moody ballad with Mark Knopfler-sounding guitar work from Robbie Blunt, provided Plant with an elusive UK hit single when it reached number 11 during the long hot summer of 1983. It also enabled him to appear on *Top Of The Pops*, the UK TV show that for years copped a version of

'Whole Lotta Love' as its theme tune.

Following an aborted live TV recording for *The Tube* (for which Queen's Roger Taylor took over on drums), Plant and his band set out on a world tour. For the North American leg Phil Collins travelled with them, after which ex-Little Feat drummer Ritchie Hayward took over for the UK and Australian legs and subsequently became a full-time member. Ex-Foreigner guitarist Bob Mayo also helped out on this tour. Although still adamant about not performing any Led Zeppelin numbers, hints of the past did emerge in Plant-penned live arrangements of 'Other Arms' and 'Slow Dancer'.

The seeds of the next major Plant project bore fruit on the US tour when, together with Phil Collins and Paul Martinez, he recorded a version of Charlie Rich's 'Philadelphia Baby' at the legendary Sun studios in Memphis. Spurred on by this session and encouraged by Atlantic supremo Ahmet Ertegun, after the tour's completion in Tokyo, a weekend of studio time was booked at the Atlantic studios, New York for March 1984. The idea was to record a batch of vintage R&B numbers with Ertegun supervising. Guest contributors included Nile Rodgers, Jeff Beck, band leader Paul Shaffer and arranger Dave Mathews.

The project was completed in London where Plant enlisted the help of Jimmy Page, who contributed solos to a cover of Phil Phillips And The Twilights' 1959 do-wop hit 'Sea Of Love' and 'I Get A Thrill'.

The resulting five-track mini-album was issued at the end of the year as 'The Honeydrippers Vol One'. Though only a minor success in the UK, it was a smash US hit shifting 100,000 copies and providing Plant with a surprise Top Five American single in 'Sea Of Love'. The Honeydrippers success gave Plant a dual career status from which to progress.

For his next touring assault he combined his conventional solo show with a special Honeydrippers segment, complete with lavish fifties Cadillac staging and backing from the Uptown Horns and singers The Queen Bees. That tour, which covered the US in the summer of 1985 and reached the UK with dates at the Birmingham NEC and Wembley Arena in September, coincided with the release of his third proper solo album 'Shaken 'n' Stirred'.

This proved to be a very difficult set both in content and construction. The sessions were anything but smooth with Robbie Blunt in particular finding it hard to come to terms with both the material and the

use of a Roland synth guitar. The results were decidedly mixed. The addition of ex-Eurythmics backing singer Toni Halliday on several tracks often obscured the main vocal track, and many of the arrangements went for atmosphere as opposed to melody. There were a couple of stand-out performances ('Little By Little' and 'Sixes And Sevens'), but overall it was a confusing affair and barely scraped into the Top 20 on both sides of the Atlantic.

The live shows of this period were, however, hugely enjoyable with The Honeydrippers section being very well received. In July 1985 the rather fragmented state of Robert's solo status was further complicated by a reunion, slap bang in the middle of the tour, with Page and John Paul Jones at *Live Aid*. For the rest of the year rumours were rife that they would reform permanently. This was further fuelled by a studio get together of

Robert with Robbie Blunt, circa 1983.

the three, plus drummer Tony Thompson near Peter Gabriel's Bath recording complex early in 1986. As it turned out there was to be no permanent reunion and instead Plant made a clean break of it all by disbanding his solo band and rebuilding his career from scratch. Relationships with Robbie Blunt had been strained for some time and the need for a new impetus was no real surprise.

It was to be a full two years before Plant re-emerged. In between times he made a few appearances under The Honeydrippers moniker (including a set with The Big Town Playboys at the 'Heart Beat' charity show at the NEC Birmingham), signed a new management deal with Who manager Bill Curbishley, and on the recommendation of Eurythmic Dave Stewart worked with German musician and ex-Psychotic Tank, Robert Crash. A couple of songs they collaborated on

would turn up on his next album. There had been talk of a second Honeydrippers album but conscious of becoming something of an American version of Shakin' Stevens, the idea was shelved.

A new record finally began to take shape in 1987 when Plant received a demo tape from Virgin Music of the production team Act Of War. Most impressed with the content, he met with the principals involved, Dave Barrett and Phil Johnstone, and immediately began working with them in the studio. With additional help from drummer Chris Blackwell (formerly with Johnstone in The Rest Is History), and bassist Phil Scragg, and Doug Boyle more than enough tracks were ready and mixed by Autumn 1987.

Encouraged by the youthful vigour of his new band members and their enthusiasm for his own heritage, for the first time since the demise of Led Zeppelin Robert Plant felt at ease with his past. The upshot of that was the inclusion of Zepp samples on the track 'Tall Cool One', the addition of Jimmy Page on the aforementioned outing and 'Heaven Knows', and the decision (highly criticised by some die-hard Zepp followers) to reinstate a handful of Led Zeppelin numbers into his new live set. These were premièred at a series of low-key UK college gigs Plant and his new group (sometimes billed as The Band Of Joy in reference to his pre-Zepp line-up), undertook in early 1988.

The completed album had originally been titled 'Wolves', a reference to Robert's new tour logo, but surfaced as the cryptic 'Now And Zen' in February 1988. It was preceded by a single 'Heaven Knows' which provided Plant with his second Top 40 hit. The album, ranging from commercially slanted songs such as 'Why' and 'Dance On My Own', rockabilly workouts 'Tall Cool One' and 'Billy's Revenge', to the superb ballad 'Ship Of Fools', was a most assured return and met with considerable critical acclaim. It made the Top 10 in the UK and US, remaining on the Billboard chart for many months.

This new phase of his solo career represented another change in image. Back came the flowing locks and the flowery waistcoats, and there was a revival of the hippy imagery of a bygone era from the backdrop stage visuals, through to the use of The Doors' 'Break On Through' on the encores. There was even a nostalgic return to the Marquee club where Plant showcased his new live set to the European press in February.

The 'Non Stop Go' tour as it was labelled,

for which bassist Charlie Jones was added to the line-up in place of the unavailable Phil Scragg, kicked off in the UK in the spring and by the time the set had weaved its way round the US twice, Robert Plant had played to nigh on one million people.

Along the way he reunited with Page for a memorable Hammersmith encore, reformed Led Zeppelin for a day at Atlantic's 40th Anniversary show, added even more Zepp songs to the American leg of the tour (namely 'Communication Breakdown', 'Immigrant Song' and 'In The Light'/'Nobody's Fault But Mine'), allowed the 'Tall Cool One' video complete with Zepp samples to be used in a lucrative advertising deal with Coca Cola (a decision he regrets now), and played shows with support from Joan Jett, The Georgia Satellites, Stevie Ray Vaughan and The Mission.

In 1989, Robert and his touring colleagues constructed songs for another album, and the actual recording sessions took Robert Plant back to Olympic studios where many of Led Zeppelin's most famous tracks were laid down. The material came together from a pool of ideas the Plant band had logged at soundchecks and other stops along the tour.

After its completion in late 1989, Robert threw a 21st birthday party for his daughter Carmen. This resulted in another loose and enjoyable jam with his former Zeppelin comrades. As the new decade dawned rumours were rife again that a permanent reunion was now a distinct possibility.

In the midst of all the rumour, Plant's fifth solo set 'Manic Nirvana' was unleashed. It garnered very favourable reviews. Harder edged than most of his entire solo output, it benefited from a polished nineties production that captured his vocals in magnificent form. As well as a hard contemporary feel, there was still room for variety, amply supplied by the very 'Led Zeppelin III' sounding acoustic throwback 'Liar's Dance' and the rootsy Kenny Dino fifties cover 'Your Ma Said You Cried In Her Sleep Last Night'. The latter included an affectionate chorus line lifted intact from 'Black Dog'.

This pull of the past, and the need to still display a commitment to the future, continued to baffle his audience. In May, Plant, Page and Jones joined Jason Bonham at his wedding reception to run through a set of Zeppelin classics, in a much publicised reunion. His 'Manic Nirvana' tour which kicked off in Europe

Now And Zen, Tall Cool One, 1988.

included no less than six Led Zepp numbers in the set as well as backdrop film footage from *The Song Remains The Same* movie.

When he was named the Silver Clef award winner for outstanding contributions to British music, he avoided the opportunity of celebrating the occasion with a speculated (and expected) full Zepp get together at the massive Award winners concert held at Knebworth in aid of the Music Therapy charity on June 30, 1990. Instead he appeared with his own line-up, bringing Jimmy Page in for a three-song Zepp finale that included the first ever live airing of the Polar recorded 'Wearing And Tearing'. Earlier, Page had sat on the sidelines as Robert and his band ran down the Page/Plant compositions 'Immigrant Song' and 'Going To California'.

Thus, Robert Plant's solo standing remains in a somewhat confused state as he takes his 'Manic Nirvana' tour through America and the world. The 'will he or won't he' saga goes on. A 1991 fully-fledged Led Zeppelin reunion is still receiving much press speculation. Whether he does decide to play the music he created from 1968 to 1980 with his former colleagues again, remains in the balance.

More certain is his undoubted enthusiasm to keep searching out new musical avenues on which to focus his extraordinary vocal talent. An exploration that has already served up a wide variety of challenging music since he resumed, in forced circumstances, the mantle of Robert Plant – Solo Artist, back in the early eighties.

Backstage with son Logan and the McCartneys, Knebworth 1990.

With Phil Johnstone and Doug Boyle, circa 1988.

Jimmy Page in the early 1980's.

Jimmy Page

It was never going to be an easy period for Jimmy Page after the death of John Bonham and the retirement of the musical vehicle he himself had created all those years ago. Being ensconced in the very house the tragedy took place did not help matters, and rumours of Page's failing health soon began to surface. Certainly for some months he did not touch a guitar. There exists the famous Page fable, that when he did eventually ask his guitar technician Tim Marten to fetch the Gibson Les Paul out of storage, to their horror it was nowhere to be found. Fortunately it had only been borrowed and was soon back with its true owner. If it had remained lost, who knows what chance the public would have had of hearing from Jimmy Page again.

His activity though, remained minimal. On March 10, 1981, coincidentally the day after Plant's live return in the Midlands, Jimmy joined his former Yardbirds sparring partner Jeff Beck for a jam on an encore version of 'I'm Going Down' at London's Hammersmith Odeon. The next few months found Jimmy holed up at his Sol studio in Cookham, playing host to such luminaries as Elton John, George Harrison, Mick Fleetwood, Bill Wyman and Alan White. He also began shifting through material for the 10th Led Zeppelin album project.

In late August he was asked by his near neighbour, film director Michael Winner, to supply the soundtrack for the Winner-produced, movie sequel *Death Wish 2*, starring Charles Bronson. Faced with coming up with a film's worth of music in just eight weeks, Jimmy rose to the challenge in a similar manner to the way he approached the tight deadlines of the 'Presence' album. Working with an early cut of the movie, Page synchronised the music to the violent footage aided by Fairport drummer Dave Mattacks, bassist Dave Paton, Gordon Edwards on piano and vocals, Dave Lawson arranging and former sixties star Chris Farlowe on vocals. This project also provided Jimmy with the opportunity to investigate the possibilities of the Roland guitar synthesiser.

The resulting soundtrack album was released in February 1982. His playing throughout was excellent, and the songs that stood out as more than mere soundtrack music, such as the string-bending 'Prelude', and the Zepp-riff inspired 'Who's To Blame', were reassuring statements of his ability to develop his guitar craft outside of Led Zeppelin. Michael Winner was obviously impressed, as he redeployed much of Jimmy's music for *Death Wish 3*.

Early in 1982 Page returned to the stage when, together with Robert, he appeared on an encore with Foreigner in Munich, helping out on a version of 'Lucille'. This period was also taken up with mixing and overdubbing the tracks that would emerge as 'Coda', the final Led Zeppelin album issued in November of that year. A month earlier Page narrowly escaped a jail sentence for drug possession. Conditionally discharged, Page stated he was launching a new group in the New Year to tour America and Japan. At the same time unfounded rumours circulated that Page might be joining a new Whitesnake line-up.

A strong pointer to Jimmy's eventual plans occurred when he joined Eric Clapton and his band at a low-key gig at the Civic Hall Guildford on May 24, 1983. Jimmy played on encore versions of 'Further On Up The Road' and 'Cocaine'.

Three months later Page answered Clapton's call to star in two special charity shows to be held on September 20 and 21 at London's Royal Albert Hall. These gigs were staged to raise money for the multiple sclerosis charity ARMS and the stricken, former Faces bassist, Ronnie Lane. His mobile studio had once recorded the epic 'Physical Graffiti' material at Headley Grange. Rehearsals for the show took place at Clapton's home.

Jimmy decided to fill his spot with material from the *Death Wish* soundtrack. At the shows, he was supported by Simon Phillips, Fernando Saunders, Chris Stainton, Andy Fairweather Lowe, Ray Cooper, John Hooker and Steve Winwood who provided vocals where required. One song he was certainly not employed for was Jimmy's moving rendition of 'Stairway To Heaven'. This was added to the set as an instrumental and proved to be a stirring highlight of both shows. Page also lined up with Beck and Clapton for the finale of 'Tulsa Time', 'Layla', and 'Goodnight Irene'. Considering it was his first major appearance in years, Jimmy's playing on the brown Fender Telecaster he now favoured was surprisingly assured.

Such was the success of the dates, it was decided to repeat the exercise in America. Nine shows were performed in Dallas, San Francisco, Los Angeles and New York. For this part of the ARMS tour, Jimmy asked Paul Rodgers to help him out in his set as Steve Winwood was not available. There had been tentative plans for Page to work with Rodgers earlier in the year, but Paul got involved with his own solo album. With that completed, he travelled with the ARMS touring party contributing to 'Who's To Blame', 'City Sirens', 'Boogie Mama' (from his solo 'Cut Loose' album) and 'Bird On A Wing' (a new Page/Rodgers composition later renamed 'Midnight Moonlight').

In the New Year, plans were laid for Jimmy and Paul to form a permanent touring band. Before that project reached fruition, Page played some dates with Ian Stewart's Rocket 88, appeared at a benefit concert for Alexis Korner at the Piotoria Blues festival in Italy (performing 'Train Kept A Rollin'' among others), and resumed his musical alliance with Roy Harper. This involved appearing with Roy at festivals in Thetford and Cambridge, being filmed for a bizarre interview on *The Old Grey Whistle Test* on Scafell Pike in the Lake District, playing a gig at London's Rock Garden and recording the 'Whatever Happened To Jugula?' album which was released in 1985.

Other Page activity in a productive year included jamming with Yes at a show in Dortmund, appearing on three tracks on Stephen Stills' 'Right By You' album, which was recorded at Page's Sol studio, guesting on two tracks for John Paul Jones' *Scream For Help* soundtrack, and appearing on Robert's 'Honeydrippers Vol. One' set.

The big project, though, was assembling a band with Paul Rodgers. Rehearsals and auditions took place in the summer at

Nomis studios. Pino Paladino was initially offered the bass position but was committed to touring with Paul Young. Jimmy then invited Tony Franklin, who had recorded and played live with Roy Harper and Page during that year, and offered him the job. The drum vacancy was filled by Chris Slade, former Tom Jones and Manfred Mann's Earth Band drummer. He accepted a spot with Dave Gilmour's band just as the Page/Rodgers offer came in, but agreed to join the line-up after completing a US tour with the Pink Floyd guitarist. Other drummers who came down to jam during this period included Bill Bruford and The Damned's Rat Scabies.

"Jimmy Page turned out to be a really nice geezer and seemed very relaxed," said Scabies who, as a high spokesman of punk, might be expected to belittle Page. "It was great. He was pouring sweat and laughing and threw himself into the solo. He plays like an old master. We played everything from country and western to heavy punk and blues, then boogie. He looks half Chinese up close, and a bottle of Grecian 2000 wouldn't go amiss."

All the auditions had been booked in as The McGregors, a name Harper was also using. When it came to seriously considering a group name, Page came up with The Firm. The new line-up made their live début in Stockholm (a favourite Page testing ground) on November 29, 1984. After further dates in Copenhagen, Lund, Frankfurt, Ludwigshafen and Hamburg, The Firm played a series of sell out gigs on home soil, kicking off in Rodgers' home town of Middlesborough on December 5, and taking in two nights at Hammersmith Odeon. The live set was respectful to both Rodgers' and Page's past catalogue, and concentrated on material from their newly recorded début album, *Death Wish 2*, and Paul's 'Cut Loose' album.

Although well received on these first gigs, The Firm ultimately promised more than they delivered. Matters were not helped by the release of their début album in early 1985. This was a lack-lustre affair, with only 'Midnight Moonlight' and the single 'Radioactive' making any lasting impression. Following a début tour of America, The Firm played further dates in the UK at Birmingham NEC, Edinburgh Playhouse and Wembley Arena. The latter show was vastly under-subscribed, and though Page played his heart out it was clear that The Firm had many short-comings. The Page/Rodgers partnership was plainly not working and they had

seriously overestimated their audience.

Undeterred, they recorded a second album at The Sol at the end of 1985. This came amid much Led Zeppelin reformation rumour after Live Aid. It was in early 1986 that Page got together with Plant and Jones to jam down in Bath. In April he was back on the road for what was to be the final Firm tour. Their second album 'Mean Business' was issued initially in the States and then in the UK to only lukewarm response, reaching number 22 in America and a lowly 46 at home.

Sessions to note during the 1985/86 period included a Page/Rodgers link up for Bill Wyman's 'Willie And The Poor Boys' album, and Page contributions to the ex-Yardbirds project, Box Of Frogs album 'Strange Land', and The Rolling Stones track 'One Hit To The Body' for their 'Dirty Work' album, and live jams with Plant, The Beach Boys and Jaco Pastorius.

When The Firm finished their tour of the US, Page returned to England with no concrete plans. In the summer of 1986 he attended and played at Les Paul's birthday bash in New York.

He then set about demoing material for a new solo project but unfortunately some of these demos were stolen from his residence. Early in 1987, Page set about planning a double solo album. The idea was to produce a side of rock 'n' roll, a side of blues, an acoustic side and an experimental side. Along the way, this plan was cut back to a single album. Musicians who guested on the album included Jason Bonham (who had supported The Firm with Virginia Wolf in America), Tony Franklin, Durban Laverde and Felix Krish on bass, and guest vocal

Mr and Mrs J. Page, attending Jason Bonham's wedding, April 1990.

appearances from John Miles, Chris Farlowe and Robert Plant. The latter returned the compliment by inviting Page to contribute to his 'Now And Zen' album.

The resulting album, entitled 'Outrider' and released in June 1988, heralded an almost phoenix-like rebirth. As well as changing management and record companies, ending a 20-year association with Atlantic by switching to the Geffen stable, on a personal level Jimmy had married and become the proud father of a son (James Patrick).

'Outrider' was the best recorded evidence of the guitarist's durable talent since 1980. Back in full control, Page dominated proceedings by returning to the diversity of his best work. Alongside splendid blues performances such as 'Hummingbird', there stood minor key inventive instrumentals like 'Emerald

On stage with Aerosmith at London's Marquee Club, August 1990.

Eyes'. And with Plant, he clocked in a high energy rocker 'The Only One'. Encompassing a whole range of guitar styles and instruments (he divided the playing amongst the Les Paul, Telecaster, Stratocaster, Roland Synth and Martin and Washburn acoustics), 'Outrider' provided the perfect vehicle for Page's renewed enthusiasm. The only disappointment was that it wasn't a double . . .

With a touring unit of John Miles, Jason Bonham and Durban Laverde, Jimmy embarked on his first solo tour, commencing in America and culminating in a series of UK dates. Perhaps influenced by his former partner, Jimmy used this tour to reinvestigate his back catalogue. 'Over The Hills And Far Away', 'Custard Pie', 'In My Time Of Dying' and an instrumental collage of 'White Summer/Black Mountain Side' and 'Kashmir' were included in a balanced set that covered every step of his career. As was a reverent instrumental version of 'Stairway To Heaven'. The whole tour was a resounding success.

Since then, Page has inevitably been a key element in various Zeppelin reunions and speculation. It appears that Jimmy would now be comfortable paying homage to the legacy of Led Zeppelin when and if the occasion arises . . . as he did at the Knebworth Silver Clef show. Time will tell if that notion becomes reality.

Jimmy commenced the nineties with a guest appearance with Bon Jovi at their Music Therapy charity show at Hammersmith. He performed 'Train Kept A Rollin'' and 'With A Little Help From My Friends' – two records he had originally played on (by The Yardbirds and Joe Cocker respectively) before Zeppelin formed. After the Jason Bonham wedding reunion, Page played with Robert at the Knebworth Silver Clef gig, and in August he showed up at the Donington 'Monsters Of Rock' event to jam with Aerosmith. Again he stepped back on the old wah-wah pedal for a stunning 'Train Kept A Rollin''. Two days later Jimmy reappeared with Aerosmith at London's Marquee for the final half hour of their set, joining them for 'Ain't Got You', 'Think About It', 'Red House', 'Immigrant Song' and 'Train Kept A Rollin''. When Page took the stage Aerosmith singer Steve Tyler respectfully introduced him as . . . "The man without whom we wouldn't be here."

Much of the summer had been taken up with further Zeppelin activity. This involved the remastering and sequencing of a 54-track compilation of Zeppelin material for a special CD box set, scheduled for autumn release.

In the light of all the Led Zeppelin reunion rumours, Jimmy was asked backstage at Donington by Mick Wall if the band would play live again. "Well you'll have to ask Robert," he said. "It's true, isn't it (laughing). I mean I love playing that stuff, it's part of me . . . a great big part of me and I love playing it."

Since the demise of Led Zeppelin, Jimmy has undergone many musical adventures – some more fulfilling than others. However, although greying a little at the edges, he remains a dazzlingly enigmatic guitar hero. He is justly proud of Zeppelin's achievements and, it would seem, well at ease paying homage to them when and if the occasion arises.

Jimmy Page is also sure to make new music in the future, attracting attention every time he picks up a piece of wood with six strings on it. The way it's been since 1963 . . .

Backstage at Knebworth, 1979.

John Paul Jones

Always the quietest personality of the four, it was no real surprise that after the retirement of Led Zeppelin, John Paul Jones would retreat from the public eye. Tucked away in the Devonshire countryside, he built his own home studio inside a building that was once a Sunday school. With his array of keyboard instruments he was content to tinker around, recording local musicians and scoring classical pieces for his own amusement. His interest in new computer technology also led him to become a member of the Electro Acoustic Music Association.

The only live appearance he made in the early eighties, was an encore jam with Robert Plant when the 'Principal Of Moments' tour played in Bristol in December 1983.

In 1984, however, he was approached on Jimmy Page's recommendation by film director Michael Winner to supply the soundtrack for his new movie *Scream For Help*. This led to his name being credited on a record in its own right for the first time in 20 years; it was way back in April 1964 that a youthful JPJ released his one and only previous solo disc. This was a single recorded when he was just about to embark on a successful career as a highly sought after session-man-cum-arranger. Fresh from a stint in the backing band of ex-Shadows Jet Harris and Tony Meehan, Jones inherited the former's six-string bass guitar sound for a typical bouncy, sixties instrumental entitled 'Baja'.

This session was produced by Rolling Stones producer Andrew Loog Oldham who was about to employ John as his musical director. In the rush to get the single out, JP tells the story that the B-side, the strangely titled 'A Foggy Day In Vietnam', did not in fact feature him at all and was the product of a Stones session at Regent Sound. This would explain the song's strong similarity to early era Stones tracks such as 'Heart Of Stone' and 'Tell Me'.

Twenty years on, John Paul Jones set about the task of completing his first post-Zeppelin recording. Much of the material found him in the role of multi-instrumentalist. He did, however, enlist various guest musicians for certain songs. Close neighbour and Page folk guitar favourite John Renbourne contributed to 'When You Fall In Love', a track that also marked JP's début as a lead vocalist. His only previous public vocal performance had been for the live version of 'The Battle Of Evermore' sung with Robert on Zeppelin's 1977 US tour dates. Godparent to his children and long-time friend Madeline Bell (he produced her 1973 'Comin' Atcha' album) sang on 'Here I Am' and 'Take It Or Leave It', and at the recommendation of Atlantic exec Phil Carson, Yes vocalist Jon Anderson helped out on 'Christie' and 'Silver Train'. Session players Graham Ward and Colin Green also contributed, while for lyrics Jones kept things in the family by asking his daughter Jacinda to help out.

That left one name. JP felt a Booker T-inspired instrumental called 'Spaghetti Junction' required a screeching guitar solo. A call to Windsor brought his former partner scurrying down to Devon, guitar army in hand. While at the Sunday School studio together, Jones and Page concocted another instrumental piece called 'Crackback'. This remains one of the most authentic Zeppelin-inspired solo tracks of any ex-member, a riveting Page exercise with a very 'Black Dog' sounding Jones bass riff which, given a set of Plant lyrics, would not have been out of place on any latter era Zeppelin album.

The soundtrack for *Scream For Help* (made up, as Jones explained at the time, of film source music i.e. music heard in the film coming from car radios etc, rather than incidental music) came out on the Atlantic label in April 1985. The film itself received poor reviews and was pulled out of the West End after a short run. The album was therefore little heard. It certainly demonstrated Jones' continued prowess as a skilful musician, and for 'Crackback' alone, remains an important post-Zepp recording.

Apart from a brief appearance in Paul McCartneys *Give My Regards To Broad Street* movie (John Paul can be seen and heard in the film and soundtrack album performing 'Ballroom Dancing' with the McCartneys, Ringo Starr, Dave Edmunds and Chris Spedding) and the famous reunion with Page and Plant at *Live Aid*, little was heard from the Jones camp until 1987.

In the wake of his number one re-issued hit 'Stand By Me', Ben E. King set about recording a comeback album. Three of the tracks on the resulting album, 'Save The Last Dance For Me', include Jones' contributions and J.P. also helped out at King's London Palladium show which was also attended by Robert Plant.

More production work followed. In the wake of the sudden upsurge in Zepp popularity, fuelled by the likes of Goth bands such as The Cult and Sisters Of Mercy naming them as a key influence, and The Beastie Boys scoring a hit album which heavily sampled original Zepp tracks, The Mission, led by ex-Sister Wayne Hussey, sought out Jones to produce their next album. Contact was made via a tape sent from the Mission camp to Jones' home in Devon.

The resulting album, 'Children', was

recorded at the Manor studios from September to November 1987. As well as producing the set, Jonesy was also responsible for keyboards and programming. The Zepp influence was well in evidence on tracks such as 'Tower Of Strength', with its swirling 'Kashmir'-sounding string effect. The Mission even coaxed the man back on stage when he joined them for the encore of 'Shelter From The Storm' at their London Astoria date in March 1988. Wayne Hussey threw in some lines from 'Rock And Roll' as an acknowledgement. This association was a short lived affair however, with Jonesy's attention to studio detail not always in harmony with the group's requirements.

In May 1988 John Paul joined Page, Plant and Jason Bonham for the Atlantic Anniversary show. Since then, there has been a distinct lack of public activity. He is now contracted to the Opal label and management stable and did have a track included on an Opal compilation entitled 'Music From Films'.

Recent Jones activity included helping out on arrangements for the new Cinderella album, and recording an industrial flamenco group in Barcelona called La Sura Dels Baus. It's safe to assume that he will continue, periodically, to commit himself to further production work, extending the vast musical talent he put to such effective use during the Led Zeppelin era.

Since 1980, John Paul Jones has slipped

On bass guitar, 1973.

back quietly into the backroom role he assumed before joining up with Page, Plant and Bonham. With no ambitions of solo stardom, it's a role he obviously feels very comfortable with. However, should his ex-colleagues decide to play together at any point in the future, when it comes to the role of keyboards and bass . . . his contribution, as it was during the years 1968 to 1980, would be irreplaceable.

On grand piano 1985.

"Something far more powerful than words can say." Plant, Jones and Page moments after their Live Aid reunion, Philadelphia JFK Stadium, July 13, 1985.

WEARING AND TEARING:
POST 1980

Led Zeppelin After Led Zeppelin

ntil Saturday July 13, 1985, the legend of Led Zeppelin appeared to be lying respectfully dormant. Both Page and Plant had carved out seemingly satisfying solo careers, built upon a conscious effort to avoid trading on past glories. Jones had just issued a soundtrack album that saw his name restored to the record racks. Stephen Davis' scurrilous observations in *The Hammer Of The Gods* had only just hit the news stands, and Kingdom Come's cloning operation was still a while off yet.

That was until *Live Aid* brought the three remaining members of Led Zeppelin back together again.

Of course prior to that celebrated day, they had kept in contact for both business and pleasure. Late in 1981 the three made their first post-Zeppelin public appearance in a strictly non-playing role at an old favourite group haunt, Fulham's Golden Lion pub. They were there with Peter Grant to hand over raffle prizes in the venue's annual charity bash.

A few months later Jimmy and Robert got back on stage together to jam with Foreigner in Munich. Also in 1982, Plant, Page and Jones oversaw the release of 'Coda', booking in studio time at The Sol studio. In 1983 they attended various meetings in the winding down of the Swan Song operation.

Any business animosity was certainly quickly cast aside as both Jimmy and Jonesy joined Plant for encore guest slots on his solo 'Principle Of Moments' tour in London and Bristol respectively. There was more ex-Zepp interaction in 1984, when Jimmy helped out on a couple of tracks apiece on Robert's Honeydrippers project, and JP's *Scream For Help* soundtrack.

Then came *Live Aid*. After missing out on the Band Aid single, Robert put his name forward to Bob Geldof in early 1985 to be considered for the giant charity concert he was organising. With the 'Shaken 'n' Stirred' tour scheduled for dates in the summer, Plant was added to the American end of the concert. At that point New

York's Shea stadium looked the likely venue. The switch to the Philadelphia JFK stadium suited Robert better as he was due in Detroit the night before the proposed July 13 date. With so many stars on the bill, the initial idea was to double up some names, and at one point Plant was down to join Eric Clapton for a blues set. The significance of the occasion had already dawned however, and he felt that the gig demanded something much more emotional.

"It seemed to be one of the two or three occasions in my life when I should consider it," Robert recalled later. "The event was far more important than my determination to steer clear of something. So I called Jimmy and said, 'Let's do it.' He went all smarmy on me by saying 'Let's do Honeydrippers material,' expecting me to say, 'No that wouldn't be right'!"

From that call things moved fast. Robert contacted ex-Chic drummer Tony Thompson, on the road with the Power Station in Virginia. Both Jimmy and Robert had been impressed with his wide screen drumming on the Power Station album, and they asked him to join them at *Live Aid*. Thompson was actually a little reluctant to agree, and it took further persuasion before he did. His initial reticence

Whole Lotta Live Aid.

centred on the lack of rehearsal time available, something that was proving a definite problem. With Plant playing in Chicago on July 10 and 11 and Detroit the next day, the only time they had to rehearse a set was the morning of the gig in a nearby recording studio. So it was that Jimmy, Robert, John Paul Jones (who had instantly agreed to join them), Tony Thompson and Paul Martinez (from the Plant band), arrived at the JFK stadium Philadelphia on July 13 as ready as they could be to fit the bill.

It had also been decided that Phil Collins, who had flown over by Concorde from the Wembley end, would assist them as a second drummer. It was after one a.m. in the UK and turning to dusk in Philadelphia when Phil Collins ended his set and swung the mike round to utter the words that would signal the reunion of the three surviving members of Led Zeppelin, exactly five years and five days after they had last shared a stage together.

"I'd like to introduce some friends of mine. Would you welcome Mr Robert Plant, Mr Jimmy Page, Mr John Paul Jones, Mr Tony Thompson, Mr Paul Martinez."

As the curtains folded back, the reality was there for the world to see. Mr Jones, ever prepared with Fender bass strapped on and ready; Mr Page, not so ready, baggy polo shirt and traditional white scarf in tow, bowing to the audience, arms outstretched, and Mr Plant, looking supremely fit, leaping over the monitors, anxious to utter the immortal words "Good Evening!"

Unfortunately, all was not entirely well. Plant was now singing for the fourth night in succession, and coupled with the rehearsal, the strain was just too much and his voice was very hoarse. The monitors were also causing problems. "There'll be a short intermission while I get some monitors," Plant told the multitudes. Jimmy was also having equipment problems and his Gibson was well out of tune. "It was so much like a lot of Led Zeppelin gigs," recalled Plant. "One-and-a-half billion people and Page is swanning around with no guitar, and I'm wondering how my voice is going to stand up and thinking, 17 years and we still can't get it right!"

Then it was one, two, three, four and off into 'Rock And Roll' with two drummers blazing. The TV drum sound was scratchy and distorted and Jimmy's guitar lurched rather than glided into the mix but, despite the technical problems, the whole emotional atmosphere of the occasion carried them through, and there was a definite sense of Zeppelin's old magic returning. After the opening number Plant teased the millions watching with a cry of "Any requests!" and Page duly obliged by pumping out a few 'Heartbreaker' riffs before switching into 'Whole Lotta Love'.

Due to the strict time limit, this was performed in a version similar in structure to the edited hit single of years back. Here we had Phil Collins anxiously following Tony Thompson for the right breaks, and Jimmy clustered with Plant in familiar pose for the chorus. The Gibson was still hopelessly out of tune but at least they got the ending right. And 90,000 present went mad. "OK that was kinda up tempo this is something that takes the mood down a little, and yet, then again, lifts everything up . . . maybe . . . who knows?"

Cue for the double-neck entry of 'that' song. In a day strewn with emotion, the sight of the ex-members of Led Zeppelin performing their most revered composition, ailments and technical problems aside, was simply very moving indeed. Joined by Paul Martinez on bass, Robert got all the lyrics off (yes, we did remember laughter), but re-entered from Page's solo a few bars too early. No matter. The satellite pictures of the final line being sung, as the camera panned high above the stadium, must be ingrained on the memories of millions of television viewers. "Thank you, see ya again."

Back in the UK the current total monies pledged by telephone stood at one million, eight hundred thousand pounds. Within an hour of the Zepp reunion being broadcast, the total had hit two million.

The actual enormity of what they had achieved just by appearing on a stage again may not have been too apparent in the initial MTV interview they did directly after the show. "Well it happened for about 20 minutes and it was great," commented Plant. Later, with hindsight, he

would admit, "I'd be lying if I said I wasn't really drunk on the whole event. The rush I got from the audience, well I'd forgotten how much I'd missed it. I'd also forgotten how Led Zeppelin and Bonzo could never be replaced. The fact that they were still chanting for us 15 minutes later, and the fact there were people crying all over the place, well it was something far more powerful than words can say."

The last word came from Jimmy: "*Live Aid* did feel like one hour's rehearsal after several years, but to be part of *Live Aid* was wonderful. It really was."

And that appeared to be that. Jimmy went back to working on a new Firm album, and Robert rejoined his band in Cleveland for the remaining 15 dates of the US 'Shaken 'n' Stirred' tour.

The sheer euphoria of July 13, though, was hard to shake off. "I kept thinking how I'd do this if I was to do it every night again," Plant commented at the time. Further Zepp excitement occurred at Meadowlands in New Jersey on July 23 when Jimmy, in the presence of Atlantic's Ahmet Ertegun, got up with Robert for an encore jam. The second time the ex-partners had been together in just over a week. Both dressed in their *Live Aid* gear, Robert repeated his "Any requests!" taunt but resisted the calls and compromised by playing old blues stand-bys 'Mean Woman Blues' and Roy Brown's 'Treat Her Right'.

C learly the pull of the past was difficult to shake off. The confused state of his solo career led Robert to rethink his whole future. On the completion of his tour in the UK in September, he disbanded the touring and recording group he'd worked with since 1981. Relationships with Robbie Blunt in particular were none too harmonious. The question in his mind was whether he could work with Jimmy and Jones again. A date was set to stage a secret get together in a village hall near Peter Gabriel's Bath studios. So in January 1986, along with Tony Thompson, Plant, Page and Jones attempted to make new music together. With Jones on keyboards, Plant allegedly handled bass parts and collectively they assembled . . . "Two or three things that were quite promising, a sort of cross between David Byrne and Husker Du."

Trying to turn the clock back, though, was particularly hard for Plant. In the intervening years he had become a lot

more decisive and forthright. Handling Jimmy Page's eccentricity was now not so easy. "For it to succeed in Bath I would have had to have been far more patient than I had been for years," Plant said later. Matters were not helped when Tony Thompson was injured in a car accident. From there it fell apart rapidly. Unable to handle Jimmy changing the batteries on his wah-wah pedal every other song, it all became too much for Plant. He left. A permanent reunion was not to be.

Instead the three picked up the pieces of their solo careers. However, their mutual appreciation society continued. In 1987 Robert invited Jimmy to play on 'Heaven Knows' and 'Tall Cool One' (at that point yet to include the Zepp sampling which Page was reportedly none too pleased about when he eventually heard it). Robert returned the compliment by adding vocals and lyrics to 'The Only One' on Page's 'Outrider' album. When Plant embarked on the 'Non Stop Go' UK tour, which included a revival of a hand-

Led Zeppelin, with Jason Bonham, at the Atlantic Records 40th Anniversary reunion, Madison Square Garden, New York, May 14, 1988.

ful of Zepp numbers, there occurred one of the most potent link-ups with Jimmy. This took place at the Hammersmith Odeon on April 17, 1988. Originally scheduled to play on three encore numbers, Page stayed on stage for a half-hour segment that included a stunning 'Trampled Underfoot', 'Gamblers Blues' (with snatches of 'I Can't Quit You Baby' and 'Since I've Been Loving You') and 'Rock And Roll'. Page looked relaxed and played brilliantly.

This was in stark contrast to their next reunion a month later.

1988 marked the 40th anniversary of the Atlantic Recording Corporation. To celebrate, a massive 12-hour concert was planned for Madison Square Garden in New York. All manner of distinguished artists past and present were invited to perform. Atlantic boss Ahmet Ertegun was very keen for Jimmy, Robert and Jones to appear. Having much admiration for Ahmet and Atlantic's long history as a pioneer independent R&B label, Robert

immediately put his name forward, and the others followed. Seeing it as a way of making amends for the shaky *Live Aid* set, this time they made ample plans for rehearsal.

It seemed natural also to call in Jason Bonham to complete the line-up. Thus, the stage was set for another celebrated Led Zeppelin return on May 14, 1988.

For Jason this was a dream come true. By that time he had carved out a career for himself as a reputable drummer, touring with Airace, and latterly Virginia Wolf who had supported The Firm. Jimmy had also enlisted his assistance in recording the 'Outrider' album and he would later take Jason on the road in his new touring unit. Jason had also played with Robert in the past, helping out on demoing his first two solo albums. He had yet to play with John Paul Jones but this proved to be no problem. The moment Page called him, Jason spent a week playing along to countless Zepp tunes. Minus Robert who was on tour in America, Jimmy, Jonesy

and Jason booked in rehearsals at London's Nomis studio. Here they ran through 15 to 20 Zeppelin numbers. It was then that JP recognised Jason's thorough knowledge of the Zepp set. ''It was like, well you just slip back to how you remembered it. I went in to a very old fill I used to do, and he's right there with me! And it's one of those things that a bass player and drummer only do when they've been married 10 years, but we went straight into it and we just looked around and both shouted 'Chicago 1975!'''

Rehearsals continued with a day in a New York studio with Robert, and a soundcheck at the Garden the day before the concert. They ran through what was to emerge as the Atlantic set, plus a version of 'I Can't Quit You Baby'. Reports from this workout indicated that this time the world would witness a Led Zeppelin reincarnated both in spirit and performance. Sadly it was not to be.

Atlantic's 12-hour 40th Anniversary concert entitled 'It's Only Rock 'n' Roll' got

The Atlantic reunion.

under way with The Coasters singing 'That's Rock 'n' Roll'. Countless acts followed including The Rascals, Crosby, Stills And Nash, Genesis, Wilson Pickett, Iron Butterfly, ELP (the last two both reformed for the day), Ben E. King and Foreigner and a solo spot from Plant and his band. There had been a plan to close the show with a greatest hits all-star jam but that idea was duly shelved. As stage organiser Bill Graham, back in harmony with the reformed Zepp stated, "No offence to anyone else on the bill but nobody could follow Zeppelin." To add to the expectation, during the day a video of Zeppelin playing 'Heartbreaker' at Knebworth was screened between band changeovers.

The trouble began when the show ran late. An extremely nervous Page arrived at the Garden around 11.30 pm. As he would note afterwards . . . "I was sitting around for an hour-and-a-half just getting wound up." Reports of his moody behaviour had been circulating since his arrival on the Wednesday. Plant too seemed uneasy, and other stories abound that up until a few minutes before they went on, he was refusing to sing 'Stairway To Heaven'. Amidst all this mayhem, Page, Plant, Jones and Bonham were ushered on to the stage just after one a.m., following an introduction from Ertegun, Phil Collins and host Robert Townsend. Jason picked out the familiar four-beat 1975 era intro on the hi-hat and Led Zeppelin 1988 were playing 'Kashmir'. It should have been a glorious moment. It was anything but.

They certainly looked the part: Robert, long flowing hair, in a smart white and black rimmed shirt; Page, a slightly broader version of the 1980 model, in extra large 'Outrider' suit, scarf, Marlboro in mouth, Dan Electro in hand; Jones, resplendent in black with the 1977 Alembic bass; and Jason playing his heart out, concentrating furiously. They did not, however, sound the part. The whole event was being televised in the US on HBO and the TV feed totally lost Jonesy's keyboards. On stage too, all was not entirely well. Robert had long since switched the verses of 'Kashmir' around from how they appeared on the studio cut. On this occasion he mixed them up entirely, missing out the 'Oh pilot of the storm' verse and being forced to sing the 'Oh father of four winds' line twice, which he acknowledged with a smile by singing 'fill my sails . . . again!'

To their credit they got through the difficult 'Kashmir' (surprisingly devoid of the regular 'Woman talkin' to ya' ad-lib) during which Plant was also struck by a blimp, and hurtled into a well intended 'Heartbreaker'. Page, jacket off and looking determined, failed miserably when it came to the solo, which lacked the fluency required to make it stand out. 'Heartbreaker' led into a truncated 'Whole Lotta Love', played in the Knebworth revamped arrangement. This provided the first real slice of sheer Zepp dynamics, as Page, Jones and Jason crunched down on the riff. After introducing Jason and getting a 'thank you' from Page, Plant swung the group through a fine 'Misty

Mountain Hop'. They now appeared much looser and more confident, and Robert clearly benefited from being familiar with this number through his solo tour. A well timed stop gap ending evoked memories of the Knebworth version of this vintage outing.

'Stairway To Heaven' inevitably closed the set. Plant had trouble with the lyrics here singing the 'Your head is humming' line twice, and Page again seemed very rusty on the solo. Then it was all over. "Thank you . . . it's been real, see you all again soon."

Opinions remain divided on this 28-minute reunion. Those that were there talk of an atmosphere and power sadly missed by the TV cameras. Certainly the small screen captured little of the Zeppelin magic that had, despite the shambolic nature of the event, been in evidence at *Live Aid*. Led Zeppelin and television had never got along well which is why they made so few appearances on TV during their prime. The Atlantic reunion seemed to justify the decision the band and Peter Grant made all those years ago to steer clear of the medium.

As for the group, well for Jason alone they were happy to have done it. The fact that the pressure affected them continues to baffle. As Plant summed it up in 1990 . . . "What happened? I can't tell you. I have no idea. I'm sitting in exactly the same spot as everyone else asking the great void why? But a lot of people thought they saw something great. The crazy thing is that at the soundcheck it was spectacular."

he erratic display at the Atlantic reunion may have made a fair case for letting sleeping dogs lie. As it turned out, it had the opposite effect. As The Who, The Rolling Stones and Pink Floyd enjoyed massive success in their respective comeback tours during the late eighties, the price for a Led Zeppelin return increased rapidly. Offers running well into the millions were bandied about. A 1990 reunion was hotly tipped from American sources. In March Plant released the well received 'Manic Nirvana' album and returned to the road with his own band, the set heavily laden with Zeppelin numbers.

Against the backdrop of all the rumours, the ex-members continued to add fuel to the fire by staging non public get togethers. The first occurred in late 1989 at the 21st birthday party of Plant's daughter Carmen. Together with various members of his own band, Plant jammed again with Jones and Jimmy. They did 'Trampled Underfoot', 'Misty Mountain Hop' and 'Rock And Roll'. With no expectations it sounded great, spurring Plant to say, "Pagey was playing so good. I had a big lump in my throat. When he plays in those circumstances it's unbelievable. That little time of playing with him gave me something that I hadn't had for a long time." The exercise was repeated on April 28, 1990, when in similar social circumstances, Page, Plant and Jones reformed with Jason at his wedding reception near Kidderminster. They did a set that featured 'Bring It On Home', 'Rock And Roll', 'Sick Again', 'Custard Pie' and Jerry Lee Lewis' 'It'll Be Me'. Those that heard it said it sounded fantastic.

A slightly bigger audience witnessed the next ex-Zepp link up. On June 22 Robert Plant attended the annual awards lunch for the Nordoff Robbins Music Therapy record industry charity. Each year the charity singles out a British performer for the prestigious Silver Clef award. For what Music Therapy chairman Andrew Miller described as, "An outstanding achievement," the 1990 award went to Plant. This made him eligible for the massive Silver Clef Award Winners charity show that had been in the planning for over a year. It paved the way for a nostalgic return to Knebworth where Robert agreed to line-up with Paul McCartney, Pink Floyd, Elton John, Cliff Richard and other distinguished British performers.

Unsurprisingly, this set the rumour machine back in motion. All during the

Eleven years gone, Knebworth reunion, 1990.

At Jason Bonham's wedding, May 1990.

week of the show, which was staged on June 30, speculation grew that another Zeppelin reunion was in the making. Many newspapers even went as far as printing their name in the list of the running order. For whatever reason, the Knebworth stage did not witness a regrouping of Plant, Page, Jones and Jason as had been widely tipped. Instead Plant invited Jimmy to join him for a jam with his band. They rehearsed on the Thursday (delving into the Zepp catalogue for a special surprise) and soundchecked at Knebworth on the Friday. Asked then if Led Zeppelin would be back on stage tomorrow, Plant replied with a curt, "No" and a huge smile.

Introduced by Radio One DJ Gary Davies as, "A singer who is no stranger to big crowds, he played to a total of 380,000 on his last visit here 11 years ago," Robert Plant strode back onto the Knebworth platform at around 4.45 pm on a windy Saturday afternoon. With his now excessively long hair blowing in the wind, Plant whipped his band into 'Hurting Kind' from the Nirvana album. It was 'Immigrant Song', a 'Led Zepp III' epic, that really burst the nostalgia floodgates wide open. Here was the singer from Led Zeppelin, belting out one of their greatest

numbers, on a stage that was the scene of one of their most memorable concerts. The mid afternoon sun also evoked memories of that festival in a field at Shepton Mallet near Bath many years back, when 'Immigrant Song' received one of its first public airings. It did seem rather absurd that the co-writer of this epic was somewhere in the wings awaiting entry. As it did when, after performing the hippy-inspired 'Tie Dye On The Highway' and going acoustic for 'Liar's Dance' (with Plant teasing with the line, 'Let's just save it for the lady who's sure . . . the lady who's sure? but she won't be back again . . . I know she won't be back again'), Plant and his band sang 'Going To California', a song that surely encapsulates the ethereal Page/Plant combination more than most and which cried out for his involvement.

After restoring the tempo with 'Nirvana' and 'Tall Cool One', Robert finally acknowledged his guest. "Well this little award was given to me last week, not particularly for anything I've done, but for what has happened between 1966, when I made my first record, and today. I've been working for four years with these guys and it's been a wonderful time and I owe a good portion of this to these chaps behind me. I also owe a major proportion of this to my good friend who has just joined me on stage . . . Jimmy Page."

And on he bounded. Looking like he'd stepped off the set of the 'Wasting My Time' video in a well cut suit, Page strapped on the cherry red Gibson and cut into a rather shaky 'Misty Mountain Hop'. However, the next number made everything else that had gone before (including the majority of past reunion efforts) look mighty insignificant. Page and Plant proceeded to storm through 'Wearing And Tearing', the Polar track issued on 'Coda' and a number never ever previously played live. The energy level was quite remarkable, Page attacking the guitar with an intensity that brought to mind the rejuvenated days of a decade previous. Here was a performance that upheld the spirit that was Led Zeppelin with devastating accuracy. After all these years the chemistry evidently remained the same.

A rousing 'Rock And Roll', with Page manically stalking the stage, ended this all too brief resurgence. Page and Plant left the Knebworth stage as they had 11 years before, arm in arm. Happy and surely content in sharing with the audience the notion that a Led Zeppelin in the nineties, could still be a very viable proposition.

Led Zeppelin

Remasters

'LED ZEPPELIN'

Atlantic 7567821441/2/4 (six albums/four CD's/four cassettes)

Whole Lotta Love/Heartbreaker/Communication Breakdown/Babe I'm Gonna Leave You/What Is And What Should Never Be/Thank You/I Can't Quit You Baby/Dazed And Confused/Your Time Is Gonna Come/Ramble On/Travelling Riverside Blues/Friends/Celebration Day/Hey Hey What Can I Do/White Summer – Black Mountain Side/Black Dog/Over The Hills And Far Away/Immigrant Song/The Battle Of Evermore/Bron-Y-Aur Stomp/Tangerine/Going To California/Since I've Been Loving You/D'yer Mak'er/Gallows Pole/Custard Pie/Misty Mountain Hop/

Rock And Roll/The Rain Song/Stairway To Heaven/Kashmir/Trampled Underfoot/For Your Life/No Quarter/Dancing Days/When The Levee Breaks/Achilles Last Stand/The Song Remains The Same/Ten Years Gone/In My Time Of Dying/In The Evening/Candy Store Rock/The Ocean/Ozone Baby/Houses Of The Holy/Wearing And Tearing/Poor Tom/Nobody's Fault But Mine/Fool In The Rain/In The Light/The Wanton Song/Moby Dick – Bonzo's Montreux/I'm Gonna Crawl/All My Love.

'REMASTERS'

Atlantic Zep 1/7567804152/4 (triple album/double CD/double cassette)

Communication Breakdown/Babe I'm Gonna Leave You/Good Times, Bad Times/Dazed And Confused/Heartbreaker/Whole Lotta Love/Ramble On/Since I've Been Loving You/Celebration Day/Immigrant Song/Black Dog/Rock And Roll/The Battle Of Evermore/Stairway To Heaven/The Song Remains The Same/D'yer Mak'er/No Quarter/Houses Of The Holy/Trampled Underfoot/Kashmir/Nobody's Fault But Mine/Achilles Last Stand/All My Love/In The Evening. Cassette and CD versions also include Misty Mountain Hop/The Rain Song.

LED ZEPPELIN
REMASTERED 1990
The Same Picture With A Different Frame

The release of these two separate Led Zeppelin retrospective collections in the space of two weeks in October 1990, rounded off a year in which the group's popularity reached heights unparalleled since the mid-seventies. The excitement, both critical and commercial, that greeted the appearance of the 'Led Zeppelin Remastered' project emphasised how much the group – and the timeless and eclectic quality of their music – had been missed during the 'disposable pop' atmosphere of the eighties.

It had been no secret that Jimmy Page was deeply unhappy with the Led Zeppelin CDs that Atlantic issued without consulting him. Originally produced for vinyl, the music suffered in transit: subtle frequencies in the sound spectrum were lost and the 'ambient' sound that Page had worked so hard to create by the placement of microphones in the studio was also lost. Small wonder, then, that when Atlantic approached him to remaster the tapes for a compilation collection, he jumped at the idea. Studio time was booked at New York's Sterling studios where Page spent a week in May 1990 with engineer George Marino digitally restoring Led Zeppelin's whole catalogue from the original two-track master tapes.

The plan was to compile a multi-track box set collection for which Page drew up a possible listing for Plant and Jones to sanction. "I really wanted to improve the overall sound spectrum," Page was quoted on the official press release. "Basically it's the same picture with a different frame."

John Paul Jones added: "The songs sound as fresh today as they did when first recorded, and the new positions in the running order seem to put them in a totally different light."

A long term reissue of the entire catalogue remastered for CD is also envisaged.

The original compilation concept was to package 54 tracks in a deluxe box with accompanying booklet of photos and essays. Atlantic's European distributors

East West also managed to clear a separate edited version of the set for Europe only. This condensed version, virtually a greatest hits package aimed squarely at the lucrative Christmas market, appeared under the title 'Remasters' as a 24-track, triple album and 26-track, double CD and cassette on October 15. A full marketing campaign including a TV advertisement was prepared as the Zepp catalogue finally succumbed to the commercial potential of the nineties. Plant, Page and Jones did retain part of their original strategy in vetoing the planned release of 'Stairway To Heaven' as a UK single.

The 'Remasters' set was scheduled for deletion on March 31, 1991, and since it contains one track not on the box set ('Good Times Bad Times'), it is sure to be a future Zepp collectable.

The real gem for Zeppelin enthusiasts was the October 29 appearance of the 54-track box set, simply entitled 'Led Zeppelin' and spread over six albums, four CD's and four cassettes.

Despite certain faults – the dearth of selections from 'Physical Graffiti', no chronological live tracks or alternate studio takes, the factual errors in the visually superb accompanying booklet (*Live Aid* in 1987 – I think not) – this set does stand as a lasting testament to the diversity of musical styles Led Zeppelin approached from 1968 to 1980.

Beautifully packaged with that typically bizarre airship shadowed, cornfield 'mystery circles' illustration, it's wonderful to hear so many tracks all at one sitting. For those very familiar with their catalogue, the new sequencing is also a joy – as 'Heartbreaker' switches instantly to 'Communication Breakdown', 'Over The Hills And Far Away' juxtaposes against 'Immigrant Song' and 'The Song Remains The Same' drifts into 'Ten Years Gone'. Note too, the slightly longer intro to 'Nobody's Fault But Mine' with an extra opening Page guitar riff, and the fact that many timings on the original albums were well out (e.g. 'Kashmir' is now correctly listed as being 8.31 in duration, and not the long

presumed 9.41).

And there are some new delights. The little heard 'Zeppelin III' era 'Hey Hey What Can I Do', previously only available on a long-deleted UK Atlantic sampler album, and as the B-side to the 1970 'Immigrant Song' US/European single, retains all its original summer of 1970 semi-acoustic warmth. It's also great to hear the spiralling blues slide of the BBC *Top Gear* 1969 radio remnant 'Travelling Riverside Blues' – a Page/Plant/Robert Johnson interpretation. Nostalgic memories also prevail on the live BBC take of 'White Summer/Black Mountain Side' from June 27, 1969.

Jimmy has also included an affectionate Bonzo tribute, an amalgamation of 'Moby Dick' and 'Bonzo's Montreux', produced with the aid of Synclavier programming at Atlantic's Synclavier suite.

All in all, the overall sound quality is greatly enhanced, with Page adding a new punch and clarity remastered from the original analogue tapes.

In the round of interviews accompanying this set, Jimmy hinted strongly that a live compilation video could well be in the offing, a statement fuelled by MTV's exclusive showing of clips from Seattle in 1977 and Knebworth 1979. Future Page plans include the recording of a second solo album and the formation of a new recording and touring unit.

Which of course leaves the final begging question. Will they reform? Certainly if Page can win over Plant it could well happen. And if the pair, alongside John Paul Jones, are able to collaborate again in producing new music of substance then a whole new chapter could well be waiting to be written.

Meanwhile, my final advice here is for you to pull out the box set, commence at track one, and return to the Ten Album Legacy section earlier in this text to monitor again the magic and memories of Led Zeppelin's music.

Reformation or not, this is a story that will run and run.

The celebration continues . . .

THE LED ZEPPELIN CHRONOLOGY

1944–1990

1944
January 9 – James Patrick Page born in Heston, Middlesex.

1946
January 3 – John Paul Jones (nee Baldwin) born in Sidcup, Kent.

1948
May 31 – John Henry Bonham born in Redditch, Worcestershire.
August 20 – Robert Anthony Plant born in West Bromwich, Staffordshire.

1962
Jimmy Page joins Neil Christian And The Crusaders.

1963
January – Jimmy Page's first appearance on record, a session for Jet Harris and Tony Meehan's 'Diamonds'.
October – Jimmy Page plays on Carter Lewis And The Southerners 'Your Mamma's Out Of Town' and gigs with them on some radio dates. John Paul Jones joins Jet Harris and Tony Meehan's backing group.

1964
April – John Paul Jones' solo single released – 'Baja'/'A Foggy Day In Vietnam'. John Paul Jones makes his name as one of the top session arrangers and Jimmy Page establishes himself as one of the top UK session guitarist's playing on countless hit records of the era. Robert Plant plays in his first groups – Andy Long And The Original Jaymen, The Black Snake Moan and The Crawling King Snakes.
John Bonham plays in his first groups – Terry Webb And The Spiders and A Way Of Life.

1965
February – Jimmy Page releases a solo single – 'She Just Satisfies'/'Keep Moving'.

1966
June – Jimmy Page joins The Yardbirds initially on bass, soon switching to dual lead guitar with Jeff Beck.
November – Page takes over as lead Yardbirds guitarist following Beck's departure.
October – Robert Plant sings lead vocal on Listen's single 'You Better Run'/'Everybody's Gonna Say'.
December – John Paul Jones arranges the strings on The Yardbirds' recording of 'Little Games' at Olympic studios.

1967
Robert Plant links up with John Bonham in The Band Of Joy.
March – Release of Robert Plant's solo single 'Our Song'/'Laughing, Crying, Laughing'.
March – Release of Jeff Beck's 'Hi Ho Silver Lining' single which has the Page composition 'Beck's Bolero' on the B-side. It was while playing on this session that Page heard Keith Moon suggest the name Lead Zeppelin as a possible title for the group they discussed forming.

August – The Yardbirds 'Little Games' album issued in the US. It includes the future Page stage showcase number 'White Summer'.
September – Release of Robert Plant's solo single 'Long Time Coming'/'I've Got A Secret'.

1968
January – Band Of Joy play regular London dates at the Middle Earth.
March – New Page/Yardbirds track 'I'm Confused' (later to be re-titled 'Dazed And Confused') aired at a session on John Peel's *Top Gear* radio show.
April – John Paul Jones performs with Jimmy on a session for Donovan's 'Hurdy Gurdy Man', and asks to be considered for a new group Jimmy is rumoured to be forming.
May – Band Of Joy split. Robert records demos at Marquee studios. John Bonham tours with Tim Rose.
June 2 – Last Yardbirds recording session at CBS studios in New York includes Page's 'Tangerine'.
June 5 – Last Yardbirds US gig in Alabama.
June 22 – Announced that Keith Relf and Jim McCarty are leaving The Yardbirds.
June – Robert Plant gigs and records with Alexis Korner.
June – Jimmy Page records with Joe Cocker at Olympic Studios.
July 7 – Final Yardbirds gig at Luton Technical College.
August – Jimmy Page, Chris Dreja and former Yardbirds manager Peter Grant see Robert Plant play with Hobstweedle at a Birmingham teacher training college. At this point B.J. Wilson from Procol Harum who Page had worked with on the Joe Cocker session and the unknown Paul Francis were being touted as possibles for the vacant drum position.

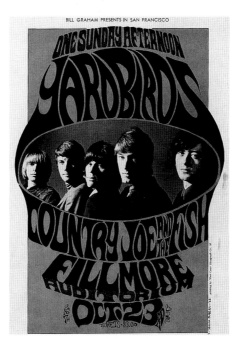

August – Plant offered vocalist job in The New Yardbirds line-up after visiting Page's Pangbourne home.
August – Chris Dreja decides not to carry on as bassist in The New Yardbirds. Page calls in John Paul Jones.
August – John Bonham completes the New Yardbirds line-up on Plant's recommendation.
September – First Page, Plant, Jones and Bonham group rehearsals, in Gerrard Street, London.
September 14 – Fulfil existing Yardbirds dates billed as The New Yardbirds on a 10-date Scandinavian tour commencing in Copenhagen.
Late September – Agreed that The New Yardbirds name will be phased out. After considering names such as The Mad Dogs, The Mad Boys and The Whoopie Cushions, Page and manager Peter Grant return to Keith Moon's Lead Zeppelin phrase, knocking out the 'a' to simplify the name for American audiences. Thus The New Yardbirds become Led Zeppelin.
October – Record first album at Olympic studios.
October 17 – First gig billed as Led Zeppelin at Surrey University.
October 18 – Play the Marquee still billed as The New Yardbirds.
October 19 – Last ever gig billed as The New Yardbirds at Liverpool University.
November 9 – Plant marries Maureen in London. The 'reception' is Led Zeppelin's first billed London show at the Roundhouse, Chalk Farm.
November – Grant clinches worldwide deal with Atlantic and forms Superhype publishing company.
December – Month of club gigs in the UK.
December 26 – Commence first American tour at the Coliseum in Denver, Colorado.

1969
January 17 – 'Led Zeppelin I' album issued in America.
February 2 – Complete US tour at New York's Fillmore East.
February – Led Zeppelin first album enters *Billboard* Top 40.
March – More club dates in the UK.
March 19 – Scandinavian tour includes 30-minute showcase on Danish TV (finally aired in the UK 20 years later!).
March 21 – One and only live UK TV appearance playing 'Communication Breakdown' on BBC2's *How Late It Is*.
March 23 – First radio session on John Peel's *Top Gear*.
March 25 – Filming session at Staines for *Supershow* movie.
March 28 – Led Zeppelin début album issued in UK.
April – More UK gigs, followed by second US visit (the first as headliners).
May – US tour continues. Début album enters *Billboard* Top 10. Recording sessions commence along the way for the second album.
June – Record session for BBC Radio One, at Aoelian Hall, London and Maida Vale.
June 13 – First proper UK tour commences at Birmingham Town Hall.
June – More sessions for second album at Morgan studios.

June 27 – Playhouse Theatre London show taped for BBC radio's *In Concert*.

June 28 – Appearance at the Bath Festival.

June 29 – Two shows at London's Royal Albert Hall Pop Proms.

July 5 – Third US tour. Over 20 dates including open air festivals (they miss out on a scheduled appearance at Woodstock). More recording takes place for the second album.

August – Third US tour ends at the Texas International Festival in Dallas.

September – Short holiday break. Second album is completed.

October 12 – Resume touring with warm-up date in Paris followed by this Sunday night showcase at London's Lyceum ballroom.

October 17 – Led Zeppelin become first rock act to play New York's Carnegie Hall when they open their fourth US tour.

October 31 – 'Led Zeppelin II' released to massive, worldwide sales.

November 8 – Fourth US tour ends at San Francisco's Winterland ballroom.

November – Initial recording for the third album commences at Olympic. 'Since I've Been Loving You' is tried out as well as 'Jennings Farm Blues'.

December 5 – Projected UK release of 'Whole Lotta Love' as an edited single halted by Peter Grant.

December 11 – Led Zeppelin's worldwide record sales recognised with a presentation of gold and platinum discs by the Parliamentary secretary to the Board Of State at London's Savoy hotel.

1970

January 7 – Seven-date UK tour opens in Birmingham.

January 9 – Royal Albert Hall gig filmed and recorded for an intended Zeppelin-financed TV documentary. The same week it is revealed Led Zeppelin have turned down an offer to appear on the *Tom Jones* TV show.

January – 'Whole Lotta Love' reaches number four on the *Billboard* chart.

February – Edinburgh gig cancelled after Plant receives facial injuries in a car accident.

February 21 – European tour kicks off in Copenhagen where the group are billed as The Nobs after threat of legal action from Count Von Zeppelin!

March 13 – European tour ends at the Montreux Jazz Festival.

March 21 – 27-date fifth American tour commences in Vancouver.

April 4 – Jimmy Page's solo appearance on the *Julie Felix* BBC2 show (he performs 'White Summer'/'Black Mountain Side') screened.

April 6 – While in Memphis, Led Zeppelin made honorary citizens.

April 19 – US tour ends in Phoenix.

May – Plant and Page write and prepare material for the third album at a cottage in Bron-Y-Aur. Later in the month the group begin recording at Headley Grange in Hampshire.

June – Recording sessions at Olympic.

June 20/21 – Warm-up dates in Reykjavik, Iceland.

June 28 – Bill-topping appearance at the Bath Festival.

July 9 – Commence short German tour in Dusseldorf.

July/Early August – Commence additional recording for the third album, this time at the newly opened Island Studios.

August 5 – Sixth American tour commences in Cincinatti.

August 17 – While in Memphis, Page completes mixing of the third album at Ardent studios.

September 19 – Final 1970 concerts at Madison Square Garden, New York.

September 27 – Back in the UK, Led Zeppelin end The Beatles' reign as Top Group in *Melody Maker*'s annual

readers' poll.
October 16 – Led Zeppelin honoured with another presentation of gold discs by Parliamentary Secretary to the Board Of State, Anthony Grant, recognising their "Substantial contribution to the country's healthy balance of exports."
October 23 – 'Led Zeppelin III' released.
November/December – Holiday break and initial fourth album sessions at Island studios.

1971

January – Led Zeppelin take The Rolling Stones' mobile studio to record the fourth album at Headley Grange.
February – Overdub sessions at Island studios. Page travels to Los Angeles to mix the tapes at Sunset Sound studios.
February 14 – All the group attend the *Disc* and *Music Echo* awards in London when they are voted the world's top band.
March 5 – Back on the road for a British tour commencing at Belfast Ulster Hall. 'Stairway To Heaven' is played live for the first time.
March 23 – The UK tour sees them returning to the club venues that first gave them a gig, and ends with a nostalgic date at London's Marquee.
April 4 – First broadcast of the much bootlegged BBC Sunday repeated on Wednesday *In Concert* radio show taped the previous month at London's Paris Theatre.
May/June – European tour dates.
July 3 – Final European tour date ends with a curtailed show at Milan's Vigorelli Stadium due to a crowd riot.
July – Fourth album mixed again in London.
August 19 – After two warm-up dates in Montreux, their seventh US tour commences in Vancouver.
September 16/17 – US tour ends with two shows in Honolulu, after which the group holiday in Hawaii.
September 28 – Five-date Japanese tour commences in Tokyo.
October – Led Zeppelin travel back to the UK. Plant and Page visit Thailand, India and Hong Kong.
November 11 – UK tour commences at Newcastle City Hall.
November 12 – 'Led Zeppelin IV' album issued.
November 20/21 – Two, five-hour 'Electric Magic' appearances at Wembley Empire Pool, with Bronco, Home and Stone The Crows.
December 15 – UK tour ends in Salisbury.

1972

February – A planned date in Singapore cancelled when the group is refused entry to the country because of their long hair.
February 16 – 10-date Australian tour commences in Perth. On the route back, Page and Plant make some experimental recordings in Bombay with the Bombay Symphony Orchestra.
April/May – Fifth album recording sessions on location at Stargroves and Olympic studios.
June 6 – Eighth American tour opens at the Cobra Hall, Detroit.
June – Mixing and recording sessions at Electric Lady studios for the fifth album.
June 28 – US tour ends at the Tueson Community Centre.
August/September – Holiday break.
October 2 – Second Japanese tour commences in Tokyo.
October 28/29 – Two dates at Montreux Casino.
November – Fifth album mixed and completed. Announcement of longest ever UK tour prompts 100,000 ticket sales in one day.
November 30 – UK tour commences at Newcastle City Hall.

December 22/23 – Two Christmas dates at London's Alexandra Palace.

1973

January 2 – Plant and Bonham only just make date at Sheffield City Hall after their Bentley breaks down. Plant comes down with 'flu and the following dates at Bradford and Preston have to be rescheduled.
January 30 – UK tour ends in Preston.
February 16 – Provisional release date of the fifth album to be titled 'Houses Of The Holy' not fulfilled due to sleeve problems.
March 3 – European tour opens in Copenhagen.
March 26 – 'Houses Of The Holy' finally released.
April 1/2 – European tour closes with two nights at the Palais de Sport, Paris.
April – Led Zeppelin rehearse a new stage rig at the Old Town studios in preparation for a mammoth two-legged US tour.
May 4 – Ninth US tour opens to 49,000 fans at the Atlanta Braves Stadium.
May 5 – An astounding 56,800 attend Led Zeppelin's second show of the tour at Tampa Stadium. This sets a record for the largest attendance for a one-act performance, previously held by The Beatles for their Shea Stadium show in 1965.
June 3 – First leg of US tour ends with a rescheduled gig at the LA Forum. This is due to Page spraining his finger.
June – Mid-tour holiday in Hawaii.
July 6 – US tour second leg kicks off in Chicago.
July 23 – Film maker Joe Massot begins shooting footage at the request of Peter Grant and the group in Baltimore.
July 24 – More screen test footage taken at the Three Rivers Stadium in Pittsburgh.
July 27/28/29 – Final nights of the US tour at Madison Square Garden – recorded and filmed for their movie project. Just before the last show, the theft from a deposit box of $203,000 of the group's money at the Drake Hotel is discovered. The crime goes unsolved.
August 1 – Led Zeppelin and entourage return to England for a well earned break. Robert holidays in South Morocco.
August 11 – Led Zeppelin offer a reward of $10,000 for the recovery of the money stolen from the Drake Hotel.
September – Robert picks up his award for Top Male Singer at the *Melody Maker* Poll Awards lunch in London.

October – Joe Massot commences filming individual sequences at the homes of Plant, Page, Jones, Bonham and Peter Grant.
November – Initial sixth album sessions at Headley Grange. Bonzo and Jimmy record an Eastern-flavoured demo instrumental, later to take shape as 'Kashmir'. Sessions break up when Jones takes a rest to think over his intention to quit the group.
December – John Paul Jones promotes Madeline Bell's 'Comin' Atcha' album (which he produced) by playing bass on her BBC2 appearance on *Colour My Soul*.
December 10 and 11 – Joe Massot and crew film Jimmy's mountain climbing sequence for the movie at Loch Ness.

1974

January – In re-signing with Atlantic, Peter Grant announces that all future Led Zeppelin recordings will appear on their own label. The label will also be signing other acts.
January – A group party at the Portman Hotel, London, results in a £1,000 bill.
January/February – Sixth album sessions resume at Headley Grange with a revitalised John Paul Jones back at the helm.
January – Slut Records rumoured to be the title of the new Zeppelin label.
February 14 – Jimmy joins Roy Harper on stage at the Rainbow London. Plant and Bonham are also in attendance.
March/April – More recording sessions. Their record label, now officially named Swan Song, sets up offices in New York and London and signs Bad Company and Maggie Bell for the US.
May 10 – Swan Song Records launched with all members in attendance at two receptions in New York and Los Angeles. During these celebrations the group attend Elvis Presley's LA Forum concert and gain an audience with him after the show.
May – On their return, Peter Grant considers offers for the group to headline a one-day festival on July 20 at Knebworth, and an August 29 date at the Munich Festival due to be relayed live to 10,000 theatres in America. Both are turned down due to the band's commitments to completing their album and 1973 concert film.
July – Mixing sessions at Olympic for the sixth album. This will now be a double set, employing tracks unused from previous albums.
July – New director for their film Peter Clifton works

with the group at Shepperton studios.

August 31 – John Paul Jones forms the backing band with Dave Gilmour and Steve Broughton for Roy Harper's free Hyde Park appearance.

September 1/4 – Jimmy Page jams with Bad Company in Austin, Texas, and Central Park, New York. Bad Company's début album will later this month provide Swan Song with its first number one.

September 14 – All the group attend the Crosby, Stills, Nash and Young Wembley Stadium show. Page and Bonzo jam with Stills, Young and Nash at an after-show party in Piccadilly.

October 31 – Swan Song officially launched with a bizarre party at Chislehurst Caves. All the group attend, plus many guests including Bad Company and first UK signings The Pretty Things.

November 6 – The Pretty Things inaugurate Swan Song in the UK with their single 'Is It Only Love'. Announcement of the planned release of Led Zeppelin's new double album 'Physical Graffiti' (slated as November 29) and their US tour scheduled to open in January 1975.

November 26 – Led Zeppelin gather at the Livewire Theatre in Ealing to commence rehearsals for their US tour.

December 21 – Jimmy and Jonesy jam with Bad Company at their Rainbow gig in London.

1975

January 11/12 – Warm-up dates in Rotterdam and Brussels. Plant records an interview with Bob Harris backstage in Brussels, later screened on *The Old Grey Whistle Test*.

January 17 – The group rehearse a revised set in Minneapolis due to Jimmy breaking his finger days before at Victoria station.

January 18 – 10th US tour opens at the Metro Sports Centre, Minneapolis.

February 3 – At the first of three Madison Square Garden shows, Page restores 'Dazed And Confused' to the set for the first time, his injured finger having forced its temporary deletion up until then.

February 14 – First leg of the tour completed with a show at the Long Island Coliseum. Plant and Page holiday on the island of Dominica.

February 24 – 'Physical Graffiti' finally issued worldwide to phenomenal sales.

March 15 – Tickets for Led Zeppelin's just-announced Earls Court shows sell out within four hours.

March 27 – Final night of the US tour at the Los Angeles Forum.

April – Jimmy, Robert and Peter Grant fly to New York on Swan Song business. Jimmy does some mixing on their film soundtrack at Electric Lady studios.

April 19 – Two extra dates are added at Earls Court due to what promoter Mel Bush describes as "Unprecedented demand in the history of rock music."

May 10 – Swan Song distribute 5,000 copies of a special limited edition UK single coupling 'Trampled Underfoot' with 'Black Country Woman'.

May 17/18/23/24/25 – 85,000 people attend Led Zeppelin's five massive shows at the Earls Court arena in London.

May 25 – All the group attend an after-show party held at the Swan Song/Earls Court restaurant.

May 26 – Robert Plant and wife Maureen leave for a holiday in Agadir. These travels would later be chronicled in the lyrics of 'Achilles Last Stand'.

June – Robert meets with Jimmy in Marakesh for the Morrocan folk festival.

June – Peter Clifton announces the near completion of the Led Zeppelin feature film.

July – Plant and Page continue their travels back through Casablanca and Tangiers, eventually meeting

up with the rest of the group at the Montreux Festival. A second US tour is announced for August. This is the start of a year of non-residency for the group for tax purposes. Page and Plant resume their holidays with their families in Rhodes.

August 3 – Page leaves for Italy, planning to reunite with the group for rehearsals five days later in Paris.

August 4 – Robert and Maureen Plant seriously injured when their rented car goes off the road in Rhodes. Both are air lifted back to the UK. Plant is forced to recuperate in Jersey due to his tax situation.

September – With the upcoming tour plans cancelled, Plant moves to Malibu. Jimmy Page follows. Songwriting commences for a new album in lieu of the tour.

September 14 – Plant, Page and Grant attend the 'Renaissance Pleasure Fair' in Novato.

September 27 – Page and Bonzo pick up the group's seven *Melody Maker* poll awards at a reception in London.

October – Rehearsals held at SIR studios in Hollywood for the recording of a new album.

November – Led Zeppelin record their seventh album at Munich's Musicland studios in a mere 18 days.

December 10 – Back in Jersey, the group make a surprise appearance at the Beehan's West Park night club.

December 24 – All the group back in England for Christmas.

1976

January 1 – In Paris, Plant takes his first unaided steps since the accident.

January – In New York Robert holds a round of interviews. Page continues mixing the soundtrack at Electric Lady. Bonzo leaps on stage at the end of Deep Purple's Radio City Hall show to proclaim, "Hi, I'm John Bonham from Led Zeppelin and we've got a new album coming out soon!"

February – Zeppelin sweep the board in the *NME* readers' poll.

March – Back in London, Page holds a series of interviews at the Swan Song office.

April 5 – The seventh Led Zeppelin album 'Presence' is released.

May 23 – Robert Plant returns to the stage with Jimmy to jam with Bad Company at the LA Forum.

May 26 – Led Zeppelin return to the UK. The flight back includes a humorous run-in with actor Telly Savalas.

May 27 – Heavily rumoured the group will play a surprise show at the Marquee. Hundreds turn up but the only Zeppelin activity is a jam between John Paul Jones and The Pretty Things.

June 5 – Led Zeppelin approached to play Wembley Stadium in July. They turn it down due to their involvement in completing their feature film which will be known as *The Song Remains The Same*.

June 19 – Robert Plant attends the Cardiff rock festival.

July – Dave Edmunds signs to Swan Song.

August – Jimmy completes the mixing of their double soundtrack album at Trident. Warner co-ordinate the distribution of the film for Autumn screening.

September 12 – Jimmy produces an all percussive track by John Bonham at Montreux studios. It eventually surfaces on 'Coda'.

September – Page is sacked by Kenneth Anger from supplying the music to his *Lucifer Rising* movie, for coming up with only 26 minutes of film music in three years.

October 5 – Led Zeppelin seen in TV action when *The Old Grey Whistle Test* shows clip of 'Black Dog' from the film.

October 9 – Tickets go on sale for the London screenings.

IN CONCERT AND BEYOND

LED-ZEPPELIN

THE·SONG·REMAINS·THE·SAME

JOHN BONHAM · JOHN PAUL JONES · JIMMY PAGE · ROBERT PLANT
CONCERT SEQUENCES FILMED AT MADISON SQUARE GARDEN

SOUNDTRACK ALBUM AVAILABLE ON **SWAN SONG** RECORDS AND TAPES
DISTRIBUTED BY ATLANTIC RECORDS

From Warner Bros ⓦ A Warner Communications Company

October 20 – The Led Zeppelin film *The Song Remains The Same* receives its world première at Manhattan's Cinema One in New York. All the group in attendance. All proceeds go to the Save The Children Fund. A party is held afterwards at the Pierre Hotel.

October 22 – *The Song Remains The Same* soundtrack double album released worldwide. The movie receives a West Coast première in Los Angeles with a party afterwards at the Bistro.

October 23 – Don Kirshner's rock concert show screens Led Zeppelin's first film clips on US TV.

October 30 – Led Zeppelin announce plans to return to live action with a projected world tour kicking off in America next February.

November 2 – Robert and Peter Grant interviewed by Michael Appleton on *The Old Grey Whistle Test*. 'Dazed And Confused' clip also shown.

November 4 – Double European première for the film at Warner West End and and ABC1 Cinema's in London. All the group attend and throw a huge post-première party at the Floral Hall in Covent Garden.

November 7 – The film opens simultaneously in Birmingham, Glasgow, Liverpool, Cambridge, Leeds, Reading and Southampton.

November/December – Group rehearsals commence in London for their 1977 touring assault. The first number they run down is 'Achilles Last Stand'.

1977

January – More rehearsals at Manticore studios in Fulham. Jimmy and Robert attend The Damned's show at The Roxy in Covent Garden.

January 21 – Robert and Bonzo attend the Eater, Generation X and Damned package at the Roxy.

February 5 – Announced that Zeppelin will commence their planned world tour in America at Fort Worth on February 27. Rumours abound that a festival date in the UK is being lined up for June.

February 24 – US tour postponed when Robert contracts severe tonsilitis. Now due to open in Toronto in April.

March – Tour dates revised again. Now opening in Dallas. UK dates now looking doubtful.

April 1 – The 11th US tour opens at the Memorial Centre Dallas.

April 30 – First leg of the tour ends with a date at the Pontiac Silverdome. In attracting 76,229, they break their own record set in Tampa in 1973, of having the largest audience for a single-act show.

May – Mid-tour break. Page holidays in Cairo.

May 12 – At the Ivor Novello luncheon at the Grosvenor Hotel in London, Peter Grant, Jimmy, Robert and J.P accept an award for Led Zeppelin's, "Outstanding contribution to British music."

May 18 – US dates resume in Birmingham, Alabama.

June 3 – Rain halts a show at the Tampa stadium after 20 minutes. Due to crowd disturbances, a planned replacement date for the next day is scrapped by local authorities.

June 7–12 – Six nights at Madison Square Garden, New York.

June 21–26 – Six nights at the LA Forum.

June 28 – Return to the UK for an 18-day break.

July – Promoter Mel Bush cancels a festival due to take place at Wrotham Park on August 25, when he fails to secure Zeppelin as the headline act.

July 17 – Third and final stretch of the US tour opens at the Seattle Kingdome.

July 23 – After a show at the Oakland Coliseum, Peter Grant, John Bonham, tour manager Richard Cole and security man John Bindon are involved in violent clashes backstage with promoter Bill Graham's staff.

July 24 – The group play a very low-key second Oakland date.

July 25 – The Oakland incident results in charges of battery against Grant, Bonham, Cole and Bindon. A civil suit asking £2 million in punitive damages is also filed against the group.

July 26 – The group move to New Orleans for a planned show at the Superdome on July 30. Here Robert learns of the sudden death of his five-year-old son Karac due to a stomach infection. He immediately flies back to England with Bonzo and Richard Cole. The remaining seven US tour dates are cancelled.

August 14 – Page plays a charity gig with Ron Wood at the Half Moon, Plumpton.

September – It is heavily rumoured that following the curtailed US tour, Led Zeppelin will split up.

September – Page jams at the WEA business conference at the Metropole Hotel, Brighton with Billy Kinsley of Liverpool Express, Carl Simmons and Phil Carson.

October – Jimmy Page holds a round of press interviews at the Swan Song office to dispel the split rumours.

1978

February 16 – The cases against Grant, Bonham, Cole and Bindon are heard in California. All incur suspended prison sentences and fines.

May – Led Zeppelin reunite at Clearwell castle in the Forest of Dean to rehearse and plan their future.

July – Strongly rumoured that the group will soon return to the UK stage, possibly at Maggie Bell's Festival Hall show. Nothing materialises.

July – Robert Plant sits in with various Midlands bands, including a date at the Wolverly Hall with Melvin Giganticus and The Turd Burglars.

August – Plant jams with Dr Feelgood in Ibiza.

September 15 – Plant, Page and Jones attend Richard Cole's wedding in Fulham.

September 16 – Plant joins Dave Edmunds for the encore at Birmingham Town Hall.

October – Jones and Bonham participate in Paul McCartney's Rockestra sessions at Abbey Road, London.

October – Led Zeppelin commence rehearsals in London for their new album.

November 1 – Plant and Jones attend the Golden Lion rock raffle in Fulham.

November 6 – Led Zeppelin travel to Stockholm to record their new album at Abba's Polar Music studio.

December – Initial recording completed at Polar studios. Page mixes some of the new material at his Plumpton home over Christmas.

1979

January 21 – Robert Plant 's wife Maureen gives birth to a son, Logan Romero.

February – Mixing sessions back at Polar. Rumoured that Zeppelin will commence touring in Europe soon.

May 8 – Jonesy and Robert attend Dave Edmunds' wedding reception.

May 17 – Reported that Jimmy conducted the opening of Phillips Harbour in Caithness Scotland, and Robert gigged with Melvin's Marauders in Stourbridge.

May 22 – Led Zeppelin announce their return to the British stage. A bill-topping show at Knebworth in August that will coincide with the release of their new album.

June 3/4 – Box offices open around the UK. Promoter Freddie Bannister reports the demand to be "The most incredible in my experience." Names being touted as possible support acts include Dire Straits, Fairport Convention, Joni Mitchell, Little Feat, Bob Seger, Van Morrison, The Boomtown Rats, B.B. King, Aerosmith and The Marshall Tucker Band.

June 9 – Robert Plant gives his first interview in two years to Radio One's *Rock On* programme.

June 26 – All the band attend the Rockpile gig at the Hammersmith Palais and after-show party at the Clarendon.

July 4 – Due to exceptional demand, Led Zeppelin confirm a second Knebworth appearance on August 11.

July 4 – The group hold intensive rehearsals at Bray studios.

July 19 – Knebworth bill confirmed. Keith Richards and Ron Wood's New Barbarians will play during the second week.

July 19 – Jimmy Page holds interviews at Swan Song in London.

July 23/24 – Led Zeppelin play two warm-up shows at the Falkoner Theatre in Copenhagen.

July 26 – Last minute line-up changes. Marshall Tucker drop out to be replaced by Commander Cody at Knebworth.

August 3 – Led Zeppelin arrive at Knebworth for an evening soundcheck.

August 4 – First Knebworth show. Fairport Convention, Commander Cody, Chas And Dave,

Southside Johnny And The Asbury Dukes, Todd Rungren's Utopia, Led Zeppelin.

August 11 – Second Knebworth show. Chas And Dave, Commander Cody, Southside Johnny And The Asbury Dukes, Todd Rungren's Utopia, The New Barbarians, Led Zeppelin.

August 20 – The new Led Zeppelin album 'In Through The Out Door' released around the world.

September 17 – Freddie Bannister's Tedoar company forced into liquidation following financial problems over Knebworth.

October 27 – The entire Zeppelin catalogue is featured in the *Billboard* Top 200 album chart. No other group or artist in American chart history has had so many albums listed during the same week.

November 10 – The Zeppelin entourage take a block booking for Abba's Wembley shows.

November 28 – Plant, Jones, Bonham and Grant attend the *Melody Maker* Poll Awards reception at the Waldorf Hotel and collect a total of seven awards.

December 2 – Jimmy attends the Paul McCartney And Wings gig in Brighton. Paul and Linda plus Denny Laine stay at his Plumpton home.

December 10 – David Lytton Cobbold, of the Knebworth estate, fined £125 for allowing Led Zeppelin to play over their allocated time at the Knebworth shows.

December 12 – Bonzo and Robert catch the Wings Birmingham show.

December 28 – Tommy Vance repeats the 1969 *In Concert* Zeppelin BBC broadcast.

December 29 – Robert, Jonesy and Bonzo attend the Paul McCartney And Wings Kampuchea benefit show at London's Hammersmith Odeon. Robert sings 'Little Sister' with Rockpile and all three join Paul and many others in the star-studded Rockestra finale.

1980

January 16 – 'The Summit', a compilation album in aid of the International Year Of The Child, put together by K-Tel and Swan Song is launched at a reception in London attended by Robert, Phil Lynott, Eric Clapton and others.

February 3 – Robert joins Rockpile at the Birmingham Top Rank.

March 4 – Bonzo travels to the Tyne Tees studio to film a live interview with Billy Connolly for the *Alright Now* TV show.

April 27 – Led Zeppelin commence rehearsals at the Rainbow Theatre in London. This is in preparation for a European tour they will shortly undertake.

May 1 – First tour itinerary formulated by Harvey Goldsmith. Ten dates due to start in Vienna on May 22.

May 5 – Rehearsals move to the New Victoria Theatre.

May 9 – Tour dates revised. Now planning to open in Paris on June 16 at the Palais de Sports.

May 11 – Final tour date revision. It's now definitely 15 dates spanning Germany, Holland, Belgium and Austria, opening in Dortmund on June 17.

May 18 – Rehearsals continue at Shepperton studios.

June 1 – Reported that Jimmy is to buy Michael Caine's Windsor home for £900,000.

June 6 – Completion of rehearsals at Shepperton.

June 17 – Led Zeppelin open their European tour at the Westfallen Halle, Dortmund.

June 27 – A show at the Messecentre Halle in Nuremburg has to be scrapped after three numbers, due to John Bonham collapsing from physical exhaustion.

July 5 – Bad Company's Simon Kirke joins the group for the encore at Munich's Olympic Halle.

July 7 – Final show of the tour at the Berlin Eisoport Halle.

August – Holiday break for Bonzo, Robert and John

Paul Jones. Jimmy moves to Windsor.

September 11 – Peter Grant announces details of the 'Led Zeppelin: The Eighties Part One' touring campaign. This will herald a return to America. Initially they will play 19 dates covering the North East and Midwest. The long term plan is to cover the South next spring. The opening date will be at the Montreal Forum on October 17.

September 18 – Jimmy Page attends technical discussions at Swan Song for the upcoming tour. He inspects a model set-up of the stage rig they plan to use for the 'Led Zeppelin: The Eighties Part One' campaign.

September 21 – Massive ticket demand reported in America.

September 24 – John Bonham leaves Worcestershire to meet up with the rest of the group at Bray studios for the first rehearsal for the upcoming US tour. After the rehearsal the entourage return to Page's Windsor home. Bonzo falls asleep after a heavy drinking bout.

September 25 – At around 1.45 pm, Zeppelin sound technician Benji Le Fevre checks Bonzo's room to see why he hasn't stirred. Checking his pulse he immediately calls a doctor. Shortly after, John Bonham is pronounced dead, having inhaled his own vomit. By seven pm, the news has leaked to the press and is carried as a major news item on every TV and radio station in the country. At the same time, as yet unaware of the tragedy, over 1,000 fans in Chicago are queueing for early copies of the *Chicago Tribune* which carries mail order ticket details of Led Zeppelin's four planned concerts at the Chicago Stadium in November.

September 26 – In the wake of the tragedy, Thames Valley Police announce there are no suspicious circumstances involved.

September 27 – Tributes pour in from across the world. The US tour is cancelled and speculation is rife that Zeppelin will now disband.

October 7 – Following an inquest, a verdict of accidental death is returned on John Bonham.

October 10 – John Bonham's funeral held at Rushock, Worcestershire.

October 18 – Rumours commence that Cozy Powell/ Aynsley Dunbar/Peter Criss/Paul Thompson/and Carmine Appice will be named as a replacement for Bonzo.

November 7 – The remaining members of Led Zeppelin travel to Jersey to discuss their future. On their return, they hold a meeting with Peter Grant at the Savoy Hotel in London to announce their intention to retire Led Zeppelin as a group.

December 4 – Led Zeppelin issue the following press statement: "We wish it to be known that the loss of our dear friend, and the deep respect we have for his family, together with the sense of undivided harmony felt by ourselves and our manager, have led us to decide that we could not continue as we were."

1981

March 9 – Robert Plant commences a series of live gigs at Stourbridge Wine bar. Playing old R&B numbers with a pick-up band known as The Honeydrippers.

March 10 – Jimmy joins Jeff Beck for three encores at his Hammersmith Odeon show.

August/September – Robert begins recording his first solo album at Rockfield studios.

September – Jimmy records the soundtrack to *Death Wish 2* at The Sol studio.

December 15 – Jimmy, Robert, John Paul Jones and Peter Grant attend the Golden Lion charity raffle and present the prizes.

1982

February 15 – *Death Wish 2* soundtrack issued on Swan Song.

March – Work commences on mixing studio out-takes for a final Zeppelin album.

May – Plant and Page join Foreigner for an encore in Munich.

June – Robert gives his first post-Zeppelin interviews and commences a promotional tour of America.

June 28 – 'Pictures At Eleven', Robert Plant's début solo album released. It enters the UK chart at number two.

July 21 – Robert performs 'Worse Than Detroit' at the Prince's Trust show at London's Dominion theatre.

September – 'Burning Down One Side', first Plant solo single for 15 years, issued.

September – Plant is interviewed on the *Whistle Test* TV show and his first video for 'Burning Down One Side' is screened.

October – Page receives a 12-month conditional discharge for drug offences.

November 22 – The 10th Led Zeppelin album 'Coda' is released.

November – John Paul Jones films a segment for Paul McCartney's film *Give My Regards To Broad Street* at Elstree studios.

1983

May 23 – Page joins Eric Clapton for the encore at a Guildford Town Hall show.

May – Robert completes the recording of his second album. Swan Song is wound up as a label.

June 22 – Robert and his new band (with Queen's Roger Taylor on drums) film a set in front of a live audience for the *Tube*'s Midsummer TV special at the Tyne Tees studio in Newcastle. Unhappy with the result, he vetoes the screening.

July 4 – 'Big Log' released as a single.

July 11 – Robert Plant's second album 'The Principle Of Moments' is released.

July 28 – As the single 'Big Log' coasts up the UK charts, Robert appears on *Top Of The Pops*.

August – Tour rehearsals at Shepperton for Robert's upcoming début solo tour.

August 29 – Robert Plant's first solo tour opens at the Rosemont Horizon, Chicago.

September 20/21 – Jimmy Page returns to the stage for two concerts in aid of the ARMS charity at London's Royal Albert Hall.

October 1 – US leg of Plant's American tour ends in Vancouver.

November – "In The Mood" released as a single to coincide with Plant's tour.

November 22 – Plant's UK tour opens at the Glasgow Apollo.

November 28/29 – The ARMS US tour dates with Jimmy commence in Dallas.

December 8/9 – ARMS tour ends in New York's Madison Square Garden.

December 4 – John Paul Jones joins Robert for an encore jam at Bristol's Colston Hall.

December 13 – Jimmy joins Robert for an encore jam at London's Hammersmith Odeon.

December 24 – Plant's UK tour ends with a date at the Birmingham Odeon. Jason Bonham joins him for the encore.

1984

February – Robert Plant's world tour takes in dates in Australia.

February 24 – The 'Principal Of Moments' tour ends in Tokyo.

March – Robert records the 'Honeydrippers Vol One' material at New York's Atlantic studios. On returning to London, he invites Jimmy to play on two tracks.

June – Page gigs with Roy Harper at the May Tree Fair in Thetford. He also records an album with Harper.

June 5 – Jimmy Page plays with Ian Stewart's Rocket 88 at Nottingham Boat Club.

June 24 – Jimmy joins Yes on stage in Dortmund.

July 16 – Page plays at the Piotoria blues festival in Italy.

July 28 – Page plays two sets with Roy Harper at the Cambridge Folk Festival.

July 29 – Jimmy Page plays at Battersea Park concert with Roy Harper.

August – Jimmy forms a new band with Paul Rodgers and commences auditions and recording at Nomis studios.

November 6 – Jimmy Page and Roy Harper are seen in a filmed segment on *Whistle Test*. It is announced that Jimmy's new group The Firm will play in the UK in December.

November 12 – 'The Honeydrippers Vol. 1' mini album released.

November 23 – Page joins Roy Harper at London's Rock Garden.

November 29 – The Firm open their European tour in Stockholm.

December 7/8/9 – The Firm play UK gigs at Middlesborough Town Hall and London's Hammersmith Odeon.

December 15 – Plant plays in a Honeydrippers line-up that features Brian Setzer on US TV's *Saturday Night Live*. On the *Billboard* chart, 'Sea Of Love' is number three.

1985

January – Plant and his band record a third album. 'Sea Of Love' issued in the UK as a single.

January 18 – Plant reforms The Honeydrippers to play a special benefit show at Rolls Hall, Monmouth.

February 11 – The Firm's début album is released.

February 28 – The Firm commence a 32-date tour of America at the Dallas Reunion Arena.

March 4 – 'Whatever Happened To Jugula?' album by Roy Harper and Jimmy Page issued.

March 22 – John Paul Jones' soundtrack album 'Scream For Help' released. Robert releases new single 'Pink And Black'.

May 9 – The Firm's US tour ends in New Jersey.

May 18 – The Firm play the NEC Birmingham.

May 20 – The Firm play the Edinbugh Playhouse.

May 20 – Robert Plant's third solo album 'Shaken 'n' Stirred' is released.

May 22 – The Firm play London's Wembley Arena.

June 10 – Robert Plant's 'Shaken 'n' Stirred' US tour commences in Vancouver.

July 13 – The remaining members of Led Zeppelin reunite to play three numbers at the *Live Aid* show at the JFK stadium in Philadelphia.

July 23 – Jimmy joins Robert for the encore of his appearance at the Meadowlands, New Jersey.

August 5 – Plant's US tour ends in New York's Madison Square Garden.

August 19 – 'Little By Little' issued as a single to

coincide with Plant's gigs.
September 8 – Plant brings the 'Shaken 'n' Stirred' tour to the NEC, Birmingham.
September 10 – Plant's final 1985 tour date at Wembley Arena. Jimmy Page attends the show and end of tour party afterwards.
October – Page starts work on a second Firm album. Plant disbands his touring and recording band of three years standing.

1986
January – The remaining members of Led Zeppelin reunite at a village hall in Bath for experimental recordings. Tony Thompson plays drums.
January – The Firm's second album issued in the States.
March 14 – The Firm's second US tour opens in Tampa.
March 13/14 – Plant plays warm-up dates with The Big Town Playboys at Leeds University and Norwich University.
March 15 – The 'Heart Beat' charity show at the NEC in Birmingham features a set with Robert Plant and The Big Town Playboys.
March 24 – 'Mean Business' released in the UK.
May 28 – The Firm's US tour ends in Detroit. Phil Carson jams on bass.
May – John Paul Jones and Robert attend Ben E. King's London Palladium show and Jones agrees to work on his new album.
July 4 – Page jams with The Beach Boys on the encore of their Washington date.
July – Page attends the 72nd birthday celebrations for Les Paul in New York.
August 9 – Plant joins Fairport Convention on stage at the Cropredy Festival in Oxfordshire for an encore.
September/October – Plant and Page begin making plans to record new albums. Plant writes material with Robert Crash. A demo of production team Act Of War comes his way and leads to a link-up with Phil Johnstone.

1987
January to September – Jimmy Page records a solo album at The Sol, calling in Robert to sing on one track.
September to November – Robert Plant records a new album with a new line-up. Page contributes solos for two of the tracks. Robert enlists Bill Curbishley as his new manager. Jimmy leaves Atlantic and signs to Geffen.
July – John Paul Jones commences production work on The Mission's new album at the Manor studio.
December 17 – Billed as The Band Of Joy, Robert débuts his new line-up at Leas Cliff Hall, Folkstone. This is the first show to feature Plant's interpretation of Led Zeppelin numbers.
December 30 – Another low-key show at the Stourbridge Town Hall.

1988
January 18 – 'Heaven Knows', Plant's first new music in two years, is released as a single.
January 23 – Plant plays a series of warm-up, low-key university dates kicking off in Leicester.
February 3 – A nostalgic return to the Marquee club as Robert plays a showcase gig for the European press.
February 4 – Robert holds press conferences for the university and overseas press.
February 29 – Robert Plant's fourth solo album 'Now And Zen' is released. On the same day, the John Paul Jones-produced Mission album is also issued.
March – Ben E. King's album with contributions from John Paul Jones is issued.
March 16 – Plant's 'Non Stop Go' tour of the UK commences in Newport.

March 27 – John Paul Jones joins The Mission for the encore of their show at London's Astoria Theatre.
April 11 – 'Tall Cool One' issued as a single.
April 17 – Jimmy Page joins Robert for an extended encore jam on the last night of Plant's UK tour at London's Hammersmith Odeon.
May – Robert commences another US tour.
May 14 – Led Zeppelin reform for the Atlantic Records 40th Birthday show at New York's Madison Square Garden.
June 14 – Robbie Blunt and Brian Setzer join Robert onstage at the L.A. Forum.
June 20 – Jimmy Page's solo album 'Outrider' released.
September – Jimmy commences a solo tour of America.
September – Plant plays two rescheduled gigs in Ireland. 'Ship Of Fools' issued as a single.
November 1 – Plant plays a further round of American shows, commencing in Columbus.
November 21 – Jimmy Page starts a five-date UK tour at the Birmingham Hummingbird.
November 23/24 – Page plays 2 dates at London's Hammersmith Odeon.
November 28 – Plant's mammoth US tour ends in Tucson.

1989
February – Robert Plant's *Mumbo Jumbo* video compilation issued. Robert records a new album at Olympic studios.
November – The remaining members of Led Zeppelin play together at the 21st birthday party of Robert's daughter Carmen, in Birmingham.
December – Robert Plant appears live with a local band at a *Day Of Awareness* charity busk held in Kidderminster shopping centre. He performs cover versions of Bryan Adams' 'Run To You', 'Spirit In The Sky', ZZ Top's 'She Loves My Automobile', The Police's 'Every Breath You Take', 'All Along The Watchtower' and Zepp's 'Rock And Roll'.

1990
January 10 – Page joins Bon Jovi for the encore at their Music Therapy gig at the Hammersmith Odeon.
January – Strong rumours persist that Led Zeppelin will reform for a summer US tour. Reports of multi-million dollar offers are also rife.
February – Robert Plant commences promotional interviews for his new album.
March 19 – Robert Plant's fifth solo album 'Manic Nirvana' is released.
March 26 – 'Hurting Kind (Got My Eyes On You)' issued as a single.
April 28 – Zeppelin to reform rumours fuelled when

Page, Plant and Jones join Jason Bonham to perform a Zeppelin set at Jason's wedding reception.
May 1 – Robert Plant begins a European tour in The Hague.
May – 'Your Ma Said You Cried In Your Sleep Last Night' issued as a single.
May – Jimmy Page re-masters the original Led Zeppelin catalogue with engineer George Marino at New York's Sterling studios. This is for a box set compilation scheduled for autumn release.
June 1 – UK tour commences at Sheffield City Hall.
June 4/5 – Plant plays two nights at the Hammersmith Odeon.
June 7 – UK tour ends at the NEC, Birmingham.
June 22 – Robert Plant receives the Silver Clef award in London and accepts an invitation to perform at the Knebworth Silver Clef show.
June 28 – Many national newspapers take it for granted that Plant will reform Led Zeppelin at Saturday's Knebworth show.
June 30 – The Knebworth Silver Clef event; no Led Zeppelin reunion, but Jimmy Page does join Plant and his band for a three-song Zeppelin finale.
July 5 – Robert Plant's US tour commences in Albany, New York.
August 6 – The Knebworth album featuring Jimmy and Robert's live work-out of 'Wearing And Tearing', is issued. The TV special is screened in the evening.
August 14 – Plant winds up his US tour with a show in Sacramento.
August 18 – Jimmy Page attends the 'Monsters Of Rock' festival at Donington and jams with Aerosmith.
August 20 – Another Page/Aerosmith jam at the Marquee club in London. Page performs five numbers, including a version of 'Immigrant Song'.
August 31 – Announcement of the formats for the upcoming Led Zeppelin compilation set. The 54-track box set, to be known simply as 'Led Zeppelin', will be released worldwide at the end of October. A condensed version, entitled 'Remasters', will be available as a triple album and double CD and cassette in Europe only. All versions will be deleted on March 31, 1991. Atlantic's plans for a December 3 release of 'Stairway To Heaven' as a single have been vetoed by Jimmy, Robert and John Paul. The single would have appeared as a 12-inch, a CD single and a limited picture disc.
September 17 – Robert Plant announces details of a short Christmas tour of the UK which includes dates in Newcastle, Wolverhampton and two nights at London's Town And Country Club.
September 20 – *Rolling Stone* magazine features Led Zeppelin on the cover and carries a lengthy interview with Jimmy Page, Robert Plant and John Paul Jones.
September – Radio One announces it is producing a three-hour *Story Of Led Zeppelin* programme to tie in with the release of the Led Zeppelin box set.
October 15 – 'Remasters' triple album and double CD/cassette package released in Europe and the UK. It enters the UK chart at number 10.
October 29 – 'Led Zeppelin' box set of six LPs, four CDs/cassettes released worldwide. It reaches the top 20 in America and in reaching number 48 in the UK becomes the most expensive album set to register a top 50 position.
November – In interviews in various publications Jimmy Page expressed his desire to write new material with Robert Plant. He also announces plans to record a new solo album and form a new touring band.
December 15 – Radio One broadcasts a two hour special, The Mighty Arms Of Atlas – The Power Of Led Zeppelin hosted by Alan Freeman.
December 18/19/20 – Robert is forced to cancel his three nights at London's Town & Country Club due to laryngitis. The dates are rescheduled for January 1991.

DISCOGRAPHY

Appendix 2A

This discography is divided into two parts. Part one covers Led Zeppelin and all other related activities during their reign. Part Two is an individual study of each group member, encompassing both pre and post Zeppelin solo activities.

Whilst not claiming to be totally complete, this discography hopefully chronicles all notable Page, Plant, Jones and Bonham records, tapes, CD's, videos and written works from 1963 to 1990.

All catalogue numbers are UK pressings unless otherwise stated. Relevant chart placings are listed where applicable.

UK DISCOGRAPHY

UK ALBUMS

Led Zeppelin
Atlantic 588 171 Original issue March 1969 with turquoise lettering on cover.
UK chart position: No. 6 – 79 weeks on chart.
Atlantic 588 171 (second issue with orange lettering).
Atlantic K40031 (reissue 1972).

Led Zeppelin II
Atlantic 588 198 Original issue October 1969.
UK chart position: No. 1 – 138 weeks on chart.
Atlantic K40037 (reissue 1972).

Led Zeppelin III
Atlantic 2401 002 Original issue October 1970.
UK chart position: No. 1 – 40 weeks on chart.
Atlantic K 50002 (reissue 1972).

Four Symbols
Atlantic 2401 012 Original issue November 1971.
UK chart position: No. 1 – 62 weeks on chart.
Atlantic (reissue 1972).
Atlantic limited lilac vinyl pressing K50008 November 1978.
HMV Classic Collection box set package (individually numbered limited edition of 3,500) issued September 1988.

Houses Of The Holy
Atlantic K50014 Original issue March 1973.
UK chart position: No. 1 – 13 weeks on chart.

Physical Graffiti
Swan Song SSK89400 Original issue February 1975.
UK chart position: No. 1 – 27 weeks on chart.

Presence
Swan Song SSK59402 Original shrink wrapped package issue April 1976.
UK chart Position: No. 1 – 14 weeks on chart.
Prime Cut reissue in single sleeve 1986.

Soundtrack From The Film *The Song Remains The Same*
Swan Song SSK89402 Original issue October 1976.
UK chart position: No. 1 – 15 weeks on chart.

In Through The Out Door
Swan Song SSK59410 Original issue as six differing sleeve designs labelled A to F, August 1979.
UK chart position: No. 1 – 16 weeks on chart.

Coda
Swan Song A0051 Original issue November 1982.
UK chart position: No. 4 – 7 weeks on chart.

Remasters
Atlantic Zep 1/756780415 2/4 October 1990. Triple album/double cassette and double CD European issue only. See chapter nine for full details.
UK chart position No. 10

Led Zeppelin
Atlantic 7567821441/2/4 October 1990 Six LP/four CD or four cassette box set. See chapter nine for full details.
UK chart position No. 48

UK COMPACT DISCS

(see also notes in US CD discography)
Led Zeppelin – Atlantic 240031, January 1987.
Led Zeppelin II – Atlantic 240037, December 1986.
Led Zeppelin III – Atlantic 250002, January 1987.
Four Symbols – Atlantic 250008, July 1983.
Four Symbols – HMV Classic Collection box set package C88 1 – 4 (individually numbered limited edition of 3,500), September 1988.
Houses Of The Holy – Atlantic 250014, January 1987.
Physical Graffiti – Swan Song 298400, January 1987.
Presence – Swan Song 259402, June 1987.
Soundtrack From The Film *The Song Remains The Same* – Swan Song 289402, February 1987.
In Through The Out Door – Swan Song 259410, January 1986.
Coda – Swan Song 7900512, July 1987.
Remasters – Atlantic 7567 80415, October, 1990.
Led Zeppelin – box set Atlantic 7567 821 44, October, 1990.

UK PROMO SINGLES

Communication Breakdown/Good Times Bad Times
Atlantic 584269. DJ only promo, April 1969.
Whole Lotta Love (edited version)/Livin' Lovin' Maid (She's Just A Woman)
Atlantic 584 309. Withdrawn from release, December 1969. This catalogue number was subsequently reallocated to another Atlantic release – 'Take It Off Him And Put It On Me' by Clarence Carter.

D'yer Mak'er/Over The Hills And Far Away
Atlantic K10296. DJ only promo, March 1973.

Trampled Underfoot/Black Country Woman
Swan Song DC1. Promo giveaway, May 1975.

Wearing And Tearing/Darlene
Swan Song intended Knebworth commemorative single – SSK 19421, shelved August 1979.

Stairway To Heaven/Immigrant Song/Whole Lotta Love/Good Times Bad Times
Atlantic LZ2 – 10-inch promo single issued to promote the 'Remasters' project, October 1990.

UK PROMO CD

Stairway To Heaven/Immigrant Song/Whole Lotta Love/Good Times Bad Times. Atlantic CD LZ 1 – 4-track promo sampler CD single issued to promote the 'Remasters' project, October 1990.

UK PROMO CASSETTE

Stairway To Heaven/Whole Lotta Love. Atlantic L2 23LC promo cassette issued to promote the 'Remasters' project, October 1990.

NOTABLE COMPILATION APPEARANCES

The Age Of Atlantic
Atlantic 2464 013 (1970). Includes 'Whole Lotta Love' and 'Communication Breakdown'.

Supertracks
Vertigo Sport One. Sport Foundation charity album released 1977 includes 'Trampled Underfoot'.

Flying High
Atlantic 588 184. Obscure Polydor distributed compilation featuring 'You Shook Me'. Issued 1969. Possible record club only release.

The New Age Of Atlantic
Atlantic K20024 – (May 1972). Features the 'Led Zeppelin III' out-take 'Hey Hey What Can I Do'.

Soundtrack To The Film *Homer*
Atlantic 2400 137 (1971). 'Features How Many More Times'.

The Summit
K-Tel NE 1067 (January 1980). Features 'Candy Store Rock'. Compiled with the aid of the group and Swan Song for the International Year Of The Child charity.

Classic Rock 1966-1988
Atlantic K78 19351 (December 1988). Double set celebrating Atlantic's 40th anniversary. Includes Dazed and Confused, Whole Lotta Love and Stairway To Heaven plus Robert Plant's Heaven Knows.

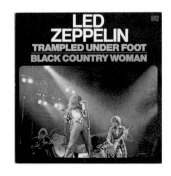

NOTABLE GUEST APPEARANCES MADE BY ZEPPELIN MEMBERS DURING THE GROUP'S CAREER 1968 – 1980.

Joe Cocker: With A Little Help From My Friends
Regal Zonophone RLRZ 1006 (1968). Features Page on the title track, Bye Bye Blackbird and Marjorine.

No Introduction Necessary
Spark SRLM 107 (1968). Features Page and Jones on unspecified tracks on this jam session release. Reissued on Thunderbolt TB007 (1985).

P.J. Proby: Three Week Hero
Liberty LBl83219E (April 1969). Features all four members on the track 'Jim's Blues'. Jones also arranges several of the tracks. Reissued on Beat Goes On CD BGOCD 87.

Al Stewart: Love Chronicles
CBS 63460 (January 1969). Features Page on unspecified tracks.

Catoone: Catoone
Atlantic 588 174 (April 1969). Features Page as guest artist on unspecified tracks.

Family Dog: A Way Of Life
Bell SB22122 1969. Features Page and Jones on unspecified tracks.

Lord Sutch And Heavy Friends
Atlantic 2400 008 (June 1970). Features Page and Bonham on six tracks recorded during the 'Led Zeppelin II' sessions at Mystic studios in LA. The story goes that Sutch asked Page and Bonham to lay down some backing tracks of old rock standards and then rewrote his own lyrics at a later date. Thus 'Thumping Beat' is taken from 'Lucille', and 'Baby Come Back' is really Roy Head's 'Treat Her Right'. Other tracks listed are 'Union Jack Car', 'Wailing Sounds', 'Cause I Love You', and 'Flashing Lights'. (Reissued as Smoke And Fire on Thunderbolt THBL022 1985)

Roy Harper: Stormcock
Harvest SHVL 789 (June 1971). Features Page on the track 'Same Old Rock'.

Roy Harper: Lifemask
Harvest SHVL 808 (February 1973). Features Page on the track 'The Lord's Prayer'.

Madeline Bell: Comin' Atcha'
RCA SF8389 (December 1973). Features John Paul Jones on bass and keyboards – recorded and produced by him at his Dormouse studios.

Jobriath: Creatures Of The Night
Elektra K42163 (1974). Features John Paul Jones – track unspecified.

Roy Harper: Flashes From The Archives Of Oblivion
Harvest SHDW 405 (November 1974). Features Page on the live tracks taken from the Rainbow St. Valentine's show in 1974 as part of the Intergalactic Elephant Band. Plant can be heard in a compère role.

Maggie Bell: Suicide Sal
Polydor 2383313 (February 1975). Features Page on the tracks 'Coming On Again' and 'If You Don't Know'.

Roy Harper: H.Q.
Harvest SHSP 4046 (June 1975). Features John Paul Jones on the track 'The Game'.

Paul McCartney And Wings: Back To The Egg
EMI/MPL PCTC 257 (May 1979). Features John Bonham and John Paul Jones as part of the Rockestra on 'Rockestra Theme' and 'So Glad To See You Here'.

The Concerts For Kampuchea
Atlantic K60153 (February 1981). Features Plant with Rockpile on 'Little Sister' and Plant, Jones and Bonham with McCartney's Rockestra on 'Rockestra Theme', 'Let It Be' and 'Lucille'.

Roy Wood: The Singles
Speed Speed 1000 (July 1982). Features John Bonham on the track 'Keep Your Hands On The Wheel'. Also available on the Roy Wood US only album 'On The Road Again' Warners BSK 3247 (1979).

NOTABLE RADIO SHOW PROMOS

BBC In Concert 1971
BBC transcription disc 129330S

US DISCOGRAPHY

US ALBUMS

Led Zeppelin
Atlantic SD 8216 (January 1969) Reissued on SD19126 (1971)
US chart position: No. 10 – 50 weeks on chart – certified Gold July 22, 1969.

Led Zeppelin II
Atlantic SD 8236 (October 1969) Reissued on SD 19128 (1971)
US chart position: No. 1 – 29 weeks on chart – certified Gold November 10, 1969.
Also Atlantic Mobile Fidelity Sound Lab pressing (1970).

Led Zeppelin III
Atlantic SD7201 (October 1970) Reissued on SD 19128 (1971)
US chart position: No. 1 – 19 weeks on chart – certified Gold October 8, 1970.

Four Symbols
Atlantic SD7208 (November 1971) Reissued on SD19129 (1971)
US chart position: No. 2 – 24 weeks on chart – certified Gold November 16, 1971.
Also Atlantic SD19129 – limited white vinyl pressing (1978).

Houses Of The Holy
Atlantic SD7255 (March 1973) Reissued on SD19130 (1973)
US chart position: No. 1 – 39 weeks on chart – certified Gold April 10, 1973.

Physical Graffiti
Swan Song SS2 200 (February 1975) US chart position: No. 1 – 15 weeks on chart – certified Gold March 6, 1975.

Presence
Swan Song SS8416 (April 1976) US chart position: No. 1 – 13 weeks on chart – certified Gold April 1, 1976.

Soundtrack From The Film *The Song Remains The Same*
Swan Song SS2 201 (October 1976) US chart position: No. 2 – 12 weeks on chart – certified Gold November 3, 1976; certified Platinum April 12, 1977.

In Through The Out Door
Swan Song SS16002 (August 1979); initial run with six differing sleeve designs. US chart position: No. 1 – 28 weeks on chart – certified Gold January 7, 1980; certified Platinum January 7, 1980; certified triple platinum October 3, 1984.

Coda
Swan Song 79 00511 (November 1982) US chart position: No. 6 – 9 weeks on chart – certified Gold February 7, 1983; certified Platinum February 7, 1983.

Led Zeppelin Box Set
Atlantic 82144 (October 1990) US chart position: No. 18

US CD's

The advent of the CD market in the mid-eighties led Atlantic to hurriedly make available all the Led Zeppelin catalogue on CD. In doing so little care was taken in the remastering of these discs. In some cases the material was taken from second and third generation tapes and consequently excessive tape hiss often mars the quality of the music. On 'Physical Graffiti' there is an unforgivable mastering error when the end spoken tag is completely left off 'In My Time Of Dying'. Updated US copies have reputedly amended this flaw, though European versions remain affected. It was this gross lack of quality control that led Jimmy Page to undertake the remastering of their material, from the original master sources, for the 1990 'Remasters' box set project.

US SINGLES

Good Times Bad Times/Communication Breakdown
Atlantic 45 2613 (1969)

Whole Lotta Love (edited version)/Livin' Lovin' Maid (She's Just A Woman)
Atlantic AT2690 (1969)

Whole Lotta Love (full length version)/Livin' Lovin' Maid (She's Just A Woman)
Atlantic 45 2690 (1969) Reissued on Atlantic Oldies OS 13116
US chart position: No. 4 – 13 weeks on chart.

Immigrant Song/Hey Hey What Can I Do
Atlantic 45 2777 (1970) Reissued on Atlantic Oldies OS 13131
US chart position: No. 16 – 10 weeks on chart.

Black Dog/Misty Mountain Hop
Atlantic 2849 (1971)
Reissued on Atlantic Oldies OS 13129 US chart position: No. 15 – 8 weeks on chart.

Rock And Roll/Four Sticks
Atlantic 2865 (1972) Reissued on Atlantic Oldies OS 13130

Over The Hills And Far Away/Dancing Days
Atlantic 2970 (1973)

D'yer Mak'er/The Crunge
Atlantic 2986 (1973) US chart position: No. 20 – 8 weeks on chart.

Trampled Underfoot/Black Country Woman
Swan Song SS70102 (1975) US chart position: No. 38 – 2 weeks on chart.

Candy Store Rock/Royal Orleans
Swan Song SS70110 (1976)

Fool In The Rain/Hot Dog
Swan Song SS71003 (1979) US chart position: No. 21 – 8 weeks on chart.

US PROMO SINGLES

Dazed And Confused/Babe I'm Gonna Leave You
Atlantic promo EP1019 (1969)

Whole Lotta Love (edit)/Whole Lotta Love (full length)
Atlantic promo 45 2690 (1969)

Immigrant Song (mono)/Immigrant Song (stereo)
Atlantic promo 45 777 (1970)

Gallows Pole (mono)/Gallows Pole (stereo)
Atlantic advance promo ST PR 157 (1970)

Black Dog (edit)/Black Dog (full length)
Atlantic promo 45 2849 (1971)

Rock And Roll (mono)/Rock And Roll (stereo)
Atlantic promo 45 2865 (1972)

Stairway To Heaven (mono)/Stairway To Heaven (stereo)
Atlantic promo PR 175 (1972)

Stairway To Heaven (stereo)/Stairway To Heaven (stereo)
Atlantic promo PR 269 (1972)

Four Symbols Juke Box EP with Rock And Roll, Black Dog and Stairway To Heaven.
Little LP's Unlimited/Atlantic promo SD 77208 (1972)

Over The Hills And Far Away (mono)/Over The Hills And Far Away (stereo)
Atlantic promo 45 2970 (1973)

D'yer Mak'er (edit)/D'yer Mak'er (full length)
Atlantic promo 45 2986 (1973)

Houses Of The Holy Juke Box EP with Dancing Days, D'yer Mak'er, The Song Remains The Same and The Crunge
Little LP's Unlimited/Atlantic promo SD 77255 (1973)

Trampled Underfoot (mono edit)/Trampled Underfoot (stereo edit)
Swan Song promo SS70102 (1975)

Candy Store Rock (mono)/Candy Store Rock (stereo)
Swan Song promo SS70110 (1976)

Fool In The Rain (edit)/Fool In The Rain (full length)
Swan Song promo SS71003 (1979)

Stairway To Heaven/Hey Hey What Can I Do
Atlantic promo picture disc PR268/9 (1979) (This pressing is claimed to be a bootleg by some sources)

Stairway To Heaven/Hey Hey What Can I Do
Atlantic promo lilac vinyl PR 268/9 (1979) (Again may be a bootleg)

What's It All About
(Promo radio interview disc with Bill Huie for public service religious broadcast) Atlantic promo MA 1841 (1981)
B-side features Larry Gatlin.

What's It All About (music and interviews)
Side one Led Zeppelin; side two The Who MA 2902

Little Sister (Rockpile with Robert Plant)/Lucille (Paul McCartney's Rockestra) including Plant, Jones and Bonham.
Atlantic PR 388 Four track 12-inch promo from the Concerts For Kampuchea live set (also includes The Who)

NOTABLE US PROMO ALBUMS

Led Zeppelin original first album advance white label test pressing.
Atlantic promo 681461 PR (1969)

Led Zeppelin/Dusty Springfield in-store sampler.
Includes 'Good Times Bad Times', 'Babe I'm Gonna Leave You', 'Your Time Is Gonna Come' and 'Communication Breakdown' on side one and selections from 'Dusty In Memphis' on side two with talk-over links.
Atlantic promo TLST 35 (1969)

Heavies For April – Sampler promo compilation with

No Quarter (edit)
Atlantic promo PR 184

NOTABLE US CASSETTE RELEASES

Immigrant Song/Hey Hey What Can I Do
Swan Song cassette single SR 4 2777 (1990)

Trampled Underfoot/Black Country Woman
Swan Song cassette single SR 4 70102 (1990)

Fool In The Rain/Hot Dog
Swan Song cassette single SR 4 71003 released (1990)

NOTABLE US RADIO SHOW PROMOS
Pressed for radio show distribution only.

Armed Forces Radio Network: Houses Of The Holy radio promo.
With The Song Remains The Same/Dancing Days/The Crunge/D'yer Mak'er P 13893

The Best Of BBC Rock Hour: For Broadcast October 26, 1980 – 1971 (London Wavelength).
Track listing: Immigrant Song/Heartbreaker/Dazed And Confused/Stairway To Heaven/Going To California/Whole Lotta Love.

London Wavelength: Maxell presents Led Zeppelin BBC Rock Hour.
1969 and 1971 BBC *In Concert* recordings on two LP set.

Led Zeppelin Interview.
July 28, 1975 Toyota Sound Communication double album of music and interviews.

Led Zeppelin – A Stairway To Heaven: Westwood One.
Three LP set of music and interviews covering their entire career broadcast November 24, 1988.

Atlantic 40th Anniversary: Superstars In Concert.
Three LP set includes Foreigner, Yes and Led Zeppelin. Live versions from May 14, 1988 of 'Heartbreaker', 'Misty Mountain Hop', 'Whole Lotta Love' and 'Stairway To Heaven'.

NOTABLE US CD RADIO PROMOS

In The Studio – (The Album Network).
Special show with Page and Plant interviews about the making of the first album.

Rarities – Precious Gems.
12 cut radio special from Radio Today. Includes Led Zeppelin's obscure non-album track 'Hey Hey What Can I Do'.

It's Been A Long Time – Tribute To John Bonham.
Music and interviews 6 cut radio show includes live tracks broadcast Sept 1990.

Led Zeppelin Profiled – radio promo
For the box set release Oct 1990. Atlantic PRCD 3629-2.

NOTABLE FOREIGN RELEASES

SINGLES

The 10 US singles were made available in most European markets as well as Australia and Japan. The following is a country by country list of additional singles and EP couplings.

Angola
Over The Hills And Far Away/Dancing Days
(Atlantic ATS 610)

Australia
This Is Led Zeppelin EP: Whole Lotta Love/Good Times Bad Times/Hey Hey What Can I Do
(Atlantic EPA 220)

Led Zeppelin Acoustically EP: That's The Way/Going To California/Stairway To Heaven
(Atlantic EPA 228)

Belgium
Whole Lotta Love/Immigrant Song
(Atlantic 10236)

France
Dancing Days/Over The Hills And Far Away
Atlantic 10328)

How Many More Times
(cardboard postcard disc)

I Can't Quit You Babe
(cardboard postcard disc)

Communication Breakdown
(cardboard postcard disc)

Germany
Whole Lotta Love/Immigrant Song
(Atlantic 10236)

The Ocean/Dancing Days
(Atlantic 10316)

Holland
Whole Lotta Love/Immigrant Song
(Atlantic 10236)

Bron-Y-Aur Stomp/Out On The Tiles
(Atlantic 2019 030)

Italy
Bron-Y-Aur Stomp/Immigrant Song
(Atlantic NP 10316)

Heartbreaker/Bring It On Home
(Atlantic NP03162)

Moby Dick/Gallows Pole
(Atlantic NP 03183)

Iran
Whole Lotta Love/Instant Karma
(John Lennon Plastic Ono Band)/Maudie (Chicken Shack) EP (Top Four EX 4338)

Japan
Whole Lotta Love/Thank You
(Atlantic Nippon DT 1139)

Livin' Lovin' Maid (She's Just A Woman)/Bring It On Home
(Atlantic Nippon DT 1146)

Immigrant Song/Out On The Tiles
(Atlantic DT 1180)

Mexico

Immigrant Song/Tangerine/Out On The Tiles EP
(Atlantic ATL 2207014)

**Whole Lotta Love/Communication Breakdown/
Immigrant Song EP**
(Atlantic Gamma GX 07 762)

**Whole Lotta Love/Livin' Lovin' Maid (She's Just A
Woman)/Heartbreaker EP**
(Atlantic 2207 002)

**D'yer Mak'er/Over The Hills And Far Away/Black
Dog/Misty Mountain Hop EP**
(Atlantic Gamma GX 07 818)

**Good Times Bad Times/Communication Breakdown/
Dazed And Confused EP**
(Atlantic ATL 2047)

New Zealand

The Ten Legendary Singles
(Atlantic/Swan Song) Special seven-inch box pack of
the 10 standard Led Zeppelin singles. (Some of these
singles are incorrectly pressed so regular A-sides
become B-sides. This occurs on the couplings of
'Candy Store Rock', 'D'yer Mak'er' and 'Whole Lotta
Love'.)

Poland

Livin' Lovin' Maid (She's Just A Woman)
(plastic postcard disc)

Immigrant Song
(plastic postcard disc)

Friends/Celebration Day
(plastic postcard disc)

Bring It On Home
(plastic postcard disc)

Whole Lotta Love
(plastic postcard disc)

Black Mountain Side
(plastic postcard disc)

Good Times Bad Times
(plastic postcard disc)

Heartbreaker
(plastic postcard disc)

Moby Dick
(plastic postcard disc)

Your Time Is Gonna Come
(plastic postcard disc)

Communication Breakdown
(plastic postcard disc)

Spain

Whole Lotta Love/Communication Breakdown
(Atlantic H 523)

Taiwan

**Custard Pie/Boogie With Stu/Night Flight/Down By
The Seaside EP**
(Track FT 204)

The Rover/Trampled Underfoot
(Track F206)

NOTABLE FOREIGN CD SINGLES

Japan

Trampled Underfoot/Black Country Woman –
Swan Song CD single (1989)

Fool In The Rain/Hot Dog –
Swan Song CD single (1989)

NOTABLE FOREIGN PROMO SINGLES

Argentina

All My Love/Hot Dog –
Atlantic promo DIF 132

Brazil

**Friends/Celebration Day/Since I've Been Loving You
EP –**
Atlantic/Swan Song promo RG 03 AB (free single with
Rock Espatular magazine 1978)

Stairway To Heaven/Stairway To Heaven (edit) –
Atlantic 12-inch promo.

Italy

Heartbreaker/Woodstock
(Mathews Southern Comfort) – Atlantic juke box
promo ATL JB 98006 (1970)

Gallows Pole
(3.58 edited version)/

You Can't Judge A Book By The Cover (Cactus) –
Atlantic juke box promo RJB JB 98025 (1970)

The Ocean
(minus count in)/

Already Gone (The Eagles) – Atlantic/Asylum juke
box promo JB 55 (1973)

Rock And Roll
(live soundtrack version)/

Disco Inferno (The Trammps) – Swan Song/Atlantic
juke box promo 028 (1977)

Fool In The Rain
(4.00 edit)/

Hot Dog – Swan Song promo 097 (1980)

Spain

Whole Lotta Love
(edit)/

Leaving On A Jet Plane (Peter Paul And Mary) –
Atlantic/Hispavox promo CP 36

D'yer Mak'er/The Crunge
– Atlantic/Hispavox promo CP 195

Over The Hills And Far Away/Dancing Days
– Atlantic/Hispavox CP 182

NOTABLE FOREIGN ALBUM VARIATIONS

Austria

Led Zeppelin II
– Atlantic 9205 This version of the second album was
leased to the RCA record club for distribution to their
subscribers. It has a completely different sleeve
design, replacing the original graphics with a live shot
circa 1969. Copies were also available to RCA record
club readers in Germany.

Germany

Two Originals Of Led Zeppelin
(Atlantic) Rare double package of the first two Led
Zeppelin albums in the Kinney/Atlantic 'Two
Originals Of' series. Sleeve has Zeppelin phallic
cover. Withdrawn soon after release.

Led Zeppelin 1 and 2
– Atlantic AK 2 35 Similar package to the above, this

time with live photos on gatefold sleeve. Withdrawn.

Italy

Led Zeppelin
– Joker SM 3721 (1974) Track listing: Immigrant Song/
Stairway To Heaven/What Is And What Should Never
Be/Whole Lotta Love medley.
Recording of the 1971 BBC *In Concert* performance.
This surfaced in the mid-seventies on the Joker label
in a semi-legal release. The Italian copyright laws are
much less stringent than those in the UK and US.

USSR

Stairway To Heaven
Melodiya C 60 27501 005 1988 Special seven-track
compilation album featuring Immigrant Song/Gallows
Pole/Since I've Been Loving You/Black Dog/ When
The Levee Breaks/Rock And Roll/Stairway To Heaven.
(Strictly speaking, this is a bootleg album insofar as it
was copied from existing records and was unlicensed
by Led Zeppelin who did not receive any royalties.
The USSR is not subject to copyright laws as
applicable in the West. Melodiya is the state owned
record label in the USSR.) The front sleeve carries a
studio picture of Zeppelin *circa* 1969, while the rear
has a lengthy biography of the band in Russian.
Available in the following pressings:
Aprelev pressing with red label 1988
Aprelev second pressing with white label 1988
Riga pressing red label 1989
Leningrad pressing with de-luxe red label 1989
Tashkent pressing
Leningrad pressing white label 1988

Yugoslavia
Two Originals Of Led Zeppelin
Scarce pressing of the German package.

NOTABLE FOREIGN CD PROMOS

Japan
Forever Young Hard Rock CD Collection –
Warners CD compilation including 'Rock And Roll'
and 'Custard Pie'

Stairway To Heaven –
ARC Productions Big Artist series. Scarce limited
16-track Japanese only compilation

INTERVIEW DISCS
With no copyright on spoken word recordings, these
items emerged in the late eighties. This is a
representation of UK releases.

Ramble series
(available on CD or picture disc)

Ramble Vol I Robert and Bonzo
Australian interview 1972.

Ramble Vol 2 Robert and Jimmy
Australian interview 1972.

Ramble Vol 3 Jimmy Page
Zig Zag Interview 1972

Ramble Vol 4 Jimmy Page
Zig Zag Interview 1972

Chris Tetley Interview
(CTI 1004) picture disc

**Led Zeppelin On Compact Disc: Box set interview
CD.**
(CID Productions CID 007)

LED ZEPPELIN ON FILM AND
VIDEO

The Song Remains The Same
(Warner Video PES 61389) released on video 1984.
"The world's most expensive home movie," as Peter

Grant once observed, originally released for the big screen in 1976.

Directed by Joe Massot and Peter Clifton. Musical sequences filmed at Madison Square Garden July 27/28 and 29 1973.

Starring John Bonham, John Paul Jones, Jimmy Page, Robert Plant, with Peter Grant, Richard Cole, Derek Skilton and Colin Rigdon.

Music: Autumn Lake/Bron-Y-Aur/Rock And Roll/Black Dog/Since I've Been Loving You/The Song Remains The Same/The Rain Song/Stairway To Heaven/Dazed And Confused/Moby Dick/Heartbreaker/Whole Lotta Love/Stairway To Heaven.

Length: 137 minutes. Director of Photography: Ernie Day; Special Effects: Shelly of Camera Effects; Make-up Effects: Colin Arthur.

The Song Remains The Same – trivia:

The backstage row involving Peter Grant was shot at the Civic Centre, Baltimore. The airport and cavalcade scenes come from the July 24 show in Pittsburgh. The concert footage was shot over three days in Madison Square Garden. Out-take footage shot in New York included an interview with Zepp attorney Steve Weiss, and a segment featuring Jonesy and wife Mo at a police firing range. Bonzo's filming included shots of him riding along Blackpool pier and drag racing at Santa Pod. The sea boat scenes in Robert's sequence were shot in Aberystwyth. Joe Massot was taken off the project in early 1974 because the group were unhappy with the early rushes of the film. Peter Clifton was brought in to oversee completion.

In 1990 there emerged in America a video from Joe Massot's original film footage titled *The First Cuts*. This seemingly legitimate release has out-take fantasy scenes plus original concert film of 'Whole Lotta Love', 'The Song Remains The Same', 'Dazed And Confused' and 'Moby Dick' – 35 minutes in total. Joe Massot is also known to be sitting on many feet of unused footage from the 1973 filming.

Supershow

Virgin Vision VVD 167 (released September 1986).

Long awaited video that includes footage of Led Zeppelin performing 'Dazed And Confused' live at Staines studios on March 25, 1969. This was part of a day's filming that included appearances by Eric Clapton, Buddy Miles, Stephen Stills and Roland Kirk. Initially issued as a feature film given limited showings in the early seventies. Premiered at the London Lyceum Nov. 1969.

NB: It's almost certain that Zeppelin performed other numbers at this session. They may be lining a vault somewhere.

Rock Aid Armenia

(Virgin Video VVD 636) released November 1989.

Charity compilation features the *Supershow* Dazed And Confused clip plus The Firm promo for Satisfaction Guaranteed.

NOTABLE UK TV FOOTAGE

After making one solitary live TV appearance, Peter Grant and the group made a conscious decision to shy away from the medium. This is a run down of the few occasions when they were seen or heard on the small screen.

How Late It Is:

BBC 2, March 21, 1969. The only live UK TV appearance on a late night pilot show. Zeppelin replaced The Flying Burrito Brothers and performed 'Communication Breakdown'. This clip is thought to have been erased as Mike Read was unable to locate it for reshowing on the *Pop Quiz* TV show in 1982.

Old Grey Whistle Test:

BBC 2, March 20, 1973. Bob Harris previews the 'Houses Of The Holy' album by playing 'No Quarter' against one of Whistle Test's abstract (non-Zepp) film clips.

Old Grey Whistle Test:

BBC 2, January 17, 1975. An interview with Robert conducted with Bob Harris backstage before their warm-up date in Brussels on January 12.

Old Grey Whistle Test:

BBC 2, February 21, 1975. Against another abstract film, previews of 'Trampled Underfoot and 'Houses Of The Holy' are aired, four days before the release of 'Physical Graffiti'.

Old Grey Whistle Test:

BBC 2, April 6, 1976. 'Achilles Last Stand' is aired a day after the release of 'Presence'.

Old Grey Whistle Test:

BBC 2, October 5, 1976. Zepp return to the small screen in action from *The Song Remains The Same* movie when a clip of 'Black Dog' is previewed.

Old Grey Whistle Test:

BBC 2, November 2, 1976. An interview with Robert and Peter Grant with Michael Appleton filmed on a boat on the Thames is screened, plus Jimmy's violin bow segment from the movie.

Tiswas:

Central TV, June 1978. Robert makes a surprise appearance on the cult Saturday morning kids' TV show filmed in Birmingham. He receives a face full of custard pie from the phantom flan flinger.

Alright Now:

Tyne Tees TV, March 4, 1980. John Bonham records an interview with Billy Connolly screened in this TV show alongside a clip of 'Moby Dick' from the film. NB – TV offers that Peter Grant turned down included invitations from *Top Of The Pops*, *This Is Tom Jones*, *The Ed Sullivan Show*, *Beat Club* and an offer of one million dollars from ABC to perform a gig in Germany that would have been beamed live via satellite to the US. In May 1970, Granada TV producer Johnny Hamp approached the group to appear in a series of half-hour showcases he was commissioning. Again they turned the offer down.

TV Themes:

'Moby Dick' was used as the theme to BBC 2's *Disco 2* rock show circa 1970/71. A big band rock instrumental version of 'Whole Lotta Love' was used as the theme tune to BBC 1's *Top Of The Pops* during the seventies. The opening riff of the original version of 'Whole Lotta Love' was used as the theme to BBC 1's children's show *Search*.

OTHER NOTABLE FOOTAGE

Danish TV:

March 19, 1969. A special mini-concert filmed before an audience during the afternoon in Copenhagen – the group went on to an evening show at the Gladsaxe Club. Tracks screened: 'Communication Breakdown', 'Dazed And Confused', 'Babe I'm Gonna Leave You', 'How Many More Times'. This footage is still in existence and after a clip was shown on BBC 2's *Arena Heavy Metal* documentary, it received a surprise full UK screening on January 1, 1990. Filmed in black and white – producer: Edmont Jensen.

Communication Breakdown:

Promo film, circa 1969. An obscure and very early clip (possibly February 1969), with the group filmed close up running down 'Communication Breakdown' most impressively. Shown years later on Japanese TV.

French TV: Tous En Scene

circa 1969.

During their visit to Paris for a one off show at the Theatre D'Olympia on October 10th 1969 – the group appeared live on the French TV show *Tous En Scene*.

Whole Lotta Love:

promo film, circa 1969/70. Screened on the German *Beat Club* TV show in 1970, this has the studio version of 'Whole Lotta Love' playing over footage that includes various psychedelic effects, an exotic topless dancer, and infrequent shots of the group playing live. The live segments look to be from the Winterland in San Francisco, April 1969.

Royal Albert Hall:

January 7, 1970. One of the landmark Zeppelin shows, commissioned by Peter Grant to be filmed for inclusion in a TV special they intended to produce themselves during 1970. This has recently turned up as an hour-long bootleg video. Track listing: We're Gonna Groove/I Can't Quit You Baby/White Summer/Communication Breakdown/Whole Lotta Love/C'mon Everybody/Long Tall Sally medley. A superb vintage visual record of Led Zeppelin growing in stature.

NB: Other footage known to have been shot for their intended documentary included film of their spring US tour in 1970, plus their visit to Iceland in June, together with various off-stage clips and interviews including early film of Jason Bonham playing drums at home with Bonzo.

Honolulu:

September, 1970. A few minutes of what looks to be professionally shot film has emerged without sound.

Dutch Film Clip.

A minute's worth of 'Immigrant Song' live from Amsterdam in May 1971.

Australian TV:

1972. Clips of 'Rock And Roll' and 'Let's Have A Party' from the Sydney Showground gig in March 1972 were screened on Australian TV.

GROUP OWNED VIDEO FILM

As well as the Royal Albert Hall and 1970 film, there are reels of original video film lining the Zeppelin archives. The author saw some of these reels (including the Seattle Kingdome show in 1977 and Knebworth August 4, 1979) at the Swan Song office in 1982.

The footage is mainly culled from the following sources:

Earls Court: May 17/18/ 23/24/25, 1975.

Full shows exist from the video film shot and beamed on to the giant screen above the stage as the group performed.

USA Tour, 1977.

Many of the dates on this tour were filmed by CEE/Europa TV for projection on the giant ediophor screens above the stage. Again full shows from this era are in existence.

Knebworth: August 4/11, 1979.

Both shows were recorded on the Rolling Stones' mobile studio with George Chkiantz engineering and filmed both for the backdrop video screen and as an intended future release by a full crew from TV International. Segments that have surfaced from this footage include the Hot Dog promo issued in the US as a marketing aid for In Through The Out Door, a clip of Heartbreaker shown during the Atlantic 40th anniversary show in May 1988 and full versions of Kashmir and Ten Years Gone aired on MTV in Nov/Dec 1990.

The Remasters Promos 1990
Travelling Riverside Blues & Over The Hills And Far Away, both directed by Aubrey Powell.
 To promote the Remasters album Aubrey Powell, (a former sleeve designer with Hipgnosis) was commissioned to produce accompanying videos for two of the tracks. Both feature cleverly synchronised montage footage. Travelling Riverside Blues includes outakes from The Song Remains The Same movie plus glimpses of Page in his home studio circa late '73, mixed with conceptual 'Riverside' footage; Over The Hills combines film from the Danish 1969 TV show plus material from Seattle in 1977 and Knebworth. Both videos were aired extensively in Europe and the US.

The Remasters TV Advertisement
Produced to support the marketing campaign for the Remasters LP in the UK, 40 and 10 second commercials were aired across the ITV network at peak times. The ad included visuals taken from '73 and Knebworth and featured a voice over by Alan Freeman.

MTV: Led Zeppelin Whole Lotta Led Weekend/ Rockumentary, December 8/9 1990.
As part of their box set release MTV prepared a weekend of Zeppelin footage. For the first time Jimmy and Robert made available from their archives previously unseen film from 1977 and 1979 which was screened in segments over November and December 1990. This culminated in the Whole Lotta Led special. As well as full versions of Ten Years Gone from Knebworth (August 4, 1979) and Kashmir (August 11) and clips from The Song Remains and Supershow movies, MTV assembled a Led Zeppelin Rockumentary with official input from Atlantic Records. It was produced by Mike Kaufman and narrated by Kurt Loder. This is how it lined up: Interview material with Jimmy, Robert and John Paul Jones, plus the following footage: How Many More Times (Danish TV, 1969), Communication Breakdown (Danish TV, 1969), Dazed And Confused (Supershow, 1969), Whole Lotta Love, Song Remains (movie, 1973), Since I've Been Loving You (Song Remains), Rock And Roll (Song Remains), Stairway To Heaven (Song Remains), Stairway To Heaven (Seattle, 1977), Over The Hills And Far Away (Aubrey Powell promo, 1990), The Song Remains the Same (Seattle, 1977), Jimmy's acoustic Kashmir chords (home studio, 1989), Kashmir (Knebworth, 1979), Ten Years Gone (Knebworth), Achilles Last Stand (Seattle, 1977), Kashmir (silent footage, Seattle, 1977), Moby Dick (Song Remains), Moby Dick (Seattle, 1977), Wasting My Time (Jimmy Page promo, 1988), Tall Cool One (Robert Plant promo, 1988), Stairway To Heaven (Live Aid, 1985), Stairway To Heaven (Atlantic reunion, 1988), Wearing and Tearing (Jimmy and Robert, Knebworth, 1990).
*The screening of the Seattle and Knebworth footage gave rise to rumours that a definitive Led Zeppelin video anthology will eventually be commercially released. Such a project would overcome the shortcomings of The Song Remains The Same movie and accurately capture the on stage magic of their peak years.

UNOFFICIAL FOOTAGE
Unofficial amateur cine film of the group has begun to appear on the bootleg market. The quality in most cases leaves much to be desired. In the absence of any post–1973 official footage however, it remains of high interest for collectors. Clips include Chicago and LA from 1975 and Birmingham, Alabama from 1977.

LED ZEPPELIN ON THE RADIO
In the wake of their decision to shun TV early in their career, Led Zeppelin employed the use of BBC Radio One's more progressive radio shows to promote their growing reputation. These broadcasts have gone on to become some of the most bootlegged performances of the group's career. The music captured contains a marvellous spirit of adventure and they remain perfect examples of the Zepp development.

BBC Session Details
March 1969 at the BBC's Maida Vale studio:
Produced by Bernie Andrews. Tracks recorded: You Shook Me/Communication Breakdown/I Can't Quit You Baby/Dazed And Confused. Originally broadcast on John Peel's Top Gear, March 23 and April 20, and again on Symonds On Sunday introduced by Chris Grant on June 22.

June 9 at Maida Vale Studio:
Producer: unknown. Tracks recorded: The Girl I Love/ Something Else/What Is And What Should Never Be/ Communication Breakdown. This session remains something of a mystery. It was never broadcast though all the tracks can be found on the Something Else bootleg EP. Something Else is a cover of the Eddie Cochran song while The Girl I Love is a group composition that may have been considered for the second album.

June 23 at the Aeolian Hall, Bond Street:
Producer: John Walters; engineer: Tony Wilson. Tracks recorded: Communication Breakdown/What Is And What Should Never Be/Travelling Riverside Blues '69/Whole Lotta Love. This session benefited from overdubs and mixing and was the source from which Page would select Travelling Riverside Blues for the 1990 box set. Original transmission dates were June 29 and October 12 1969, and January 11 1970 – all on John Peel's Top Gear.

June 27, 1969: Playhouse Theatre, London:
Led Zeppelin In Concert special. This was the first of a Radio One showcase series. Broadcast live, the complete original running order was: Communication Breakdown/I Can't Quit You Baby/Interview by Alan Black with Jimmy and Robert/Dazed And Confused/ Interlude with Liverpool Scene's Adrian Henri/White Summer/Black Mountain Side/You Shook Me/How Many More Times.
 This show was repeated on September 5, 1969.

March 25, 1971: Paris Theatre, London:
Led Zeppelin in concert. This special show was originally broadcast as an hour-long programme on Sunday April 4, 1971, and repeated the following Wednesday. Original running order: John Peel intro/ Immigrant Song/Dazed And Confused/Stairway To Heaven/Going To California/That's The Way/What Is And What Should Never Be/John Peel intro/Whole Lotta Love – medley: Let That Boy Boogie/That's Alright/A Mess Of Blues/Honey Bee/Lemon Song.
 Those numbers were drawn from a full length set. The following numbers were performed at the recording but not broadcast: Heartbreaker/Black Dog/ Since I've Been Loving You/What Is And What Should Never Be false start/Communication Breakdown/ Thank You.

DOCUMENTARY RADIO PROGRAMMES

Two notable radio documentary series have been broadcast in recent years. The Mighty Arms Of Atlas was a one-hour programme, devoted to Led Zeppelin and aired in 1988 on Radio One as part of their Story Of Atlantic Records series. Narrated by Andy Peebles, it included new interviews with Robert, Jimmy and John Paul.
 In 1990 to tie in with the 'Remasters' release, Radio One put together a two-hour Power Of Led Zeppelin, written by Pete Frame and narrated by Alan Freeman. Aired December 15, 1990.

LED ZEPPELIN IN PRINT

Tour Books/Programmes
Texas
International Pop Festival 1969– with Zeppelin on the bill.

Bath Festival
of Blues June 28, 1969 – with Zeppelin on the bill.

Pop Proms
Royal Albert Hall, June 29, 1969 – bill topping appearance by Zeppelin.

1969 Tour Book
For the autumn 1969 tour – hardback book/ programme by the Visual Thing.

Bath Festival
Of Blues and Progressive Music, June 28, 1970 – bill topping appearance.

Japan Tour 1971.

Japan Tour 1972.

Australian Tour 1972.

USA Tour 1975.

Earls Court May 1975.

USA Tour 1977.

Knebworth August 1979.
 NB: In place of a programme for the 'Electric Magic' Wembley 1971 shows and the 1972/3 UK tour, special posters were made available. A programme was planned for the 1980 Europe tour by Martin Goldsmith Enterprises, but shelved in place of two tour posters. Bootleg programmes were sold at the Alexandra Palace 1972 dates and the Knebworth shows.

MUSIC BOOKS

Led Zeppelin
(Warner Bros Music) 1971.

The Combined Led Zeppelin 1 And 2
(Kinney/Music Sales) 1972.

Led Zeppelin Complete
(Superhype) 1974 – features the first five albums.

In Through The Out Door
(Swan Song/Warner Bros) 1980.

Off The Record
(Warners) 1987 – detailed transcriptions of five tracks.
 NB: A music book for 'Physical Graffiti' and 'Presence' was planned by Jimmy Page before the 1977 US tour to be illustrated by a series of Neal Preston photos. This project was never completed.

BOOKS

Led Zeppelin Rock Fun Photo Gallery
(Japanese Rock Fun 1976).

Rock On The Road – Mick Gold
(Futura 1976 includes section on Zepp at Earls Court).

Led Zeppelin Biography – Richie Yorke
(US Methuen 1976).

Led Zeppelin – Howard Mylett
(Panther 1976 updated 1981).

Led Zeppelin – Alain Dister
(French Rock and Folk 1980).

Led Zeppelin – Ongaku Senka
(Japanese 1980).

Led Zeppelin Viva Rock Vol 3 1980 Europe tour special – Ongaku Senka
(Japanese Viva Rock 1980).

Led Zeppelin In The Light (1968 – 1980) – Howard Mylett and Richard Bunton
(Proteus/Savoy 1981).

Led Zeppelin In Their Own Words – Paul Kendall (Omnibus Press 1981).

Led Zeppelin A Visual Documentary – Paul Kendall (Omnibus Press 1982).

Led Zeppelin HM Photo Book – (Omnibus Press 1983).

Led Zeppelin On Stage Action – Howard Mylett/Carl Dunn (private publication 1983).

Led Zeppelin Portraits – Neal Preston (Mirage 1983, two editions published).

Led Zeppelin The Final Acclaim – Dave Lewis (Babylon Books 1983).

Led Zeppelin The Book – Chris Welch (Proteus 1984).

Jimmy Page And Robert Plant The Power And The Glory – Chris Welch (Zomba 1985).

Hammer Of The Gods – Stephen Davis (Sidgewick and Jackson 1985).

Led Zeppelin The Legend Lives On – Robert Kamin (US Robus Books 1986).

Led Zeppelin Poster Book – Roger Holland (Atlanta Press 1987).

The Illustrated Collector's Guide To Led Zeppelin – Robert Godwin (Hot Wacks Press – Third edition 1990).

Led Zeppelin Live In Japan Bootleg Book Etc – (Naniawa Print, Japanese 1990).

Led Zeppelin Comic Book (US Rock Fantasy 1990).

NB: Other books touted for release that have yet to see the light include the Zepp memoirs of their one-time publicist B.P. Fallon (projected title – *Over The Top*), and original *The Song Remains The Same* movie director Joe Massot's factual account of the making of the movie (*Led Zeppelin In Motion*).

LED ZEPPELIN FANZINES

In the absence of an official fan club this author created the original UK fanzine *Tight But Loose* which published for six issues up to 1981. Since then a whole host of fanzines have appeared and disappeared. *Pure Blues* led the way followed by *Proximity, The Rover, Rock And Roll, Runes And Feathers In The Wind, The Crunge, Music Creations, In The Mood* (all US), *Hot Led, Winds Of Thor* (UK), *Storm Window, Thank You, Led Swan Press, Keep Movin'* (Japan) and *Oh Jimmy* (Italy/US).

Fanzines currently operating include the aforementioned *Oh Jimmy* (PO Box 80287, Lansing MI 48908, USA), *The Ocean* (46 Brairwood Drive, Westwood, MA 02090, USA) and *Zozo* – an informative Zepp magazine published monthly from 41 Sutter Street, Suite 1495, San Francisco, California 94104, USA.
For further information contact Dave Lewis at 14 Totnes Close, Bedford, England, MK40 3AX. S.A.E.

EARLY DAYS AND LATTER DAYS

A new UK collectors magazine is available quarterly from Andy Adams, 10A Cavendish Road, Croydon CR0 3LB.

RECOMMENDED PUBLICATIONS

Disc And Music Echo, March 7, 1970 – Anatomy Of A Wondergroup by Caroline Boucher.

Melody Maker, November 27, 1971 – Zapped by Zeppelin – Electric Magic review by Roy Hollingworth.

Zig Zag, issues 27 and 28, December 1972, February 1973. Two part interview with Jimmy Page by Pete Frame.

Melody Maker, July 1, 1972 – Led Zeppelin The Forgotten Giants? US tour report by Roy Hollingworth.

New Musical Express, June 16, 1973 – Zeppin' Out – US tour report by Charles Shaar Murray.

New Musical Express, March 1974 – Looking Back – Led Zeppelin The Noble Art Of Dynamics by Charles Shaar Murray.

New Musical Express, December 7, 1974 – The Graffiti Of The Physical . . . interview with Page and album preview by Nick Kent.

Rolling Stone, March 13, 1975 – Robert Plant and Jimmy Page in conversation with Cameron Crowe – cover story.

The Observer, May 18, 1975 – Led Zeppelin Bigger Than The Beatles? by Tony Palmer.

Melody Maker, February 14, 1976 – Plantations – Lengthy interview with Robert Plant conducted in New York by Chris Charlesworth.

Trouser Press, September/October/November issues 1977. Interview with Jimmy Page by Dave Schulps.

Melody Maker, August 4, 1979 – Interview with Jimmy Page by Michael Watts and Copenhagen warm-up review.

Rolling Stone, September 29, 1990 – Led Zeppelin – The Seventies 'I Thought It Was The Greatest Band In The World' – Jimmy Page, Robert Plant and John Paul Jones talk to J.D. Considine. Ten Years On. Cover story.

COVER VERSIONS

Though few cover versions of their material surfaced in the seventies, after 1980 the Zeppelin imitation game began to gain momentum.

Its origins can be traced back to the early eighties and an LA based group The White. Led by Plant soundalike Michael White (later to release records in his own right), The White specialised in looking and sounding like Led Zeppelin and took their musical tribute to Zeppelin on the road. Fellow tribute bands bearing original names such as Kashmir and Physical Graffiti followed in their wake. The Zepp influence later began to be felt by the likes of The Cult and The Sisters Of Mercy in the UK and was blatantly sampled by Rick Rubin for The Beastie Boys' album (which led in turn to Robert using Zepp samples as a retort on the 'Now And Zen' album). In 1988, Kingdom Come built a whole album around sounding like Zeppelin and enjoyed massive, if short lived, success.

The whole Zeppelin imitation game took on bizarre proportions at the turn of the decade with the emergence of Dread Zeppelin. Led by the larger than life Tortelvis, this unlikely outfit played Led Zeppelin covers to a reggae beat with an obese Elvis Presley impersonator singing vocals. An extremely well executed satire, that proved a hit even with Robert Plant as well as a legion of followers.

Listed below is a round up of cover versions known to exist. It does not claim to be comprehensive but hopefully lists various artists who, in the absence of the real thing, have made sure the songs remain . . . not necessarily the same.

'Good Times Bad Times': Nuclear Assault

'Babe I'm Gonna Leave You': Joan Baez/Quicksilver Messenger Service/Great White.

'Dazed And Confused': Jake Holmes, The Yardbirds (both when the song was known as 'I'm Confused').

'Your Time Is Gonna Come': Sandie Shaw/Dread Zeppelin.

'Communication Breakdown': Paul Stanley (live)/ Dread Zeppelin/The Dickies/Iron Maiden.

'Whole Lotta Love': CCS/Top Of The Pops Orchestra/ The Ventures/King Curtis/Tina Turner/London Symphony Orchestra/ Blonde On Blonde/Wonder Band/Vicious Club Rumour/Love Child Orchestra/ Kazoo Orchestra/Iron Fist/John Lennon (rehearsal out-take from the 'Rock 'n' Roll' sessions).

'Heartbreaker': Iron Fist.

'Moby Dick': Dread Zeppelin/Drum Madness (Jason Bonham, Tico Torres, Mickey Currie, Jim Vallence).

'Immigrant Song': Minimal Compact/The Osmonds/ Great White/ Aerosmith (live).

'Black Dog': CCS/Dread Zeppelin/Bonham (live).

'Rock And Roll': Heart/Bonham (live)/April Wine (live)/Tent Poles/Great White (live)/Triumph/Beastie Boys (sample)/Jam – live from the Moscow Peace Festival 1989 – Skid Row/Motley Crue/Zakk Wiyde/ Jason Bonham and Sam Brown (live).

'The Battle Of Evermore': Heart (live).

'Stairway To Heaven': Patricia Paay/London Symphony Orchestra/Vienna Symphony Orchestra/ Far Corporation/Wonder Band/Elkie Brooks/Justin Hayward/Reverberi/Dread Zeppelin (live)/Frank Zappa (live).

'Misty Mountain Hop': Dread Zeppelin (live).

'When The Levee Breaks': Beastie Boys (sample)/ Memphis Minnie/Kanzas Joe McCoy/Sisters Of Mercy (live).

'D'yer Mak'er': Voice Of The Beehive.

'No Quarter': I Love Ethyl.

'The Ocean': Beastie Boys (sample).

'Custard Pie': Beastie Boys (sample).

'The Rover': Heart (live).

'Trampled Underfoot': Then Jericho (live).

'Kashmir': John Lydon (live)/The Ordinaires.

'Nobody's Fault But Mine': Innocence (sample on 'Let's Push It' – Big Beat mix).

'In The Evening': Twice Shy.

'Hey Hey What Can I Do': – Dread Zeppelin.

Notable Led Zeppelin spoofs:
The most infamous spoof (pre-Dread Zeppelin) send up of Led Zeppelin is 'Stairway To Gilligan' by Gilligan's Island. A send up of 'Stairway To Heaven', this surfaced in the US in 1978. It did not go down well with the band and Peter Grant slapped an injunction on it.

A more affectionate spoof can be heard on the B-side of Roy Wood's Wizard 1972 single 'Angel Fingers'. His 'You Got The Jump On Me Baby' is a deliberate and accurate heavy handed Zepp *à la* 'Black Dog' take-off. After all 'Does Anybody Remember Laughter?' as somebody once put it.

A cleverly sampled Zep bootleg montage appears on a bootleg single known as The Slog – coupled with a fake acoustic take of Black Dog (New Cross Skyline NCI).

DISCOGRAPHY OF SOLO ACTIVITIES

Appendix 2B

JIMMY PAGE
PRE AND POST
ZEPPELIN RECORDINGS

PRE ZEPPELIN

As one of the most sought after studio session guitarists on the London scene *circa* 1963 to 1966, Jimmy Page appeared on countless records issued during that era. These range from famous contributions to singles such as Them's 'Here Comes The Night' and The Kink's 'You Really Got Me', through banalities like Val Doonican's 'Walk Tall' to little heard obscurities such as Bobby Graham's 'Zoom Widge And Wag'. A good representation of his work during this period is captured on the album 'James Patrick Page Session Man'.

Initially compiled as a double bootleg in 1979, it can now be found on two seemingly legal US releases as follows:

James Patrick Page Session Man: Vol 1
Archive Productions International AIP 10041 Also available on CD.

James Patrick Page Session Man: Vol 2
Archive Productions International AIP 10053 Also available on CD.

In 1965 Jimmy cut a solo single for Fontana on which he sings and plays all instruments except drums:

She Just Satisfies/Keep Moving
Fontana TF 533 (February 1965)

Later in the year Jimmy became house producer at Andrew Loog Oldham's Immediate label. A representation of his work during this period can be found on the following singles and albums:

SINGLES

Fifth Avenue: Bells Of Rhymney/Just Like Anyone Would
Immediate IM 002 (1965)

Les Fleurs De Lys: Moondreams/Wait For Me
Immediate IM 20 (1965)

Glyn Johns: Mary Anne/Like Grains Of Sand
Immediate IM 013 (1965)

John Mayall's Bluesbreakers: I'm Your Witchdoctor/Telephone Blues
Immediate IM 012 (1965) Features Page as producer.

Nico: The Last Mile/I'm Not Saying
Immediate IM 003 (1965)

ALBUMS

Anthology Of British Blues Vol 1
Immediate IMAL 03/04

Anthology Of British Blues Vol 2
Immediate IMAL 05/06 Both of the above include blues jams between Page and Eric Clapton. Also available on White Boy Blues (Castle CCSLP 103) also available on CD.

Chris Farlowe: 14 Things To Think About
Immediate IMPL 0050 (1966)

Twice As Much: Own Up
Immediate IMLP 007 (1966)

The Immediate Alternatives
Sequel NEX LP 110 (1990) Available on CD.

Other notable Page activity captured on record during this era include the following:
Jimmy Page and Sonny Boy Williamson
BYG 529908. Also available as 'Jimmy Page Special Early Works' (Springboard SPB 4038).1964 jam session.

John Williams: The Maureeny Wishful Album
Moonshine Music WO 23880 (1965) Acoustic album with six tracks published by James Page Music and with Page on sitar on the tracks 'Dream Cloudburst' and 'Early Bird Of Morning'.

Jeff Beck: Beck's Bolero
Available as the B-side to 'Hi Ho Silver Lining' (Columbia DB 8151) and on the albums 'The Most Collection' (MFP 50015) and 'Jeff Beck: Truth' (SCX 6293). A Page instrumental composition recorded in 1966 with Keith Moon, Nicky Hopkins, John Paul Jones and Jeff. This session concluded with talk of Moon hitching up with Page in a line-up that would, as Moon put it, go down like a lead balloon, or even a lead Zeppelin . . .

The Rolling Stones: Metamorphosis
Decca SKL 5212 (1975)
This 1975 compilation of sixties Stones' out-takes acknowledges Page's assistance but does not specify which tracks.

JIMMY PAGE WITH THE YARDBIRDS

SINGLES

Happenings Ten Years Time Ago/Psycho Daisies
UK Columbia DB 8024; (October 1966)

Happening Ten Years Time Ago/The Nazz Are Blue
(non Page track) US Epic 10094 (November 1966)

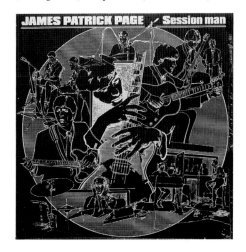

Little Games/Puzzles
UK Columbia DB 8164; US Epic 10156 (April 1967)

Ha Ha Said The Clown/Tinker, Tailor, Soldier, Sailor
US Epic 10204 (July 1967)

Ten Little Indians/Drinking Muddy Water
US Epic 10248 (October 1967)

Goodnight Sweet Josephine/Think About It
UK Columbia DB 8368 quickly withdrawn; US Epic 10303 (February 1968)

ALBUMS

Little Games
US Epic BN 26313 1967; reissued in the UK on EMI Fame 4131241). Tracks: Little Games/Smile On Me/White Summer/Tinker, Tailor, Soldier, Sailor/Glimpses/Drinking Muddy Water/No Excess Baggage/Stealing Stealing/Only The Black Rose/Little Soldier Boy. Extra tracks on UK reissue: Think About It and Remember The Night.

Live Yardbirds With Jimmy Page
US CBS special Products P 13311 released 1971. Later issued in a second pressing on Epic E 30615. Withdrawn due to injunction from Page. Tracks: The Train Kept A Rollin'/You're A Better Man Than I/I'm Confused/My Baby/Over Under Sideways Down/Drinking Muddy Water/Shapes Of Things/White Summer/I'm A Man.

Blow Up – Original Soundtrack
MGM SE 4447 (March 1967) features Page and Beck on 'Stroll On', as seen in the club scene in the film.

SOLO SOUNDTRACK ALBUM

Kenneth Anger's *Lucifer Rising*
Boleskine House Records BHR 666 (1987) USA issue. Pressed at 45 rpm on blue vinyl.
This album surfaced in America in the mid-eighties as a release of questionable legality. It contains the 23 minutes of soundtrack music Page provided for the Kenneth Anger movie in 1973/4. In a blaze of publicity, Anger took Page off the project in 1976 for coming up with so little music.

POST-LED ZEPPELIN RECORDINGS

ALBUMS

***Death Wish 2* Original Soundtrack**
Swan Song SSK 59415 (February 1982) Tracks: Who's To Blame/The Chase/City Sirens/Jam Sandwich/Carole's Theme/The Release/Hotel Rats And Photostats/A Shadow In The City/Jill's Theme/Prelude/Big Band/Sax And Violence/Hypnotising Ways (Oh Mamma).
UK chart position: No. 40 – 4 weeks on chart.

The Firm: The Firm
Atlantic 781 239 1 (February 1985) Tracks: Closer/Make Or Break/Someone To Love/Together/ Radioactive/You've Lost That Lovin' Feeling/Money Can't Buy/Satisfaction Guaranteed/Midnight Moonlight.
UK chart position: No. 15 – 5 weeks on chart.

The Firm: Mean Business
Atlantic WX 43 (April 1986) Tracks: Fortune Hunter/
Cadillac/All The King's Horses/Live In Peace/Tear
Down The Walls/Dreaming/Free To Live/Spirit Of
Love.
UK chart position: No. 46 – 3 weeks on chart.

**Roy Harper And Jimmy Page: Whatever Happened
To Jugula**
Beggars Banquet Bega 60 (March 1985) Tracks:
Nineteen Forty-Eightish/Bad Speech/Hope/Hangman/
Elizabeth/Frozen Moment/Twentieth Century Man/
Advertisement.
UK chart position: No. 44 – 4 weeks on chart.

Jimmy Page: Outrider
Geffen WX 155 (June 1988) Tracks: Wasting My Time/
Wanna Make Love/Writes of Winter/The Only One/
Liquid Mercury/Hummingbird/Emerald Eyes/Prison
Blues/Blues Anthem.
UK chart position: No. 27 – 6 weeks on chart.

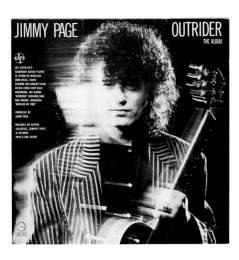

SINGLES

The Firm: Radioactive/Together
Atlantic A 9586 (February 1985)

The Firm: Radioactive/Together
Atlantic A 9586P Picture disc (February 1985)

**The Firm: Radioactive/Together/City Sirens (live)/
Live In Peace (live)**
Atlantic A 9586TE 12-inch single (February 1985)

**The Firm: Radioactive/City Sirens (live)/Live In Peace
(live)**
Atlantic A 9586T 12-inch single (February 1985)

The Firm: All The King's Horses/Fortune Hunter
Atlantic A 9458 (April 1976)

Jimmy Page: Wasting My Time/Writes Of Winter
Geffen Gef 41 (Scheduled for release June 1988 –
subsequently shelved).

**Roy Harper And Jimmy Page: Elizabeth/
Advertisement**
Beggars Banquet Beg 131 (1985) 12-inch – Beg 13T –
has live version of 'White Man'.

US ALBUMS

***Death Wish 2* – Original Soundtrack**
Swan Song SS 8511 (February 1982)

The Firm: The Firm
Atlantic 81239 (March 1985) US chart position: No. 17
– 16 weeks on chart – certified Gold April 11, 1985.

The Firm: Mean Business
Atlantic 81628 (January 1986) US chart position: No. 22
– seven weeks on chart.

Outrider
Geffen 23888 (June 1988) US chart position: No. 26 – 6
weeks on chart – certified Gold August 23, 1988.

NOTABLE US RELEASES

SINGLES(alternate couplings to UK issues)

The Firm: Satisfaction Guaranteed/Closer
US Atlantic 7 89561 (1985)

The Firm: Live In Peace/Free To Live
Atlantic 7 89421 (1986)

Jimmy Page: Wasting My Time/Writes Of Winter
Geffen 9278217 (1988)

NOTABLE US PROMO ITEMS

SINGLES

The Firm:
Satisfaction Guaranteed/Satisfaction Guaranteed
Atlantic 7 89561 radio promo (1985)

All The King's Horses/All The King's Horses
Atlantic PR 834 promo 12-inch single (1986)

All The King's Horses/All The King's Horses
Atlantic 7 89458 radio promo (1986)

Live In Peace/Live In Peace
Atlantic PR 878 promo 12-inch single (1986)

Tear Down The Walls/Live In Peace (live)
Atlantic PR 894 promo 12-inch single (1986)

Someone To Love/Someone To Love
Atlantic PR 735 promo 12-inch single (1985)

Radioactive/Radioactive
Atlantic PR 698 promo 12-inch single (1985)

Radioactive/Radioactive (extended mix)
Atlantic PR 714 promo 12-inch single (1985)

Jimmy Page:
Wasting My Time/Wasting My Time
Geffen DJ promo single (1988)

PROMO ALBUMS

The Firm:
The Firm Talk Business
Atlantic PR 883 promo interview album (1985)

PROMO CD'S

Wasting My Time (4.28)/**Wasting My Time** with
interview intro (4.40)
Geffen PRO CD 3083 promo CD (1988)

Prison Blues (edit)/**Prison Blues** Geffen PRO CD 3276
promo CD (1988)

Outrider: An Interview With Jimmy Page
Geffen PRO CD 3099 53-minute interview and album
extracts promo CD (1988)

Outrider Promo Lunch Box:
Includes promo interview video, interview CD plus
promo cassette of the album.

PROMO CASSETTE

Outrider
Geffen cassette sampler Includes The Only One/
Wanna Make Love/Prison Blues.

NOTABLE US RADIO SHOW PROMOS

The Firm Live From The Hammersmith Odeon 1984
Westwood One Superstars In Concert SS86 02. Three
album set.

The Firm Live 1985
Westwood One Superstars In Concert. Live US tour
three album set.

Off The Record With Mary Turner
Westwood One OTRSP85 16. Music and interviews
two album set.

Outrider Tour Live 1988
Westwood One Superstars In Concert SS88 25.

Jimmy Page Up Close
Neer Perfect 8823. Music and interviews two CD set.
Media Radio promo 1988.

NOTABLE FOREIGN RELEASES

Japan:
Who's To Blame (*Death Wish* **Title)/Carole's Theme**
Swan Song P1673 (1982) Japanese only seven-inch
single features alternative *Death Wish* tracks on both
sides. A-side has instrumental opening titles version
of 'Who's To Blame'. B-side is an electric slide take of
'Carole's Theme'.

GUEST APPEARANCES

Stephen Stills: Right By You
Atlantic 780 177 (1984) Features Page on the tracks
'50/50' and 'Right By You'.

The Honeydrippers Vol 1
Atlantic 790220 1 (1984) Features Page on the tracks
'Sea Of Love' and 'I Get A Thrill'.

John Paul Jones: Music From The Film *Scream
For Help*
Atlantic 780 190 1 (1985) Features Page on the tracks
'Spaghetti Junction' and 'Crackback'.

Box Of Frogs: Strange Land
Epic 26375 (1986) Features Page on the track 'Asylum'.

The Rolling Stones: Dirty Work
Rolling Stones Records/CBS 86321 (1986) Features
Page on the track 'One Hit (To The Body)'.

Willie And The Poorboys: Willie And The Poorboys
Decca Bill 1 (1985)
Features Page on the tracks 'Wasting My Time' and
'Slippin' And Slidin''. 'These Arms Of Mine' also
available on a 10-inch single (Decca/Ripple T 880 917 7)
and as a seven-inch Dutch release (Decca 880917 7).

Robert Plant: Now And Zen
Es Paranza WX 149 (1988) Features Page on the tracks
'Tall Cool One' and 'Heaven Knows'.

Roy Harper: In Between Every Line
Harvest EN 5004 (1986) Features Page on the tracks
'Short And Sweet', 'Referendum' and 'Highway
Blues'.
Recorded live 1984.

VIDEO APPEARANCES

Royal Albert Hall ARMS Concert Part 2
Videoform VFV 17 (1984) Features Page on 'Prelude',
'Who's To Blame', 'City Sirens', 'Stairway To Heaven'
and with Clapton, Beck etc on 'Layla' and 'Goodnight
Irene' and Tulsa Time.

Five From The Firm
Atlantic Home Video – US only
Features promo videos of 'Tear Down The Walls',
'Satisfaction Guaranteed', 'All The King's Horses',

'Radioactive' and 'Live In Peace'. This home video was slated for US issue in 1986, but was never widely available.

The Firm Live At Hammersmith 1984
Atlantic promo video. Filmed over the two Hammersmith dates in December 1984 for promo use only.

Wasting My Time
Geffen promo video (1988). Filmed at Shepperton for promo use only.

OTHER PAGE FOOTAGE

Other notable Page footage that has surfaced includes the following:
   An archive piece of film (circa 1958/9) from the BBC. This had a very young Page playing rhythm guitar and being interviewed by Huw Weldon. Page tells him he would like to be a biological researcher.
Page can be clearly seen with The Yardbirds playing a Fender Telecaster guitar in the film *Blow Up*. The number being performed is 'Stroll On' a variation of 'The Train Kept A Rollin'.
In March 1970, Jimmy was filmed for a solo spot on BBC 2's *Julie Felix Show*. He performed 'White Summer/Black Mountain Side'.
Jimmy and Roy Harper appeared in an interview segment for *The Old Grey Whistle Test* on November 6, 1984 – filmed up on Scafell Pike in the Lake District. As well as answering questions from Mark Ellen, the pair played 'Same Old Rock' and 'Hangman'.
On March 10/11 1985, Page took part in the filming of a video of 'These Arms Of Mine' with the Willie And The Poorboys line-up at Fulham Town Hall.
In 1988 Page performed an acoustic 'White Summer/ Black Mountain Side' with additional snatches of 'Midnight Moonlight' and 'Kashmir', during an interview for the BBC *Arena* documentary on Heavy Metal screened in 1989.
The music Jimmy composed for Michael Winner in September 1981 can be heard in the films *Death Wish 2* and *Death Wish 3*.

TOUR PROGRAMMES/MUSIC BOOKS/RECOMMENDED PUBLICATIONS

TOUR PROGRAMMES

ARMS concert programmes for September 20 and 21, 1983.
The Firm tour programme 1984.
The Firm tour programme 1985.
Outrider tour programme 1988.

MUSIC BOOKS

Jimmy Page: Super Rock Guitarist Vol 1
Jimmy Page: Super Rock Guitarist Vol 2
Jimmy Page: Outrider (Geffen 1988)

BOOKS

Jimmy Page: Tangents Within A Framework –
Howard Mylett
(Omnibus 1983)

RECOMMENDED PUBLICATIONS

Sounds Guitar Heroes
(UK November 1982) Full low down on Page's guitar collection.

Kerrang!
(UK December 27, 1984) Firm Handed. Cover story and interview by Chris Welch.

Guitar World
(US July 1986) Special issue devoted to Jimmy Page.

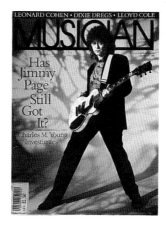

Musician
(US July 1988) Has Jimmy Page Still Got It? Cover story and interview by Charles M. Young.

Kerrang!
(UK June 25, 1988) Turn The Page: Jimmy Rides Out. Cover story and interview by Mick Wall.

Musician
(US November 1990) Jimmy Page: Living in Led Zeppelin – Interview with Max Resnicoff

Guitar World
(US October 1988) The Resurrection Of Jimmy Page. Cover story and interview by Bud Scoppa and Max Kay.

Musician
(US November 1990) Jimmy Page: Living in Led Zeppelin – Interview with Matt Resnicoff

ROBERT PLANT
PRE AND POST ZEPPELIN SOLO RECORDINGS

PRE-ZEPPELIN SOLO SINGLES

With Listen:
You Better Run/Everybody's Gonna Say
UK CBS 202456; US Columbia 4 43967 (October 1966)

Robert Plant:
Our Song/Laughing, Crying, Laughing
CBS 202656 (March 1967)

Long Time Coming/I've Got A Secret
CBS 2858 (September 1967)

The Band Of Joy with Robert Plant and John Bonham:
Although this pre-Zeppelin line-up never secured a record deal, they did record a number of tracks at Regent Sound studios early in 1968. Tracks recorded included 'Memory Lane', 'Adriatic Sea View', 'Hey Joe' and 'For What It's Worth'. Acetates of this session were pressed for band personnel. Some 21 years later it was from this source that Plant donated the track 'Adriatic Sea View' to ex-Band Of Joy member Kevyn Gammond (now a college lecturer) for use on a fund raising cassette compilation for Kidderminster College.

In The Forest
Forest Music cassette compilation (1989). Features The Band Of Joy playing 'Adriatic Sea View'.

ALBUMS

Alexis Korner: Bootleg Him
Rak SRAK 514 Also available as 'Alexis Korner And . . .'
Castle Collector series CCSLP LP/CD (Original issue 1971; reissue 1986). Features Robert Plant on the 1968 recording 'Operator'.

POST ZEPPELIN RECORDINGS
SINGLES

Burning Down One Side/Moonlight In Samosa
Swan Song SSK 19429 (September 1982) UK chart position: No. 73 – 1 week on chart

Burning Down One Side/Moonlight In Samosa/ Far Post
Swan Song SSK 19429T 12-inch single (September 1982)

Big Log/Messin' With The Mekon
Es Paranza B 9848 (June 1983) UK chart position: No. 11 – 10 weeks on chart.

Big Log/Messin' With The Mekon/Stranger Here . . . Than Over There
Es Paranza B 9848T (June 1983)

In The Mood/Pledge Pin (live)
Es Paranza B 6970 (November 1983)

In The Mood/Pledge Pin (live)/Horizontal Departure (live)
Es Paranza B 6970T (November 1983)

The Honeydrippers: Sea Of Love/Rockin' At Midnight
Es Paranza YZ 33 (January 1985) UK chart position: No. 56 – 3 weeks on chart.

Pink And Black/Trouble Your Money
Es Paranza B9640 (May 1985)

Little By Little (remix)/Doo Doo A Do Do/Easily Lead (live)/Rockin' At Midnight (live)
Es Paranza B9621F seven-inch limited edition double pack (August 1985)

Little By Little (remix)/Doo Doo A Do Do
Es Paranza B9621 (August 1985)

Little By Little (remix long version)/Easily Lead (live)/Doo Doo A Do Do
Es Paranza B9621T 12-inch single (September 1985)

Heaven Knows/Walking Towards Paradise
Es Paranza A9373 (January 1988) UK chart position: No. 33 – 5 weeks on chart.

Heaven Knows (extended remix)/Walking Towards Paradise/Big Log
Es Paranza A 9373T 12-inch single (January 1988)

Heaven Knows (extended remix)/Walking Towards Paradise/Big Log
Es Paranza A 9373CD three-inch CD single (February 1988)

Heaven Knows (extended remix)/Walking Towards Paradise/ Heaven Knows (Astral mix)
Es Paranza A 9373TB special 12-inch single limited edition box set (February 1988)

Tall Cool One (remix)/White Clean And Neat
Es Paranza A 9348 (April 1988)

Tall Cool One (extended version)/Tall Cool One (remix)/White Clean And Neat
Es Paranza A 9348T 12-inch single (April 1988)

Tall Cool One (remix)/White Clean And Neat/Tall Cool One (extended version) Little By Little (remix)
Es Paranza A 9348B three-inch CD single (April 1988)

Ship Of Fools/Helen Of Troy
Es Paranza A9281 (September 1988)

Ship Of Fools/Helen Of Troy/Heaven Knows (live)
Es Paranza A 9281TF 12-inch single limited edition with free poster (September 1988)

Ship Of Fools/Helen Of Troy/Heaven Knows (live)
Es Paranza A 9281T 12-inch single (September 1988)

Ship Of Fools/Helen Of Troy (live)/Dimples (live)
Es Paranza A 9281 CDB three-inch CD single in limited box package (September 1988)

Ship Of Fools/Helen Of Troy (live)/Dimples (live)
Es Paranza A 9281 CD0 three-inch CD single (September 1988)

Hurting Kind (I've Got My Eyes On You)/I Cried
Es Paranza A 9348 (March 1990) UK chart position: No. 45 – 4 weeks on chart.
Also available on cassette single:

Hurting Kind (I've Got My Eyes On You)/I Cried/ Oompah (Watery Bint)/One Love
Es Paranza A 8985T 12-inch single (March 1990)

Hurting Kind (I've Got My Eyes On You)/Don't Look Back/Oompah (Watery Bint)/One Love
Es Paranza A 8985 five-inch CD single (March 1990)

Hurting Kind (I've Got My Eyes On You)/I Cried
Es Paranza A 8995P. Limited edition cut to shape picture disc. (March 1990)

Your Ma Said You Cried In Your Sleep Last Night (new mix)/She Said
Es Paranza A 8945 (June 1990). Also on cassette single.

Your Ma Said You Cried In Your Sleep Last Night (new mix)/Your Ma Said You Cried In Your Sleep Last Night (album version)/One Love
Es Paranza A 8945T 12-inch single (June 1990)

Your Ma Said You Cried In Your Sleep Last Night (new mix)/Your Ma Said You Cried In Your Sleep Last Night (album version)/She Said/One Love
Es Paranza A 8945CD CD single (June 1990)

ALBUMS

Pictures At Eleven
Swan Song SSK 59418 (June 1982) Tracks: Burning Down One Side/Moonlight In Samosa/Pledge Pin/ Slow Dancer/Worse Than Detroit/Fat Lip/Like I've Never Been Gone/Mystery Title
UK chart position: No. 2 – 15 weeks on chart.

The Principle Of Moments
Es Paranza 79 0101 1 (July 1983) Tracks: Other Arms/In The Mood/Messin' With The Mekon/ Reckless Love/ Thru' With The Two Step/Horizontal Departure/ Stranger Here . . . Than Over There/Big Log
UK chart position: No. 7 – 14 weeks on chart.
N.B. Promo advance tapes have the track 'Thru' With The Two Step' listed under the title 'For Better Or Worse'.

The Honeydrippers: The Honeydrippers Vol 1
Es Paranza 79 0220 1 (November 1984) Initial copies pressed in 10-inch format.
Tracks: I Get A Thrill/Sea Of Love/I Got A Woman/ Young Boy Blues/Rockin' At Midnight
UK chart position: No. 56 – 10 weeks on chart.

Shaken 'N' Stirred
Es Paranza 790 265 1 (May 1985) Tracks: Hip To Hoo/ Kallalou Kallalou/Too Loud/Trouble Your Money/Pink And Black/Little By Little/Doo Doo A Do Do/Easily Led/Sixes And Sevens
UK chart position: No. 19 – 4 weeks on chart.

Now And Zen
Es Paranza WX 149 (February 1988) Tracks: Heaven

Knows/Dance On My Own/Tall Cool One/The Way I Feel/Helen Of Troy/Billy's Revenge/Ship Of Fools/ Why/White, Clean And Neat
Extra track on CD and cassette – 'Walking Towards Paradise'.
UK chart position: No. 10 – 7 weeks on chart.
N.B. Promo advance tapes have the track 'Dance On My Own' listed under the title 'Radioshape'.

Manic Nirvana
Es Paranza WX 339 (March 1969) Initial pressing in individually numbered limited gatefold sleeve WX 339X.
Tracks: Hurting Kind (I've Got My Eyes On You)/Big Love/S S S & Q/I Cried/Nirvana/Tie Dye On The Highway/Your Ma Said You Cried In Your Sleep Last Night/Anniversary/Liar's Dance/Watching You
Extra track on CD and cassette only – 'She Said'.
UK chart position: No. 15 – 7 weeks on chart.
N.B. Left over material from this album includes A Date With The King, Selling Fire, and Johnny's Turning Green.

NOTABLE UK PROMOS

SINGLES

In The Mood (edited version)/In The Mood (long version)
Es Paranza SAM 179 seven-inch radio promo (November 1983)

The Honeydrippers: Sea Of Love/Rockin' At Midnight
Es Paranza SAM 220 seven-inch radio promo (December 1984)

Little By Little (12-inch remix)/Little By Little (album version)
Es Paranza white label 12-inch promo SAM 2570 (August 1985)

CD SINGLE

Tie Dye On The Highway/Nirvana
Es Paranza Sam 736 promo CD for radio stations (December 1990)

ALBUMS

Pictures At Eleven – Interview album
Swan Song SAM 154 promo radio interview album (June 1982) Side A – Interview with Alan Freeman. Side B – open ended interview.

The Principle Of Moments – Interview album
Swan Song SAM 169 promo radio interview album (July 1983) Side A – interview with Ray Coleman. Side B – open ended interview.

Shaken 'N' Stirred – Interview cassette
Es Paranza PRO 654 promo radio interview cassette (May 1985) Tracks: Side 1 – Interview between Robert Plant and Andy Peebles/Too Loud/Interview/Pink And Black/Interview/Little By Little; repeated on Side 2.

Non Stop Go! – Double record interview disc.
Es Paranza PR 2244 promo interview European pressing/US sleeve (April 1988) Tracks: Side 1 – Dan Neer Interview Q & A; Side 2 – Dan Neer Interview Answers Only (for Album Orientated radio); Side 3 – Chuck Young Interview Q & A; Side 4 – Chuck Young Interview Answers Only (for College and Alternative radio). Pressed on two 45rpm discs.

Manic Nirvana Promo Presentation Box Set
Es Paranza promo package with 'Manic Nirvana' CD and album plus 12x12 booklet (March 1990).

Excerpts From 'Manic Nirvana'
(Es Paranza SAM 645) Promo CD.
Tracks: Hurting Kind (I've Got My Eyes On You)/Tie Dye On The Highway/Liars Dance/Watching You

Manic Nirvana
Es Paranza advance black label promo album in plain black sleeve (March 1990) Label plainly inscribed 'Plant Manic Nirvana'.

US ALBUMS

Pictures At Eleven
Swan Song SS 8512 (June 1982) US chart position: No. 5 – 14 weeks on chart – certified Gold August 28, 1982.

The Principle Of Moments
Es Paranza 90101 (June 1983) US chart position: No. 8 – 18 weeks on chart – certified Gold July 10, 1983 – certified Platinum January 12, 1984.

The Honeydrippers Vol 1
Es Paranza 90220 (October 1984) US chart position: No. 4 – 18 weeks on chart – certified Gold December 13, 1984 – certified Platinum December 13, 1984.

Shaken 'N' Stirred
Es Paranza 90265 (May 1985) US chart position: No. 20 – 8 weeks on chart – certified Gold July 18, 1985.

Little By Little Collectors Edition
Es Paranza 90485 1 US only mini-album (1985) Tracks: Little By Little (remix long version)/Easily Lead (live)/ Rockin' At Midnight (live)/Sixes And Sevens

Now And Zen
Es Paranza 790 8631 (March 1988) US chart position: No. 6 – certified Gold April 19, 1988 – certified Platinum September 5, 1988.

Manic Nirvana
Es Paranza 91336 (March 1990)

Manic Nirvana
US Es Paranza 913612 Special CD package with exclusive photos and red satin banner (1990)

SINGLES

Burning Down One Side/Moonlight In Samosa
Swan Song SS 7 99979 (1982)

Pledge Pin/Fat Lip
US Swan Song SS 99527 (1982)

Big Log/Far Post
US Es Paranza 79 98447 (1983) US chart position: No. 20 – 9 weeks on chart

In The Mood/Horizontal Departure
US Es Paranza 79 98207 (1983) US chart position: No. 39 – 5 weeks on chart

The Honeydrippers: Sea Of Love/Rockin' At Midnight
Es Paranza 7 997010 (1984) US chart position: No. 3 – 14 weeks on chart

The Honeydrippers: Rockin' At Midnight/Young Boy Blues
Es Paranza 7 99686 (1985) US chart position: No. 25 – 6 weeks on chart

Little By Little/Trouble Your Money
US Es Paranza 7 99644 (1985) US chart position: No. 36 – 4 weeks on chart

Too Loud/Kallalou Kallalou
Es Paranza 7 99622 (1985)

Heaven Knows/Walking Towards Paradise
Es Paranza 7 99348 (1988)

Tall Cool One/White Clean And Neat
Es Paranza 7 99348 (1988) US chart position: No. 25 – 5 weeks on chart

Dance On My Own/Billy's Revenge
Es Paranza (1988)

Ship Of Fools/Helen Of Troy
Es Paranza (1988)

Hurting Kind (I've Got My Eyes On You)/I Cried
Es Paranza (1988)

Your Ma Said You Cried In Your Sleep Last Night/ She Said
Es Paranza (1990)

NOTABLE US PROMO ITEMS

SINGLES

Burning Down One Side (mono)/Burning Down One Side (stereo)
Swan Song radio promo SS 7 99979 (1982)

Pledge Pin (mono)/Pledge Pin (stereo)
Swan Song radio promo SS 7 99952 (1982)

Pledge Pin (long version)/**Pledge Pin** (short version)
Swan Song radio promo SS 7 99952 (1982)

Big Log (3.45 short version)/**Big Log** (5.03 long version)
Es Paranza radio promo 7 99844 (1983)

Big Log/Messin' With The Mekon/Stranger Here . . . Than Over There
Es Paranza 12-inch promo PR 518 (1983)

In The Mood (3.44 short version)/**In The Mood** (5.19 long version)
Es Paranza radio promo 7 99820 (1983)

The Honeydrippers: Sea Of Love/Sea Of Love
Es Paranza radio promo 7 99701 (1984)

The Honeydrippers: Rockin' At Midnight/Rockin' At Midnight
Es Paranza 12-inch promo PR 671 (1984)

Too Loud/Too Loud
Es Paranza radio promo 7 99622 (1985)

Too Loud/Too Loud
Es Paranza 12-inch promo PR 762 (1985)

Little By Little/Little By Little
(short version)
Es Paranza 12-inch promo PR 720 (1985)

Little By Little/Little By Little
(short version)Es Paranza radio promo 7 99644 (1985)

The Way I Feel/Dimples (live)
Es Paranza 12-inch promo (1988)

Dance On My Own/Ship Of Fools (live)/Tall Cool One (live)
Es Paranza 12-inch promo (1988)

Tall Cool One (remix)/Heaven Knows (Astral mix)
Es Paranza 12-inch promo (1988)

Heaven Knows:
Es Paranza 12-inch white label one sided. PR2175 (1988).

Heaven Knows/Heaven Knows
Es Paranza radio promo 99373 (1988)

Ship Of Fools/Ship Of Fools
Es Paranza radio promo 99333 (1988)

CD'S

Walking Towards Paradise
Es Paranza promo CD single

Heaven Knows (4.03 version/**Heaven Knows** (3.57 edit) Es Paranza promo only CD PR21 2

Atlantic 40th Anniversary
Atlantic PR 2436. Compilation CD includes 'Ship Of Fools' long and short versions.

Hurting Kind (I've Got My Eyes On You) (4.04)/**Hurting Kind (I've Got My Eyes On You)**
Es Paranza promo CD single

Your Ma Said You Cried In Your Sleep Last Night (3.57)/**Your Ma Said You Cried In Your Sleep Last Night** (4.17)
Es Paranza PRCD 33492 CD single

Robert Plant Profile
Es Paranza Manic Nirvana radio promo CD Tracks: Profile Interview (25.19)/Answers Only (13.15)

NOTABLE US RADIO SHOW PROMOS

Promo albums pressed for radio show distribution only.

Off The Record with Mary Turner – Interview and music
Westwood One OTRSP 85 – 87 aired 1983. Two LP set.

BBC Rock Hour – Interview with Richard Skinner
450 – aired week of December 11, 1983.

ABC Rock Radio Network: King Biscuit Flower Hour Live 1983
From Houston, Austin and Dallas. Two LP set.

Robert Plant: The Source Broadcast
– Six LP set aired August 6, 1982.

London Wavelength An Authorised 90-Minute Special:
Two LP Principle radio special 1983.

Superstars In Concert: Shaken 'N' Stirred Tour Live:
Three LP set. Westwood One.

Superstars In Concert:
Three LP set Westwood One (March 2, 1986).

Superstars In Concert:
Three LP set Live Wembley Arena Westwood One (1985).

Superstars In Concert:
Three LP set Live Westwood One (June 2, 1988).

Up Close: Parts 1 and 2.
Four LP set music and interviews (February 1988).

NOTABLE RADIO SHOW CD PROMOS

In The Studio: Now And Zen.
Music and interview on CD (October 31, 1988).

Up Close: Parts 1 and 2.
Four CD music and interview (1990).

In The Studio: Manic Nirvana World Première (March 15, 1990).
Es Paranza/Album Network PRCD 3301-2 promo CD.

NOTABLE FOREIGN RELEASES

SINGLES
Alternate couplings to regular UK/US/European releases.

Canada:
In the Mood
(3.44 edit/

Horizontal Departure
Es Paranza 7 998207 (1983)

Germany:
The Honeydrippers: Sea Of Love/Young Boy Blues
Es Paranza 799686 7 (1984)

Japan:
Big Log/Far Post
Es Paranza P 1786 (1983)

Other Arms/Thru' With The Two Step
Es Paranza P 1856 (1984)

NOTABLE FOREIGN PROMOS

Japan
Slow Dancer/Burning Down One Side
Swan Song promo PS 1018

Little By Little/Little By Little
(short version)Es Paranza promo PS 1034 (1985)

Italy
Burning Down One Side/Pieno D'Amore by L. Goggi
Swan Song Promo 161 Juke Box single (1982)

Spain
Big Log/Messin' With The Mekon
Atlantic 79 9848 7 Disco Promo single (1983)

Pink And Black/Trouble Your Money
Es Paranza S 799640 7 promo with two-page biography (1985)

Heaven Knows/Heaven Knows
Es Paranza Promo (1988)

GUEST APPEARANCES/COMPILATIONS ALBUMS

Porky's Revenge Soundtrack
CBS 70265 (1985) Features 'Philadelphia Baby' by The Crawling King Snakes: Plant under the pseudonym of one of his earliest groups. Recorded at the Sun Studios Memphis with Phil Collins and Paul Martinez in July 1983. It was this session that sparked 'The Honeydrippers Vol 1' project.

White Nights Soundtrack
Atlantic K781273 1 (1985) Features 'Far Post' – leftover from 'Pictures At Eleven' and previously used as a bonus cut on the UK 'Burning Down One Side' 12-inch.

Jimmy Page: Outrider
Geffen WX 55 (1988) Plant returns a compliment by helping Jimmy out and singing vocals on 'The Only

One', the first Page/Plant composition for 10 years. Jason Bonham adds more Zepp influence on drums.

The Prince's Trust Collection: Various Artists
Telstar 2275 (1985) Double charity album including 'Little By Little' and Jimmy's *Death Wish 2* extract 'Prelude'.

The Last Temptation Of Elvis: Various Artists
NME (1990) Special charity album compiled for distribution through the *NME* UK music paper, featuring a string of acts interpreting Elvis Presley songs. Plant and guest musicians romp through a manic 'Let's Have A Party'.

Knebworth – The Album: Various Artists
Polygram 8439211 (1990) Recorded live at the Silver Clef Winners show June 30, 1990. Features 'Hurting Kind (I've Got My Eyes On You)', 'Liar's Dance', 'Tall Cool One' and 'Wearing And Tearing' (last track with Jimmy Page).

VIDEO APPEARANCES

Prince's Trust Rock Gala
MGA/UA SMV 10179 (1984) Features Plant performing 'Worse Than Detroit' with Robbie Blunt and the Prince's Trust Allstars, plus Plant on vocals and tambourine for the encore Allstars finale 'I Wanna Take You Higher'. Recorded July 21, 1982 at the London Dominion.

Mumbo Jumbo
Warner Video 750121 3 (1989) Robert Plant home video compilation includes 'Heaven Knows', 'Big Log', 'Little By Little', 'In The Mood' and 'Tall Cool One' and additional link footage.

Knebworth: The Event Vol 3
Castle Video CMP 6008 Features 'Hurting Kind (I've Got My Eyes On You)', 'Tall Cool One', 'Wearing And Tearing' and 'Rock And Roll' (last two tracks with Jimmy Page).

Hard 'n' Heavy Vol 9
Virgin Vision VVD 784 (October 1990) Video magazine contains Robert Plant interview.

PROMO VIDEOS

Specially commissioned promo videos have been filmed for the following tracks:

Burning Down One Side (1982)
Big Log (1983)
In The Mood (1983)
Sea Of Love (1984)
Rockin' At Midnight (1984)
Pink And Black (1985)
Little By Little (1985)
Heaven Knows (1988)
Tall Cool One (1988)
Ship Of Fools (1988)
Hurting Kind (I've Got My Eyes On You) (1990)
Nirvana (1990)

OTHER NOTABLE FOOTAGE

Robert Plant TV/video appearances to note include the following:

The Tube
(June 22, 1983) Filmed at Tyne Tees Studios to a specially invited audience this was to have been screened on *The Tube's* Midsummer Night special. Plant was less than happy with his performance and had it shelved. Numbers filmed: Little Sister/Treat Her Right/Sea Of Love/Pledge Pin/Other Arms/In The Mood/Big Log/Like I've Never Been Gone/Worse Than Detroit/Other Arms (take 2)/In The Mood (take 2)/Big Log (take 2)/Fat Lip/Burning Down One Side.

Italian TV

(September 1982) Mimed performance of 'Burning Down One Side'.

Top Of The Pops, BBC
(July 27 1983) Plant and band mime to 'Big Log'.

Dutch TV
(July 1983) Plant and band (with mysterious drummer) mime to 'Big Log' and 'In The Mood'.

Saturday Night Live, US TV
(December 1984) Plant with a Honeydrippers line-up that includes Brian Setzer perform live versions of 'Rockin' At Midnight' and 'Santa Claus Is Coming To Town'.

Honeydrippers Live At Rolls Hall Monmouth:
The Skinneydrippers (as they were known on the night) benefit show on January 18, 1985 semi-professionally shot on video. Track listing: Move It/Jailhouse Rock/Going Down/Every Little Bit Hurts/Crosscut Saw/All Your Love/I Need Your Loving Every Day/Your True Love/Georgia On My Mind/Mystery Train/Born Under A Bad Sign/Roll Roll Roll/The Young Ones/Save The Last Dance For Me/Can't/Great Balls Of Fire/Little Sister

Norwegian TV
(September 1985) Plant and band mime to 'Little By Little'.

Spanish TV
(circa September 1985) Bizarre clip of Plant on one of the last appearances with the 1982–85 line-up. In front of a strictly MOR seated, supper club audience they mime 'Big Log', 'Sea Of Love' and 'Little By Little'.

Heartbeat Benefit Show: NEC Birmingham
(March 15 1986) Plant live with the Big Town Playboys on Central TV – tracks screened 'Mellow Saxophone', 'Come On', 'She Walks Right In'. Plant is also seen playing guitar in the all-star finale.

Fairport Convention at Cropredy
(August 9 1986) Plant joins Fairport for the old blues chestnut 'Nineteen Years Old'. Two other blues standards were also aired on this jam.

The Roxy, UK TV show
(January 1988) Plant and band back at Tyne Tees Studios for a mime of 'Heaven Knows'.

Wired, UK TV show
(June 1988) Led Zeppelin feature: Plant is interviewed and live segment of 'Tall Cool One' screened. This was filmed on April 13 at a special film session for *Wired*. Also filmed at the sessions but not screened in the UK: 'Ship Of Fools', 'Heaven Knows', 'Billy's Revenge' and 'Helen Of Troy'. The full show was aired in New Zealand.

Coca Cola, US TV ad
(1988) Employs 'Tall Cool One' video extracts.

Atlantic 40th Anniversary, US HBO TV cast
(May 14 1988) Plant's solo spot includes 'Heaven Knows', 'Tall Cool One' and 'Ship Of Fools'.

Knebworth '90, UK Central TV
(August 1990) Plant from the June show performing 'Hurting Kind (I've Got My Eyes On You)', 'Liar's Dance', 'Tall Cool One' and 'Rock And Roll' (last track with Jimmy Page).

TOUR PROGRAMMES/MUSIC BOOKS/NOTABLE PUBLICATIONS

TOUR PROGRAMMES

Prince's Trust Rock Gala (1982)

The Principle Of Moments tour programme (1983)

The Principle Of Moments Australian tour programme (1983)

Shaken 'N' Stirred tour programme (1985)

Heartbeat Benefit show programme (1986)

Non Stop Go! tour programme (1988)

Non Stop Go! tour programme – second edition with Plant in desert front cover (1988)

Atlantic 40th Anniversary It's Only Rock 'n' Roll concert programme (1988)

Manic Nirvana tour programme (1990)

Knebworth Silver Clef Winners concert programme (1990)

MUSIC BOOKS

Pictures At Eleven (1982)

Now And Zen (1988)

BOOKS

Robert Plant Led Zeppelin's Golden Boy – Michael Gross

Circus Publications (1975)

Robert Plant: Phil S. Tene – Robus Books (1984)

RECOMMENDED PLANT MAGAZINE FEATURES

Kerrang, June 17, 1982: Interview with Steve Gett.

Sounds, September 25, 1982: The Evolution Of Plant – Interview with Geoff Barton.

Sounds Robert Plant Fan Magazine: complete magazine devoted to Robert with interviews by Steve Gett, June 1983.

Sounds, August 31, 1985: Trans – Plant From Zeppelin to solo . . . and back again? Interview with Hugh Fielder.

Record Magazine, August 1985; Robert Plant in *The Record* Interview by John Hutchinson.

Kerrang, January 23, 1988: Percy's Back! Interview with Chris Welch.

Q, March 1988: Robert Plant – The Survivor's Guide To Led Zeppelin. Interview by Tom Hibbert.

Rolling Stone, March 24, 1988: Robert Plant in the *Rolling Stone* Interview by David Fricke. Special collector's edition with Led Zeppelin Tribute To A Rock Legend.

Musician, March 1988: Zen And The Art Of Led Zeppelin. An interview with Charles M. Young.

Record Collector, October 1989: Robert Plant discography feature by Dave Lewis.

Q, May 1990: Turn It Up! Robert Plant's Record Collection – interview with Mat Snow.

Musician, June 1990: Robert Plant – The Thief Of Kashmir. Interview with Charles M. Young.

JOHN PAUL JONES
PRE AND POST ZEPP DISCOGRAPHY

PRE ZEPPELIN RECORDINGS

While working as a member of the Jet Harris and Tony Meehan backing group John Paul Jones began to drift into the London session scene. Meehan was already doing freelance production work for the Decca label and he began employing the young Jones on bass. As the session work increased, JP began to establish himself on the London circuit, linking up with Andrew Loog Oldham for some of his early Decca production work.

In April 1964 John Paul Jones had a stab at solo stardom with a single on Pye. Cut at Regent Sound, 'Baja' was a bouncy, six-string bass instrumental typical of the beat boom era. The B-side was a strange Oldham/Mike Leander composition 'A Foggy Day In Vietnam'. In the rush to get the single out, Jones later revealed that Oldham offered this track to save time and money. A track that Oldham turned out under the guise of The Andrew Loog Oldham Orchestra, it does not feature Jones at all. Sounding very much like a Rolling Stones' backing track in a similar vein to 'Tell Me' or 'Heart Of Stone', it may even feature some of The Stones on it.

PRE ZEPPELIN SOLO SINGLE

Baja/A Foggy Day In Vietnam
Pye 7N 15637; US issue on Parkway P 915 (April 1964) 'A Foggy Day In Vietnam' can also be found on a budget sampler album 'The Hitmakers', issued in 1969 on the Marble Arch label (Mal 1259).

PRE ZEPPELIN SESSIONS/ARRANGING

Back in the mid-sixties, John Paul Jones' musical talent had assured his promotion from being a mere session man to becoming musical director and arranger. He

took on the role of musical director for Mickie Most and handled countless sessions. Artists that he worked with during this era included: Cliff Richard, Alma Cogan, Barry Ryan, Lulu, Dave Berry, Dusty Springfield (he also played bass at some shows she gave at London's Talk Of The Town), Donovan, Rod Stewart, The Mighty Avengers, Barry St John, The Mindbenders, Del Shannon, The Yardbirds, Herman's Hermits, The Downliners Sect, Graham Gouldman, Jeff Beck and many more. On many of the sessions Jones came in to contact with Jimmy Page, then one of the most sought after session guitarists. Below is a representative selection of John Paul Jones' work from this era:

SINGLES

Rod Stewart: Good Morning Little Schoolgirl
Decca F 11996 (1964)

Herman's Hermits: Silhouettes
Columbia DB 8504 (1965)

Jeff Beck: Hi Ho Silver Lining/Beck's Bolero
Columbia DB 8151 (1967)

The Yardbirds: Little Games/Puzzles
Columbia DB 8165 (1967) An early link-up with Page – this has a string arrangement by Jones on the A-side.

The Yardbirds: Ha Ha Said The Clown
US Epic 10204 (1967)

The Yardbirds: Ten Little Indians
US Epic 10248 (1967)

Donovan: Hurdy Gurdy Man
Pye 7N 17537 (1968) This single is said to feature Jimmy Page, and Jones recalls that it was during this session that he asked to be considered for the new group he had heard Jimmy was forming.

ALBUMS

Downliners Sect: Country Sect
Columbia SX 17390 (1965) Jones is credited as playing 'jangle' piano on 'Rocks In My Bed and 'ethereal' piano on 'Waiting In Heaven'.

The Rolling Stones: Their Satanic Majesties Request
Decca TXS 103 (1967) John Paul Jones arranged the strings on 'She's A Rainbow'.

The Yardbirds: Little Games
US Epic 26313 reissued in the UK on MFP 4 3112 41

Jeff Beck: Truth
Columbia SCX 6293 (1968) Features Jones playing Hammond organ on the track 'Old Man River'.

Dusty Springfield: Dusty . . . Definitely
Fontana SBL 7864 (1968)
It's worth noting that when Atlantic supremo Jerry Wexler was considering Peter Grant's proposal to sign Led Zeppelin, Dusty Springfield, then signed to Atlantic in the US, gave a strong recommendation of Jones to Wexler, a contributing factor to the deal's conclusion.

The Rolling Stones: Metamorphosis
Decca SKL 5212 (1975) This compilation of Stones' out-takes acknowledges Jones' involvement on the sleeve notes, but does not specify which tracks he was involved in.

OTHER PRODUCTION WORK

Madeline Bell: Comin' Atcha
RCA SF 8393 (December 1973) This was JP's way of winding down from the madness of the 1973 Zeppelin American tour. He retreated to his Dormouse Studios and produced, played and sang backing vocals on this album by his long-time friend Madeline Bell. Aside from two songs cut without Jones at Morgan studios,

the rest of the album was recorded at Jones' home studio in the autumn of 1973. Jones even appeared as part of Madeline's band for a TV appearance on BBC 2's *Colour My Soul*.

Madeline Bell: I'm So Glad/Another Girl
RCA 2240 single from the above album (December 1973)

POST ZEPPELIN RECORDINGS

Music From The Film *Scream For Help*
Atlantic 780190 1 (March 1985) Tracks: Spaghetti Junction/Bad Child/Silver Train/Crackback/ Chilli Sauce/Take It Or Leave It/Christie/When You Fall In Love.

UK PROMO SINGLE

Here I Am/Christie
Atlantic SAM 246 seven-inch radio promo (1985)

NOTABLE US RELEASES

Music From The Film *Scream For Help*
Atlantic 7 80190 1 (March 1985) Track listing as above. The sleeve design differs from the UK version, featuring a photo of John Paul Jones on the back cover.

US PROMO

Spaghetti Junction
(remixed from the soundtrack album)/

Silver Train.
Atlantic promo 12-inch single PR 795 (1985)

GUEST APPEARANCES/ COMPILATIONS/ PRODUCTION WORK

NB: For guest appearances during the Zeppelin era see Led Zeppelin discography.

Paul McCartney: Give My Regards To Broad Street – Original Soundtrack
EMI/MPL PCTC 2 (October 1984) Features John Paul Jones on bass on the track 'Ballroom Dancing'.

Ben E. King: Save The Last Dance For Me
EMI Manhattan MTL 1013 (March 1988) John Paul Jones involvement on the following tracks: 'Because Of Last Night' – produced by Jones for JPJ Communications Ltd., recorded at CBS Studios with JP on bass; 'Whatever This Is (It Ain't True Love)' – produced by John Paul Jones for JPJ Communications

Ltd., recorded at Obus Studios, Devon; 'Two Loves' (written by JP Jones/Chris Gibbons) – recorded, engineered and mixed by John Paul Jones at Obus Studios, Devon with JP on 'all other instruments'.

The Mission: Children
Mercury Mish 2 (March 1988) Tracks: Beyond The Pale/Wing And A Prayer/Heaven On Earth/ Tower Of Strength/Kingdom Come/Breath/Shamara Kye/Black Mountain Mist/Heat/Hymn (For America).
All tracks produced by John Paul Jones who is also responsible for keyboards and programming.
Mission singles produced by John Paul Jones:

Tower Of Strength
MYTH 4 (February 1988)

Beyond The Pale
MYTH 6 (April 1988)

Beyond The Pale CD single
MYTHCD 62 also includes Jones' produced 'Tower Of Strength' (Bombay edit).
Mission CD Video:

Tower Of Strength
Mercury 0805262 (1988) Includes Jones' produced 'Tower Of Strength' and 'Dream On'.
Mission promo items with John Paul Jones involvement:

The Mission: Children interview cassette
Mercury PROC 3 Features interview with John Paul Jones.

Kingdom Come (Heavenly mix)/Child's Play (live)
MTYTHDJ 712 (1988) Promo with Jones produced A-side.

Sounds Machine
Four-track single given free with *Sounds* (1988).
Includes live version of 'Shelter From The Storm' (with a verse from 'Rock And Roll') recorded by The Mission at the Astoria Theatre, London, March 27, 1988, and featuring John Paul Jones on keyboards.

Music From Films 3
Opal Land CD 04 (1988) CD compilation of acts signed to the Opal label. Includes John Paul Jones on a composition entitled 'Three Minute Warning'. A droning instrumental with 'In The Light' type keyboard work. Written and performed by John Paul Jones at Obus Studios Devon 1985.

Cinderella: Heartbreak Station
Mercury 8480181 (1990). String arrangements by JP on the tracks 'Winds Of Change and Heartbreak Station.'

JOHN PAUL JONES VIDEO APPEARANCES

Give My Regards To Broad Street
CBS Fox 144850 (1988) McCartney movie with John Paul Jones on the 'Ballroom Dancing' segment.
Other notable Jones footage:

Madeline Bell – Colour My Soul
BBC 2 screened December 1974 JP is featured playing bass in Madeline's backing band.

Wired
Channel 4, screened June 1988 Special feature on Led Zeppelin, includes interview with John Paul Jones backstage with Wayne Hussey, plus footage of his guest spot with The Mission at the Astoria in March 1988.

RECOMMENDED PUBLICATIONS

Interviews with John Paul Jones are a rare commodity, however the following contain some revealing Jones comments.

New Musical Express, February 1970: 'Ask In' with a Led Zeppelin – interview with Ritchie Yorke.

Guitar Player, July 1977: aside from a lengthy Page piece, this issue carries an excellent interview with John Paul Jones by Steve Rosen.

Kerrang, May 2, 1985: Scream Dream: John Paul Jones interviewed at the time of the release of *Scream For Help* by Dave Dickson.

JOHN BONHAM

PRE ZEPPELIN
There is little recorded evidence of the developing drum style of the young John Bonham. Never a serious scholar, one of his early school reports included the summary: ''He will either end up as a dustman or a millionaire.''
John joined his father in the building trade when he left school. By then he had already made up his mind to play drums, practising on a rusted kit his father had bought him. Bonzo soon developed the reputation of being one of the best (and loudest!) drummers in the Midlands, enjoying stints with Terry Webb And The Spiders, A Way Of Life, The Crawling King Snakes (his first meeting with one Robert Anthony Plant), The Nicky James Movement and Steve Brett And The Mavericks. In 1967 he settled in to The Band Of Joy with Plant on vocals.
The Band Of Joy demo cut at Regent Sound studio (see Plant discography for full details) captured the first studio rumblings of his inventive style. Tracks like 'Adriatic Sea View' were already benefiting from his unusually fast bass pedal control, soon to become a trademark of the Led Zeppelin sound. Before that flowering of talent exploded into action, following The Band Of Joy's split, Bonzo joined Tim Rose on a UK tour. Word was spreading fast of this more than competent drummer from the Midlands. Joe Cocker wanted him for his band, and another reputable vocalist, Chris Farlowe, was also interested.
Then his old mate Robert Plant got back in touch urging him to join The New Yardbirds line-up, with the promise of an album and US tour. Page was already convinced of his potential, having checked him out with Tim Rose at London's Country Club. Bonzo was less sure. Hadn't The Yardbirds had their day? Luckily he weighed up the opportunity to rejoin Plant and play with Page, whom he knew to be a much respected guitarist, and finally replied to Peter Grant's endless stream of telegrams. With John Bonham on the drum stool The New Yardbirds, soon to become Led Zeppelin, had their percussive engine room well and truly covered.

GUEST APPEARANCES ETC
John Bonham's spasmodic work outside of Led Zeppelin is covered in the Zeppelin part of this discography. However, two sessions are worth emphasising again here.

Lord Sutch And Heavy Friends
Atlantic 2400 008 This 1970 recording has six forceful backing tracks cut by Page and Bonham during the recording of 'Led Zeppelin II'. The track Sutch dubbed as 'Baby Come Back' is based on Roy Brown's 'Treat Her Right', later to be employed on more than one Plant/Page reunion jam.

Roy Wood: Keep Your Hands On The Wheel
(taken from the US album 'On The Road Again').
Warners BSK3247 Recorded in 1978, Bonzo is given a free hand here, achieving a wide screen large sound from the Ludwig that drives the song along.
Unmistakably John Henry Bonham.

NOTABLE JOHN BONHAM PUBLICATIONS

New Musical Express , June 28, 1970: Happier Than Ever – an interview with Roy Carr on the eve of the Bath Festival.

Sounds, July 27, 1974: John Bonham in the *Sounds* Talk-In. An interview with Steve Peacock.

Melody Maker, June 21, 1975: Bonham Over The Hills And Far Away – Chris Welch visits John Bonham at home.

Modern Drummer, July 1984: John Bonham Tribute by T. Bruce Wittet.

JOHN BONHAM: A CELEBRATION

At the time of compiling this discography the 10th anniversary of John Bonham's death was upon us. The intervening years since his passing have done nothing to diminish his lasting reputation as one of the great percussionists of all time. Indeed his sound and influence can be heard on countless samples, through scores of imitating rock drummers, and is upheld in name by the continuing career of his son Jason.

To complete this discography, listed below are the 10 John Bonham performances that, in the author's opinion, best illustrate the importance of his contribution to the legacy of Led Zeppelin's music. These are performances that confirm that Led Zeppelin ceased to exist on Thursday, September 25, 1980. But how the memory lingers on . . .

1 – **Moby Dick**
2 – **Whole Lotta Love**
3 – **Poor Tom**
4 – **Rock And Roll**
5 – **When The Levee Breaks**
6 – **D'yer Mak'er**
7 – **In My Time Of Dying**
8 – **No Quarter (live)**
9 – **Achilles Last Stand**
10 – **Hots On For Nowhere**

SWAN SONG DISCOGRAPHY

Appendix 2C

hen Peter Grant renegotiated Led Zeppelin's contract with Atlantic Records early in 1974, a deal was set up whereby all future business affairs for the group and Grant's management interests would be handled by their own record label. This seemed a logical move as the group had long since displayed a desire for total control of their affairs, both musical and financial. Thus in the spring of 1974, Swan Song Records came into being. The name came after much deliberation (Eclipse, Slut, Slag, Deluxe, Stairway and the name of their publishing company Superhype were all rumoured to be under consideration) and came from the working title of an in-progress, lengthy instrumental (possibly an early version of 'Ten Years Gone'). Asked in the studio what he intended calling it, Page replied "Swan Song." The name was carried over as a possible album title, and then as as the label name. A sub-company owned by the group known as Cullderstead was registered for Swan Song as a business name.

The artistic intention of the label was to sign a small roster of acts. Initially Bad Company and Maggie Bell were contracted for the US, while in the UK The Pretty Things recharged their career through the new Zeppelin outlet. (Roy Harper was also sought but remained with EMI.) Launch parties were held in America in April and at Chislehurst Caves in England on October 31. New York publicist Danny Goldberg was installed as Vice-President and offices were opened in Manhattan's Rockefella Plaza, and at World's End in the King's Road, London. Over the years these were manned by Mitchell Fox and Nancy Gurskik in the US and Carole Browne, Unity Maclean and Sian Meridith in the UK.

Swan Song found instant success in Bad Company whose début album topped the US charts. In March 1975, four Swan Song albums (from Zeppelin, Bad Co, Maggie Bell and The Pretty Things) were on the *Billboard* chart. After this initial early surge, however, the label became less active.

In the UK Dave Edmunds (a Plant signing in 1976) provided a measure of success, and Michael Des Barres' Detective enjoyed some acclaim. Ultimately Grant found sustaining Zeppelin at the top too time consuming to sign other acts (he passed on managing Queen in 1975 and an early demo tape of Iron Maiden joined the scores of others lining the Swan Song shelves).

After Zeppelin's retirement in 1980, the label was eventually wound down. The last act to be signed was Bad Company drummer Simon Kirkes' outfit Wildlife. What remains is a diverse and often underrated collection of singles and albums, and of course a beautiful logo (based on a William Rimmer painting 'Evening Fall Of Day') that is regarded as one of the most distinctive rock symbols of the era.

UK DISCOGRAPHY
(excluding Led Zeppelin recordings)

SINGLES

Pretty Things: Is It Only Love/Joey
Swan Song SSK 19401 (November 1974)

Pretty Things: I'm Keeping . . ./Atlanta
Swan Song SSK 19403 (May 1975)

Pretty Things: Joey/Bridge Of God
Swan Song SSK 19401 (July 1975)

Pretty Things: Sad Eye/Remember That Boy
Swan Song SSK 19405 (January 1976)

Pretty Things: Tonight/It Isn't Rock 'n' Roll
Swan Song SSK 19406 (May 1976)

Dave Edmunds: Here Comes The Weekend/As Lovers Do
Swan Song SSK 19408 (July 1976)

Dave Edmunds: When Or Where/New York's A Lonely Town
Swan Song SSK 19409 (October 1976)

Dave Edmunds: Ju Ju Man/What Did I Do Last Night
Swan Song SSK 19410 (April 1977)

Dave Edmunds: I Knew The Bride/Back To Schooldays
Swan Song SSK 19411 (June 1977)

Maggie Bell: Hazell/Night Flighting
Swan Song SSK19412 (March 1988)

Dave Edmunds: Deborah/What Looks Best On You
Swan Song SSK 19413 (September 1978)

Dave Edmunds: Television/Never Been In Love
Swan Song SSK 19414 (November 1978)

Bad Company: Rock 'n' Roll Fantasy/Crazy Circles
Swan Song SSK 19416 (March 1979)

Dave Edmunds: A1 On The Juke Box/It's My Own Business
Swan Song SSK 19417 (April 1979)

Maggie Bell: Hazell/Night Flighting
Swan Song SSK 19412P (special picture disc reissue, May 1979)

Dave Edmunds: Girls Talk/Bad Is Bad
Swan Song SSK 19418 (July 1978 – also issued as a limited clear vinyl disc)

Dave Edmunds: Queen Of Hearts/Creature From The Black Lagoon
Swan Song SSK 19419 (September 1979)

Dave Edmunds: Crawling From The Wreckage/As Lovers Do
Swan Song SSK 19420 (November 1979)

Dave Edmunds: Singing The Blues/Boys Talk
Swan Song SSK19422 (January 1980)

Midnight Flyer: Rough Trade/Midnight Love
Swan Song SSK 19423 (March 1981)

Dave Edmunds: Almost Saturday Night/You'll Never Get Me Up
Swan Song SSK 19424 (March 1981)

Dave Edmunds with The Stray Cats: The Race Is On/(I'm Gonna Start) Living If It Kills Me
Swan Song SSK 19425 (June 1981)

B.A. Robertson and Maggie Bell: Hold Me/Spring Greens
Swan Song BAM 1 (October 1981)

Midnight Flyer: Waiting For You/Rock 'n' Roll Party
Swan Song SSK 19426 (April 1982)

Maggie Bell: Goosebumps/Key To Your Heart
Swan Song SSK 19428 (September 1982)

Robert Plant: Burning Down One Side/Moonlight In Samosa
Swan Song SSK 19429 (September 1982)

Robert Plant: Burning Down One Side/Moonlight In Samosa/Far Post
Swan Song SSK 19429T 12-inch (September 1982)

Maggie Bell: Crazy/All I Have To Do Is Dream
Swan Song MB 1 (January 1983)

Wildlife: Somewhere In The Night/Sun Don't Shine
Swan Song B9842 (September 1983)

SWAN SONG UK ALBUMS
(excluding Led Zeppelin)

Pretty Things: Silk Torpedo
Swan Song SSK 59400 (November 1974)

Pretty Things: Savage Eye
Swan Song SSK 59401 (December 1975)

Dave Edmunds: Get It
Swan Song SSK 59404 (April) 1977)

Detective: Detective
Swan Song SSK59405 (July 1977)

Detective: It Takes One To Know One
Swan Song SSK59406 (April 1978)

Dave Edmunds: Trax On Wax
Swan Song SSK 59407 (September 1978)

Bad Company: Desolation Angels
Swan Song SSK 59408 (March 1979)

Dave Edmunds: Repeat When Necessary
Swan Song SSK 59409 (June 1979)

Midnight Flyer: Midnight Flyer
Swan Song SSK 59412 (February 1981)

Dave Edmunds: Twangin'
Swan Song SSK 59411 (April 1981)

Dave Edmunds: The Best Of Dave Edmunds
Swan Song SSK 59413 (November 1981)

Jimmy Page: Death Wish 2 – The Original Soundtrack
Swan Song SSK 59415 (February 1982)

Robert Plant: Pictures At Eleven
Swan Song SSK 59418 (June 1982)

Bad Company: Rough Diamonds
Swan Song SSK 59419 (August 1982)

Wildlife: Wildlife
Swan Song B9842 (April 1983)

US SWAN SONG NON-LED ZEPPELIN ALBUM CATALOGUE

Bad Company: Bad Company
Swan Song SS 8410 (1974)

Pretty Things: Silk Torpedo
Swan Song SS 8411 (1974)

Maggie Bell: Suicide Sal
Swan Song SS 8412 (1975)

Bad Company: Straight Shooter
Swan Song SS 8413 (1975)

Pretty Things: Silk Torpedo
Swan Song SS 8414 (1975)

Bad Company: Run With The Pack
Swan Song SS 8415 (1976)

Detective: Detective
Swan Song SS 8417 (1977)

Dave Edmunds: Get It
Swan Song SS 8418 (1977)

Bad Company: Burning Sky
Swan Song SS 8500 (1977)

Detective: It Takes One To Know One
Swan Song SS 8504 (1978)

Dave Edmunds: Tracks On Wax 4
Swan Song SS 8505 (1978)

Bad Company: Desolation Angels
Swan Song SS 8506 (1979)

Dave Edmunds: Repeat When Necessary
Swan Song SS 8507 (1979)

Midnight Flyer: Midnight Flyer
Swan Song SS 8509 (1981)

Dave Edmunds: Twangin'
Swan Song SS 16034 (1981)

Midnight Flyer: Rock 'n' Roll Party
Swan Song mini-LP SS 11002 (1981)

Dave Edmunds: The Best Of Dave Edmunds
Swan Song SS 8510 (1982)

Jimmy Page: Death Wish 2 – Original Soundtrack
Swan Song SS 8511 (1982)

Robert Plant: Pictures At Eleven
Swan Song SS 8512 (1982)

Bad Company: Rough Diamonds
Swan Song 7900011 (1982)

Wildlife: Wildlife
Swan Song 7900781 (1983)
N.B. Other artists considered for Swan Song included black blues guitarist Bobby Parker, who Jimmy saw in Virginia but was subsequently never signed, and singer/songwriter Mirabai, who was signed in the US in 1974 and was due to have her first album produced by Dylan/Cash producer Bob Johnson but again nothing materialised. After Phil May left The Pretty Things in June 1976, the remaining members changed their name to Metropolis. Jimmy was keen for them to record an album but they eventually split in December 1977. Pretty Things/Metropolis keyboard player Gordon Edwards later assisted Page on the *Death Wish 2* soundtrack, playing piano on three tracks and singing on 'City Siren'.

NOTABLE SWAN SONG PROMO ITEMS

Dave Edmunds: College Radio Presents Dave Edmunds
Swan Song PR 230 (1978)

Detective: Live From The Atlantic Studios
Swan Song LAAS 002 (1978)

Robert Plant: Pictures At Eleven – Interview With Alan Freeman
Swan Song SAM 154 (1982)

BOOTLEG DISCOGRAPHY

Appendix 2D

long with Dylan, The Stones and The Beatles, Led Zeppelin were among the first acts to be boot-legged. A live audience recording of their appearance at the Los Angeles Forum on September 4, 1970 surfaced on a double album on the Blimp label a few months after the show under the title 'Live On Blueberry Hill' which was her-alded by a front page story in *Melody Maker*.

Since then there have emerged over 400 bootleg packages of Zeppelin material. These range from shoddy, poor quality live albums, to top quality mixing desk tapes and rare out-takes (reputedly stolen from Jimmy Page's possession) trans-ferred to CD.

Over the years the moral implications of such 'releases' has meant that they have been much condemned, not least in the early days of bootlegs by Peter Grant, who took it upon himself to destroy a stack of 'Blueberry Hill' albums at the Chancery Lane premises of a London record dealer and appeared on BBC TV's *24 Hours* news programme to state his dis-taste for such products.

For the dedicated fan, however, bootlegs offer the opportunity to hear the act developing on stage and in the studio. In Led Zeppelin's case, since much of their reputation was built on their live perfor-mance, their bootlegged material contains some essential listening. Such interest now extends to the group members them-selves who are all known to have requested copies of the more famous items. The unceasing flood of Zepp boot-legs is also probably one of the reasons Page has never got around to compiling that much touted chronological live project.

Not surprisingly, the Zepp bootleg cata-logue is something of a maze, containing a mass of reissues of original bootleg per-formances that vary dramatically in content and quality. At least one book has been published on the subject.

As a reference guide, what follows is a representative list of bootleg titles that covers key Zepp performances boot-legged on album and CD. Relevant historical notes are listed where applicable:

LIVE SHOWS

Alpha Omega
(RSR 241) Four album set with tracks from Spokane 1968 and Oakland 1977.

Fillmore West 1969
(GLC D545) Double set from the Fillmore April 27, 1969.

White Summer
(Swinging Pig TSP 019) Famous BBC *In Concert* June 27, 1969 show from the Playhouse Theatre. Also on CD.

Live At The London Lyceum
(LZ LLL 1 – 4) Double set from October 1969, one-off London show.

Mudslide
(TMQ) Classic early single bootleg from an FM broad-cast from Vancouver, March 21, 1970. Also on CD.

Bath Festival 1970 (Krishna)
Compilation from Bath includes 'Heartbreaker' and 'The Boy Next Door'. (A.K.A. 'That's The Way')

Live On Blueberry Hill
(Blimp/TMQ) Famous live double set from the LA Forum, September 4, 1970. Also on CD.

BBC Transcription Services
(BBCTS 152400) Best quality set from the much boot-legged BBC March 25, 1971 *In Concert* recording. Also on CD.

Live In Copenhagen
(RSR 55) Single album 10-inch pressing. Of major interest due to the inclusion of the rarely played live versions of 'Gallows Pole' and 'Four Sticks'. Also includes the Staines supershow 'Dazed And Con-fused' take from March 1969.

Going To California
(TMQ) Double album from Berkeley, Sept 14, 1971.

Live In Japan 1971
(LZL 1 – 4) Double from Osaka, Sept 29, 1971.

LA Forum – A Night At The Heartbreak Hotel
(Artemis 7199) Single album highlights from June 25, 1972.

My Brain Hurts – Live In Japan 1972
(Idle Mind 115) Single album reissue of 'Japanese Live'. Includes great cover version of 'Stand By Me'.

Quantient
(Sad Song SS 7319) Three album box set of the record breaking Tampa Stadium show, May 5, 1973.

Bonzo's Birthday Party
(TMQ 72007) Double set from the LA Forum, May 31, 1973.

Persistence
(Rune Dog R100) Double live from Kezar June 2, 1973. Clever cover sleeve parody of 'Presence'.

Three Days After
(TMQ 72016) More from LA Sept 4, 1970 and LA June 3, 1973. Includes superb encores of 'The Ocean', 'Communication Breakdown' and 'Thank You'.

Led Zeppelin Five-And-A-Half
(HH 1 – 4) Double set from Seattle, July 17, 1973.

Live At The Chicago Stadium
(Digger 2675) Notable double set from January 21, 1975 – includes the little played live tracks 'When The Levee Breaks' and 'The Wanton Song'. This is also the only 1975 bootleg to include the encore version of 'Communication Breakdown'.

Live In Dallas, Texas
(Toasted TRW 1998) Double from March 4, 1975 – defi-nitive USA 1975 performance.

214
(RSR 246) Double album from the Seattle March 21, 1975 show. Nearly 40 minutes of 'Dazed And Confused'.

Earls Court Vol 1
(Europe LZ19775) Impressively packaged single album from May 23, 1975.

Earls Court Vol 2
(Europe LZ1977511) Volume 2 from the same source as above.

Rock And Roll
(Waggle 1934) Superb double from Earls Court, May 24, 1975. Soundboard mono recording. Also on CD.

Destroyer
(DRGM 501 1 – 8) Four album box set, excellent sound. An alternative version came packaged in a car-rying case but is an inferior sound recording. Also on CD.

Listen To This Eddie
(RSR 202) Double album from LA Forum, June 21, 1975. Excellent sound and performance.

For Badgeholders Only
(Dragonfly LZ1234) Double set from LA Forum, June 23, 1977.

For Badgeholders Only Vol 2
(Dragonfly LZ7) Second half of the above show. Fea-tures Keith Moon on 'Moby Dick'.

Copenhagen Warm Ups
(Geiko Sukul 3ZC 07249) Triple album from the Falkoner Theatre Copenhagen, July 24, 1979.

Knebworth Complete And Uncut
(Amazing Stork LZ 4879) Four album set from the opening Knebworth show and the best version of the various Knebworth bootlegs.

Cologne 1980
(Hot Dog XL 1538 40) Triple set, June 18, 1980.

Bonzo's Last Ever Gig In Berlin
(Amazing Stork 7780) Reissue of a rare Japanese pressing. Triple set from the final show in Berlin, June 7, 1980.

Strange Tales From The Road
(RSR 243) Massive 10-album box set with a variety of performances including the Royal Albert Hall 1970, Osaka 1971, Tampa 1977, New York 1977 and Jimmy with Ian Stewart in Nottingham in 1984.

Led Zeppelin
(RSR 105 to 2290) Ten album bootleg compilation of various live shows 1969 to 1977, from the RSR series of albums. Packaged in a tin case.

SESSIONS/REHEARSALS/OUT-TAKES

In The Light '69 – 85
(Zip Zap Page) Double set includes majority of the BBC 1969 radio session tracks, plus live in Vancouver 1970 and *Live Aid* 1985 recordings.

Something Else
(Archive MZ 616) EP includes 'Something Else', 'The Girl I Love', 'What Is And What Should Never Be' and 'Communication Breakdown' – rare unaired BBC radio sessions from June 1969.

Hiawatha Express
(Stash 2304) Double set includes third album rehearsal material from May 1970, plus three minutes of a soundcheck at Southampton University in January 1973, and the Plant Band Of Joy demos. Also on CD.

The Making Of Friends
Recently surfaced EP containing more third album rehearsals ('Immigrant Song', 'Out On The Tiles', 'Poor Tom', 'Hey Hey What Can I Do', 'Bron-Y-Aur Stomp'), plus Plant and Page running through 'Friends' with the Bombay Symphony Orchestra. March 1972.

Studio Rehearsals May 1970
(Rock Live) Single album of material from Headley Grange, early 1971. Not May 1970 as listed.

Inedits Studio Rehearsals
(LZ 1 – 2) Single album of illuminating fourth album rehearsals including 'Black Dog', 'No Quarter', 'Stairway To Heaven' etc. All from Headley Grange early 1971.

Tangible Vandalism
(TV A – D) Another enlightening collection of rehearsals for 'Physical Graffiti' from Headley Grange in early 1974. Fair quality only but essential listening. Also on CD. Superbly packaged in 'Physical Graffiti' parody sleeve.

Out Through The Back Door
(Amazing Stork ITT A – D) Double album of alternative mixes from the Polar sessions, November 1978. Similar package to the 'In Through The Out-Takes' bootleg material but includes extra take of 'Carouselambra'. Also on CD.

The Last Rehearsal: Bonzo's Last Stand
(Oznob A – B) A single album taken from the 1980 tour rehearsals held at the Rainbow Theatre in May 1980 – not September 24 at Windsor as listed on the sleeve.

BOOTLEG CD'S

The acceptance of the Compact Disc in the late eighties brought a whole new catalogue of bootleg material. With extended playing time and superior quality, bootleg CD's proved even more desirable for the keen collector. However, this medium also gave rise to the unscrupulous tactic of transferring old bootleg titles directly from the vinyl version to CD.

While Led Zeppelin have not been exempt from this problem, many of the new Zepp titles that have sur-faced on bootleg CD do offer the enthusiast an opportunity to enjoy prime rare material with top quality sound.

There are already nearly 100 Zepp CD bootlegs. As with albums, this has already given rise to the duplication of the same material on different labels, and often with varying quality. The following is a list of the best CD bootleg releases:

LIVE BOOTLEG CD'S

San Francisco 27/4/69 Vol 1
(Kaleidoscope Music KMCD 3) Soundboard recording from the second US tour.

San Francisco 27/4/69 Vol 2
(Kaleidoscope Music KMCD 4) More from the above show.

White Summer
(Swinging Pig TSP CD 019) Superb quality recording of the BBC 1969 *In Concert* show of June 27, 1969. Also available on 'Classics Off Air Vol 2' (Neutral Zone NZCD 89005) with 1971 *In Concert* BBC material.

Live On Blueberry Hill Vol 1
(Neutral Zone NZCD 89019)

Live On Blueberry Hill Vol 2
(Neutral Zone NZCD 89020) Contains all the material from the LA 1970 show with improved sound quality.

Classics Off Air Vol 3
(Neutral Zone 89005) 72 minutes from the BBC 1971 *In Concert* with great sound quality.

Live In Stoke Vol 1
(Pageboys LZ07)

Live In Stoke Vol 2
(Pageboys LZ08) Recently surfaced good quality soundboard recording from the UK tour, January 15, 1973.

April Fools Day
(Pageboys LZ05) Not the Paris 1973 show as listed but taken from Hamburg Musichalle on March 21, 1973.

Dallas '75 Vol 1
(Rock Records LZCD 101)

Dallas '75 Vol 2
(Rock Records LZCD 102) Superb mono soundboard recording of a truly excellent show on March 4, 1975.

Over The Hills And Far Away
(Great Dane GRDR CD 8914) 75-minute condensed version of above show minus 'Moby Dick'. Superb.

Rock And Roll
(Toasted Condor 1979) Brilliant soundboard CD of three marathon performances ('Trampled Underfoot', 'Dazed And Confused', 'No Quarter') from Earls Court May 24, 1975.

Silver Coated Tails
(Toasted Condor 1981) More wonderful soundboard quality represented by three tracks from Earls Court May 23, 1975, three from Madison Square Garden June 11, 1977 and three from Zurich in 1980 including a stunning 'Heartbreaker'.

Destroyer
(Archive Productions LZ 69801) Best version of the Cleveland 1977 show on two CD's. Also on Swinging Pig.

Live In Rotterdam 1980
(Neutral Zone NCZD 89006) Excellent soundboard CD from 'Over Europe'.

Tour Over Europe 1980
(Twin Eagle CD 8803)

One of the first bootleg CD's and still one of the best – great sound – cooking show from June 29, 1980. Double CD package.

Moonlight
(Toasted Condor 1984) Another excellent 1980 soundboard quality CD this time from Frankfurt on June 30, 1980. Also available on 'Hotter Than The Hindenburg' (Rockin' LZ03).

Dinosaur
(Toasted Condor 1985) More prime 1980 live material from Frankfurt and Bremen.

Last Stand
(Toasted Condor 1999)

Final Touch
(Toasted Condor 1998) Chronicles much of the final show in Berlin – soundboard again.

BOOTLEG CD'S – STUDIO/REHEARSALS ETC:

Classics Off Air Vol 1
(Neutral Zone NZCD 88001) Brings together the two BBC sessions plus live in Vancouver 1970. Also available minus Vancouver on 'Winterland' (Living Legend LLRCD 043)

Jennings Farm Blues
(Scorpio JFB 640 10 1 70) Includes several run throughs of the remarkable out-take 'Jennings Farm Blues'. Cut in October 1969, this turns out to be an electric version of 'Bron-Y-Aur Stomp'. Superb sound quality. This CD also has an hour live from Toronto, September 4, 1971.

Studio Daze
(Scorpio SD 64 10 171) Possibly the single most essential recording of any unauthorised Zeppelin issue. In wondrous quality we hear a different vocal mix of 'Since I've Been Loving You', a six-minute blues medley out-take from the 'Hats Off To (Roy) Harper' session, five instrumental takes plus an alternative vocal version of 'No Quarter' and a priceless extended take of 'All My Love' from Polar in 1978. All this, plus 'What Is And What Should Never Be' and 'Dancing Days' live from Long Beach, June 26, 1972.

SOLO BOOTLEGS
A representative selection:

JIMMY PAGE
ALBUMS

Jimmy Page Session Man
(Slipped Disc Hoff 1098) Enjoyable double set of session era oddities.

The Royal Albert Hall Concert
(ARMS 1 A – F) Triple set from September 21, 1983 – full Page set plus Clapton, Winwood etc.

Rock Of Ages
Double album from the ARMS show in San Francisco, December 2, 1983.

European Tour 1984
(691813 A – D) Double album of The Firm in Frankfurt, December 12, 1984.

The Return Of The Led Gremlin
(Kornyfone STA 412) Double set from the 'Outrider' tour, July 10, 1988.

ROBERT PLANT
ALBUMS

The Blue Note
(XL 1559/60) Double set featuring The Honeydrippers at the Blue Note club Derby, March 13, 1981.

Just To Know What He's Doing: Live At The Tube
(Spit At Journalists Productions) Single album of the
aborted *Tube* TV recording, June 22, 1983.

Starting Over
(Dick Tracy 84 83) Good quality recordings taken from
the shows at Houston and Austin, Texas, from
Robert's début solo tour in September 1983. Double
album.

1983 Hammersmith Odeon
(MS 3003) Includes Jimmy on 'Treat Her Right', Hammersmith Odeon, December 13, 1983.

For Badgeholders Vol 3
(RSR 221) Double set from the LA Forum, June 17,
1985.

Now And Zep
(Toasted TSTD 1911) Double set from Colchester,
Essex University, January 30, 1988.

After The Crash Vol 1
(Toasted TRW 1920)

After The Crash Vol 2
(Toasted TRW 1921) Vol 1 is from the Hammersmith
Odeon, April 11, 1988. Volume 2 is more from the
same show including the 20-minute Page jam plus the
Live Aid and Atlantic reunion sets. Both on double
albums.

Non Stop Go Tour 1988
(Underground UND 257) Double set from an FM
Westwood One broadcast of the Philadelphia show on
May 23, 1988.

JOHN BONHAM
ALBUM

John Henry Bonham: Session Man
(RSR 112) Includes the Lord Sutch, P.J. Proby, Roy
Wood and Rockestra session appearances.

LED ZEPPELIN
LIVE COVER VERSIONS

Throughout their many live shows, Led Zeppelin
included a host of live workings of cover version
material. The bulk of these songs were inserted into
the rock 'n' roll medleys employed on closing finales
of 'How Many More Times' and 'Whole Lotta Love'.
Other items were included in lengthy marathons such
as 'Dazed And Confused' and 'No Quarter'.
 The following is a list of non-original numbers
known to have been played in full or as short snippets
during their live concerts from 1968 to 1980. Where
possible, the artist whose arrangement these versions
were taken from is also listed.

As Long As I Have You
(Garnett Mimms),

Fresh Garbage
(Spirit),

Long Tall Sally/Rip It Up/Lucille
(Little Richard),

Rave On/Think It Over/Peggy Sue
(Buddy Holly),

**C'mon Everybody/Summertime Blues/Something
Else**
(Eddie Cochran),

It'll Be Me/Great Balls Of Fire/Whole Lotta Shakin'
(Jerry Lee Lewis),

Tobacco Road
(Nashville Teens),

Stand By Me/We're Gonna Groove
(Ben E. King),

Blueberry Hill
(Fats Domino),

Money
(Barrett Strong),

Woodstock
(Joni Mitchell),

Take It Easy
(The Eagles),

For What It's Worth
(Buffalo Springfield),

I Saw Her Standing There
(The Beatles),

San Francisco
(Scott Mackenzie),

**Jailhouse Rock/Mystery Train/Heartbreak Hotel/
Lawdy Miss Clawdy/Let's Have A Party/A Mess Of
Blues/I Need Your Love Tonight/His Latest Flame/
Baby I Don't Care/My Baby Left Me/That's Alright
Mamma/Surrender/Frankfurt Special**
(Elvis Presley),

Hello Mary Lou
(Rick Nelson),

Be Bop A Lula
(Gene Vincent),

Johnny B. Goode/No Money Down
(Chuck Berry),

Gotta Move
(Otis Rush),

Twist And Shout/It's Your Thing
(Isley Brothers),

Don't Play That Song For Me
(Aretha Franklin),

Train Kept A Rollin'/For Your Love/I'm A Man
(The Yardbirds),

Killing Floor
(Spirit),

La Bamba
(Ritchie Valens),

Everybody Needs Somebody To Love
(Solomon Burke),

I Just Wanna Make Love To You
(Willie Dixon),

Some Other Guy
(Larry Williams),

Long Distance Call/Honey Bee
(Muddy Waters),

Eyesight To The Blind
(Sonny Boy Williamson),

Here We Go Round The Mulberry Bush
(Traffic),

Cat's Squirrel
(Cream)

**Boogie Chillin'/Let That Boy Boogie/Sittin' Here
Thinkin'/Fixin' To Die**
(John Lee Hooker),

Rock 'n' Roll Is Here To Stay
(Sha Na Na),

The Hunter
(Albert King),

I'm Goin' Down
(Freddie King),

Shake
(Sam Cooke),

Bags Groove
(Milt Jackson),

Smoke Gets In Your Eyes
(The Platters),

Shape I'm In
(The Band),

**Movin' On Down The Line/Evil Woman/Stay/Woody
Woodpecker Song/Pennies From Heaven/Suzie Q/Oh
Rosie/Season Of The Witch/Hush Little Baby/Fought
My Way Out Of The Darkness/I Gotta Know.**

JOHN PAUL JONES:
LIVE SOLO SHOWPIECES

During his solo on 'Thank You', JP threw in
versions of:

'Amazing Grace'
(Judy Collins). During his 'No Quarter' solo he
performed

'Nut Rocker'
(B. Bumble And The Stingers),

Louie Louie
(The Kingsmen) and

The Nutcracker Suite
(Tchaikovsky).

JIMMY PAGE:
LIVE SOLO SHOWPIECES

59th Street Bridge Song
(Simon And Garfunkel),

Lute Suite No. 1
(Bach) – both used during 'Heartbreaker'.

West Side Story
(Bernstein/Sondheim),

Theme From Shaft
(Isaac Hayes) both used during 'Dazed And
Confused'.

The Star Spangled Banner
(Jimi Hendrix arrangement),

Walk Don't Run
(The Ventures).
The following numbers are known to have been used
to warm up in rehearsals and soundchecks:

Shakin' All Over/I'll Never Get Over You
(Johnny Kidd And The Pirates),

Move It/Dynamite/Please Don't Tease
(Cliff Richard),

**Hail Hail Rock 'n' Roll/Nadine/Around And Around/
Reelin' 'n' Rockin'**
(Chuck Berry),

Hungry For Love.
Many other cover versions were tried at soundchecks/
rehearsal sessions.

THE CONCERTS
1968 – 1980
Appendix 3

The following is a chronological list of concerts performed by Led Zeppelin from 1968 to 1980. In collating such a list it is difficult to obtain and verify details of certain shows. Thus, this listing cannot claim to be fully complete or 100 per cent accurate. It does, however, include the vast majority of Led Zeppelin gigs performed during their 12-year career and is, to the best of the author's knowledge, the most comprehensive list so far published.

1968

September 14 – Copenhagen (opening night of 10-date Scandinavian tour as The New Yardbirds)
September 20 – Stockholm Koncerthaus
September 23 – Oslo, Norway
October 15 – Surrey University (UK début)
October 18 – London Marquee Club (support from Sleepy)
October 19 – Liverpool University
November 11 – London, Roundhouse, Chalk Farm (all night show with John Lee Hooker, The Deviants, John James and Tyres, fee: £150).
November 16 – Manchester College of Science and Technology (fee £225)
November 23 – Sheffield University
December 10 – London Marquee Club (support from Bakerloo Blues Line)
December 16 – Bath Pavilion (fee £75)
December 19 – Exeter City Hall (fee £125)
December 20 – London, Wood Green Fishmongers Hall
December 26 – Denver Coliseum (opening show of first US tour; the gate fees on this début tour range from $200 to $1,500).
December 27 – Seattle Center Arena
December 28 – Boston Tea Party (third on the bill to Vanilla Fudge and The MC5)
December 29 – New York
December 30 – Washington, Spokane Gonzaga University
December 31 – Portland

1969

January 2/3/4/5/6 – Los Angeles, Whiskey A Go Go, (residency with Alice Cooper)
January 9/10/11 – San Francisco, Fillmore West, (second on the bill with Country Joe And The Fish and Taj Mahal).
January 13 – San Diego
January 14 – Fort Worth
January 15 – Houston
January 16 – New Orleans
January 17 – Miami Image Club
January 18 – Atlanta
January 20 – Baltimore
January 21 – Pittsburgh
January 22 – Cleveland
January 23/24 – Chicago Kinetic Circus

January 25/26 – Detroit Grande Ballroom
January 27 – Toronto Rockpile
January 28 – Boston Tea Party (the legendary four-hour show that signalled the first wave of Zepp US hysteria)
January 29 – Philadelphia
January 31/Feb 1 – New York, Fillmore East (second on the bill with Iron Butterfly and Porter's Popular Preachers; end of first US tour).
March 3 – London, Wood Green Fishmongers Hall (start of a series of UK gigs: fees range from £60 against 60 per cent of the gate to £140 flat).
March 3 – Plymouth
March 5 – Cardiff
March 7 – Hornsey, Bluesville '69 Club, Wood Tavern
March 10 – London, Cooks Ferry Inn, Edmonton
March 12 – Leicester
March 14 – Stockholm Koncerthaus
March 19 – Danish TV appearance followed by evening show at Copenhagen Gladsaxe Teen Club.
March 21 – London *How Late It Is* TV appearance.
March 22 – Birmingham, Mothers Club (support from Blodwyn Pig)
March 25 – Staines, Supershow film recording.
March 28 – London Marquee Club (support from Eyes Of Blue)
March 30 – Potters Bar, Farx Club, Southall (support from Smokey Rice)
April 1 – West Hampstead, Klooks Kleek Club (support from The End/Pale Green Limousine)
April 5 – Dagenham Roundhouse
April 8 – Welwyn Garden City, Cherry Tree
April 12 – Tolworth Toby Jug
April 14 – Stoke On Trent
April 17 – Sunderland
April 24 – San Francisco, Fillmore West (start of second US tour; co-host some dates with Vanilla Fudge).
April 25/26 – San Francisco Winterland
April 27 – San Francisco, Fillmore West (all four shows with support from Julie Driscoll, Brian Auger And The Trinity and Colwell Winfield Blues Band).
April 29 – Los Angeles
April 30 – San Diego
May 2/3/4 – Pasadena Rose Palace (support from Julie Driscoll, Brian Auger And The Trinity).
May 6/7 – Honolulu
May 9 – Portland
May 10 – Vancouver
May 11 – Seattle Aquatheater
May 12 – Detroit Grande Ballroom
May 13 – Athens
May 14 – Minneapolis Guthrie Theatre
May 16/17 – Chicago Kinetic Circus
May 19 – Boston Gardens
May 21 – Syracuse
May 23/24 – Chicago Kinetic Playground
May 25 – San Jose, Santa Clara Pop Festival (other acts on the bill included The Jimi Hendrix Experience, Canned Heat, Muddy Waters, Chuck Berry, Taj Mahal and Jefferson Airplane).
May 26 – Pittsburgh
May 28 – Philadelphia
May 30/31 – New York, Fillmore East (top of the bill

SCENIC SOUNDS PRESENTS

LED ZEPPELIN and **Julie Driscoll, Bryan Auger and the Trinity**

doors open 7:00 movies

MAY 2 & 3 8:00 to 1:00

R34   R34   ⊕H

LIGHTS by Thomas Edison

SOUND by Black Gold

TICKETS: $3.50 Advance $4.00 Door

Tickets at Wallich's, Free Press Bookstores, Sound Spectrum & all Mutuals.

835 S.Raymond - The Rose Palace - Pasadena

go to the end of the Pasadena Freeway, turn left, go one block, turn right..

NEXT WEEK: The Filmed Farewell Performance of CREAM

over Woody Herman and his Orchestra and Delaney And Bonnie and Friends; end of second US tour).
June 13 – Birmingham Town Hall (start of first proper UK tour with Liverpool Scene and Blodwyn Pig supporting).
June 15 – Manchester Free Trade Hall
June 20 – Newcastle City Hall
June 21 – Bristol Colston Hall
June 26 – Portsmouth Guildhall
June 27 – London Playhouse Theatre (BBC broadcast)
June 28 – Bath Festival Of Blues, Bath Recreation Ground (also on the bill: Fleetwood Mac, John Mayall, Ten Years After, The Nice, Taste, Keef Hartley; att: 12,000).
June 29 – London, Royal Albert Hall (two shows; first night of the Pop Proms ends with a wild jam of 'Long Tall Sally' with members of Blodwyn Pig and Liverpool Scene after the houselights had gone up).
July 5 – Atlanta Pop Festival (start of third American tour)
July 6 – Newport Festival
July 11 – Laurel Festival (with Johnny Winter, B.B. King, Jeff Beck, Roland Kirk).
July 12 – Philadelphia Jazz Festival
July 13 – New York, Flushing Meadow Singer Bowl (this show ends with a jam session featuring Jeff Beck, Rod Stewart, Rick Lee from Ten Years After and Glenn Cornick from Jethro Tull powering through

'Jailhouse Rock'; att: 25,000).
July 16 – Boston
July 17 – Montreal
July 18 – Toronto
July 19 – Detroit Grande Ballroom
July 20 – Pittsburgh
July 21 – New York, Central Park (two shows with
B.B. King).
July 23 – Chicago
July 25 – Milwaukee, West Allison, Wisconsin State
Fair
July 26 – St. Paul
July 27 – Seattle, Woodinville Festival, Goldkreek Park
(with The Doors)
July 29 – Vancouver
July 30 – Portland
July 31 – Eugene
August 1 – Santa Barbara Arena (with Jethro Tull and
Fraternity Of Man)
August 2 – Los Angeles Coliseum
August 3 – Houston Music Hall
August 4 – San Diego
August 7 – Sacramento
August 8 – Berkeley
August 9 – Anaheim Convention Centre (with Jethro
Tull)
August 10 – Salt Lake City
August 11 – San Francisco, Fillmore West
August 13 – Phoenix (N.B. – this was the weekend of
the famous Woodstock Festival which Zeppelin were
originally billed to appear at on August 16).
August 17 – Wallingford Oakdale Theatre
August 18 – Toronto Rockpile (two shows)
August 30 – New York, Flushing Meadow Singer Bowl
Music Festival (with Buddy Guy and Larry Coryell)
August 31 – Dallas, International Pop Festival (also on
the bill: Sam And Dave, B.B. King, Incredible String
Band, Herbie Mann, Chicago Transit Authority and
Delaney And Bonnie; for this date the group earn
their largest fee to date – $13,000; end of third US
tour).
Sep/Oct – Dutch dates were reported in the music
press over this period but no confirmation of this has
come to light.
October 10 – Paris, Olympia Theatre (one-off European
warm-up date)
October 12 – London Lyceum Ballroom (special one-
nighter with Audience and Frosty Moses supporting;
for this show Zeppelin receive reputedly the highest
fee for one concert for a British act).
October 17/18 – New York, Carnegie Hall (first rock
group to play the prestigious venue since The Rolling
Stones in 1964; start of fourth US tour)
October 19 – Detroit
October 20 – Chicago
October 21 – Cleveland
October 22 – Philadelphia Spectrum
October 23 – Boston Gardens (their largest indoor
audience to date – 17,000 – and largest fee – $45,000).
October 24 – Buffalo
October 25 – Providence Rhode Island
October 26 – Syracuse Anadaga War Memorial
October 28 – Anaheim Convention Centre
October 29 – Seattle
October 30 – St. Louis Kleinman Music Hall
October 31 – Kansas City
November 1 – Denver
November 2 – Toronto O'Keefe Centre (two shows with
support from Edward Bear)
November 4 – Kitchener Memorial Auditorium (with
support from The Cooper Penny)
November 5 – Vancouver
November 6/7/8 – San Francisco Winterland (with sup-
port from Isaac Hayes, Roland Kirk and Wolf Gang;
end of fourth US tour).

1970
January 7 – Birmingham Town Hall (start of second UK
tour; for this tour the group went out with no support
act, a trend that would continue on the majority of
their gigs from this point on).
January 8 – Bristol Colston Hall
January 9 – London Royal Albert Hall (filmed and
recorded by the group for their intended TV
documentary)
January 13 – Portsmouth Guild Hall
January 15 – Newcastle City Hall
January 16 – Sheffield City Hall
January 24 – Leeds Town Hall
February 7 – Scheduled date at Edinburgh Usher Hall
is cancelled when Plant suffers cuts in a car smash on
the way back from a Spirit concert.
February 21 – Copenhagen KB Hallen (under the name
The Nobs after complaints from Countess Eva Von
Zeppelin over their use of the family name; start of
first proper European tour).
February 24 – Helsinki
February 25 – Gottenburg
February 26 – Stockholm
February 28 – Copenhagen KB Hallen
March 7 – Geneva Victoria Concert Hall
March 8 – Munich
March 9 – Vienna
March 10 – Frankfurt
March 11 – Düsseldorf
March 12 – Hamburg
March 13 – Montreux Jazz Festival
March 21 – Vancouver (att: 19,000, breaks the previous
record held by The Beatles; start of fifth US tour).
March 22 – Seattle Centre Arena
March 23 – Spokane
March 25 – Denver Coliseum
March 26 – San Diego Sports Arena
March 27 – Los Angeles Forum (att: 20,000, gross
$71,000).
March 28 – Dallas Memorial Auditorium
March 29 – Houston University Pavilion
March 30 – Boston Gardens
March 31 – Montreal Forum
April 1 – Toronto Maple Leaf Gardens
April 2 – Detroit
April 3 – Pittsburgh
April 4 – Philadelphia Spectrum
April 5 – Baltimore Civic Centre
April 6 – Memphis (during their stay the group are
made honorary citizens of Memphis)
April 7 – Raleigh
April 8 – Atlanta
April 9 – Tampa Curtis Nixon Hall
April 11 – St. Louis
April 12 – Chicago
April 13 – Milwaukee
April 14 – Minneapolis
April 15 – Winnipeg
April 17 – Salt Lake City
April 18 – Phoenix
April 19 – A date at the Las Vegas Convention Centre
is cancelled due to Robert's voice giving out (end of
fifth US tour).
June 20/21 – Iceland, Reykjavik (warm-up dates)
June 28 – Bath Festival Of Blues And Progressive
Music, Shepton Mallet (bill also includes Jefferson Air-
plane, Frank Zappa and The Mothers Of Invention,
The Moody Blues, The Byrds, Flock, Santana,
Dr John, Country Joe and Hot Tuna; att: 150,000).
July 9 – Dusseldorf Sporthalle
July 10 – Essen Grugehalle
July 11 – Frankfurt Festhalle (11,00 attend the first ever
rock show at the Festhalle)
July 12 – Berlin Deutschlandhalle
August 5 – Cincinnati (start of sixth US tour – no sup-
port act – minimum fee $25,000).

August 6 – Detroit
August 7 – Cleveland
August 8 – Pittsburgh
August 10 – Hampton Coliseum
August 11 – Charlotte
August 12 – Jacksonville
August 13 – Tallahassee
August 14 – Atlanta
August 15 – Birmingham
August 17 – Memphis
August 18 – New Orleans
August 19 – San Antonio
August 20 – Fort Worth
August 21 – Tulsa
August 22 – Albuquerque
August 24 – St. Louis
August 25 – Chicago
August 26 – Milwaukee
August 27 – St. Paul
August 28 – Minneapolis
August 30 – Seattle
August 31 – Portland
September 2 – San Francisco Oakland Coliseum
September 3 – San Diego Sports Arena
September 4 – Los Angeles Forum (the famous Blue-
berry Hill show)
September 5/6 – Honolulu
September 14 – Rochester
September 15 – New Haven
September 16 – Boston Gardens
September 17 – Philadelphia Spectrum
September 19 – New York, Madison Square Garden
(two shows; first appearances at the Garden gross
over $100,000; end of sixth US tour).

1971
March 5 – Belfast Ulster Hall (start of third UK tour)
March 6 – Dublin Boxing Stadium (Atlantic executive
Phil Carson joins them on bass for an encore of 'Sum-
mertime Blues').
March 9 – Leeds University
March 10 – Canterbury, Kent University
March 11 – Southampton University
March 13 – Bath Pavilion
March 14 – Stoke, The Place, Hanley
March 16 – Liverpool Stadium (cancelled)
March 18 – Newcastle, Mayfair Fillmore North
March 19 – Manchester University
March 20 – Birmingham Stepmothers
March 21 – Nottingham Boat Club
March 23 – London Marquee Club
March 25 – London, Paris Theatre (BBC broadcast; a
rearranged date from the previous week when Plant
had voice problems).
March (date unknown) – Sutton Coldfield Belfry
May 10 – Liverpool Stadium (rescheduled from can-
celled date on March 16)
June – Copenhagen (start of second European tour –
individual dates unconfirmed), Stockholm, Hamburg,

Berlin, Frankfurt, Munich, Vienna, Rome, Turin.
July 3 – Milan Vigorelli Stadium (this gig with 12,000 in attendance was abandoned when police used teargas to break up 'rioting' fans).
August – Montreux Casino (two shows; actual dates unconfirmed).
August 19 – Vancouver Maple Leaf Garden (start of seventh US tour)
August 20 – Seattle
August 21/22 – Los Angeles Forum
August 23 – Fort Worth
August 24 – Dallas
August 25 – Houston
August 26 – San Antonio
August 28 – St. Louis
August 29 – New Orleans
August 30 – Chicago
August 31 – Orlando
September 1 – Miami
September 2 – Pittsburgh
September 3 – New York, Madison Square Garden
September 4 – Toronto Maple Leaf Gardens
September 5 – Chicago
September 7 – Boston Gardens
September 9 – Hampton Beach
September 10 – Syracuse
September 11 – Rochester Auditorium
September 13/14 – Berkeley Community Centre
September 16/17 – Honolulu
September 23 – Tokyo Budokan Hall (start of first Japanese tour)
September 24 – Tokyo Budokan Hall
September 27 – Hiroshima Shiel Tallkukan
September 28/29 – Osaka Festival Hall

November 23 – Preston Town Hall
November 24 – Manchester Free Trade Hall
November 25 – Leicester University
November 29 – Liverpool Stadium
November 30 – Manchester, Kings Hall Belle Vue
December 2 – Bournemouth, Starkers Royal Ballroom
December 15 – Salisbury City Hall

1972
February 14 – Planned Singapore concert cancelled when the group are refused entry into the country due to their long hair.
February 16 – Perth Oval (start of Australian and New Zealand tour)
February 18 – Adelaide Memorial Drive
February 20 – Melbourne Kooyong Stadium
February 25 – Auckland Western Spring Stadium (att: 25,000)
February 29 – Brisbane Festival Hall
March 4 – Sydney Showground (att: 26,000)
March 10 – Sydney Showground
June 2 – Brussels (unconfirmed)
June 6 – Detroit Cobo Hall (start of eighth US tour)
June 7 – Montreal Forum
June 9 – Charlotte Coliseum
June 10 – Buffalo Memorial Auditorium
June 11 – Baltimore Civic Theatre
June 14/15 – New York, Long Island, Nassau Coliseum
June 17 – Portland Memorial Coliseum
June 18/19 – Seattle Coliseum
June 21 – Denver Coliseum
June 22 – San Bernardino Swing Auditorium
June 23 – San Diego Sports Arena
June 25 – Los Angeles Forum

December 7/8 – Manchester Hardrock
December 11/12 – Cardiff Capital
December 16/17 – Birmingham Odeon
December 20 – Brighton Dome
December 22/23 – London Alexandra Palace

1973
January 2 – Sheffield City Hall
January 7 – Oxford New Theatre
January 14 – Liverpool Empire
January 15 – Stoke On Trent, Trentham Gardens
January 16 – Aberystwyth Kings Theatre
January 18 – Bradford St. Georges Hall (rescheduled from cancelled show on January 5)
January 20 – Southampton University ('How Many More Times' is performed on this specially added show and is also professionally recorded by the group).
January 21 – Southampton Gaumont
January 25 – Aberdeen Music Hall
January 27 – Dundee Caird Hall
January 28 – Edinburgh Kings Theatre
January 30 – Preston Guild Hall (rescheduled from cancelled show on January 4)
March 3 – Copenhagen (start of third European tour)
March 4 – Gothenburg
March 6/7 – Stockholm Tennishallen
March 10 – Oslo
March 11 – Rotterdam
March 12 – Brussels
March 13 – Frankfurt
March 14 – Nuremberg Messenhalle
March 16 – Vienna Konzerthaus
March 17 – Munich Olympiahalle
March 19 – Berlin Deutschlandhalle
March 21 – Hamburg Musichalle
March 22 – Essen Grugenhalle
March 23 – Cologne
March 24 – Offenbach Arberrheinhalle
March 26 – Lyons
March 27 – Nantes
March 29 – Marseilles
March 31 – Lille
April 1/2 – Paris Palais De Sport
May 4 – Atlanta Braves Stadium (att: 49,236 – total gross $246,180; start of ninth US tour which heralds the introduction of their first sophisticated light show – including the use of mirror balls and dry ice effects).
May 5 – Tampa Bay Stadium (56,800 people pay $301,000, a figure that tops the previous highest gate and gross held by The Beatles for their Shea Stadium date. This feat earns Led Zeppelin a place in the *Guinness Book Of Records*).
May 6 – St. Petersburg
May 7 – Jacksonville
May 9 – Tuscaloosa
May 11 – St. Louis
May 13 – Mobile
May 14 – New Orleans Municipal Auditorium (during their stay at the Royal Orleans Hotel, Jones is involved in an incident described in their song of the same name – later to appear on the 'Presence' album).
May 16 – Houston
May 18 – Dallas Memorial Arena
May 19 – Fort Worth Convention Centre
May 22 – San Antonio
May 23 – Albuquerque
May 25 – Denver
May 26 – Salt Lake City Salt Palace
May 28 – San Diego Sports Arena
May 30 – First date at the Los Angeles Forum is cancelled due to Page spraining a finger on a fence at LA Airport.
May 31 – Los Angeles Forum
June 2 – San Francisco Kezar Stadium (also on the bill: Roy Harper, The Tubes and Lee Michaels; att: 49,304 –

November 11 – Newcastle City Hall (start of fourth UK tour which heralds the introduction of the four symbols designs on their stage equipment).
November 12 – Sunderland Locarno
November 13 – Dundee Caird Hall
November 16 – Ipswich St. Matthews Baths
November 17 – Birmingham Kinetic Circus
November 18 – Sheffield University
November 20 – London, Wembley Empire Pool (five-hour Electric Magic show incorporating circus acts and support from Bronco and Stone The Crows).
November 21 – London, Wembley Empire Pool (second Electric Magic show – circus acts plus Home and Stone The Crows).

June 27 – Long Beach Arena
June 28 – Tucson Community Centre
October 2/3 – Tokyo Budokan Hall (start of second Japanese tour)
October 4 – Osaka Festival Hall
October 5 – Nagoya
October 9 – Osaka Festival Hall
October 10 – Kyoto Kalikan Hall
October 28/29 – Montreux Casino
November 30 – Newcastle City Hall (start of fifth UK tour which is sold out within four hours of the tickets going on sale at box offices around the UK).
December 1 – Newcastle City Hall
December 3/4 – Glasgow Greens Playhouse

gross $325,000, a new record for California).
June 3 – Los Angeles Forum (rescheduled date)
July 6/7 – Chicago Stadium
July 9 – Minnesota St. Paul
July 10 – Milwaukee Arena
July 12/13 – Detroit Cobo Hall
July 15 – Buffalo War Memorial Auditorium
July 17 – Seattle Coliseum
July 18 – Vancouver Coliseum
July 20 – Boston Gardens
July 21 – Providence Civic Centre
July 23 – Baltimore Civic Centre
July 24 – Pittsburgh Three Rivers Stadium (att: 38,000, beating the previous record held by Alice Cooper).
July 27/28/29 – New York, Madison Square Garden

1975

January 11 – Rotterdam
January 12 – Brussels Forest National
January 18 – Minneapolis Metro Sportscentre (start of tenth US tour for which whole new stage show is prepared, including a massive neon Led Zeppelin sign that is lit during the finale; Bonzo's drums are now mounted on a rostrum and lasers are introduced for Jimmy's violin bow sequence).
January 20/21/22 – Chicago Stadium
January 26 – A date in St. Louis is cancelled due to Plant's 'flu.
January 29 – Greensboro Coliseum
January 31 – Detroit Olympia Stadium
February 1/2 – Pittsburgh Civic Arena
February 3 – New York, Madison Square Garden
February 4 – New York, Long Island, Nassau Coliseum (this date was inserted after a planned show at the Boston Gardens was cancelled by local authorities when 3,000 fans rioted while waiting to buy tickets).
February 6 – Montreal Forum
February 7 – New York, Madison Square Garden
February 8 – Philadelphia Spectrum
February 10 – Landover Capitol Centre
February 12 – New York, Madison Square Garden
February 13/14 – New York, Long Island, Nassau Coliseum
February 28 – Baton Rouge State University
March 1 – New Orleans Municipal Auditorium
March 3 – Fort Worth Tarrent Convention Centre
March 4/5 – Dallas Memorial Auditorium
March 7 – Austin (Bad Company drummer Simon Kirke joins them for the 'Whole Lotta Love' encore).
March 8 – This was the date Zeppelin should have topped, a one-day festival at West Palm Beach Speedway in Florida before 150,000 fans. The show was cancelled due to site problems.
March 10 – San Diego Sports Arena
March 11/12 – Long Beach Pacific Arena
March 17 – Seattle Coliseum
March 19 – Vancouver Coliseum
March 21 – Seattle Coliseum
March 24/25/27 – Los Angeles Forum (Linda Lovelace introduces the band on stage).
May 17/18/23/24/25 – London Earls Court Arena (total attendance 85,000; DJ's Johnny Walker, Kid Jensen, Nicky Horne, Bob Harris and Alan Freeman introduce them on stage each night; a giant 24 × 30 foot ephidor video screen is erected above the stage and at three-and-a-half hours, these are some of Zeppelin's longest shows).
August 23/24 – Two dates at the Oakland Stadium which were to have featured Zepp plus Joe Walsh and The Pretty Things are cancelled due to Robert's August 4 car smash.
September 6 – Pasadena Rose Bowl is another announced show that has to be cancelled. Plans for other US dates and a trip to South America are also shelved.

LED ZEPPELIN
1975 U. S. TOUR

December 10 – Jersey, St. Helier, Beehans West Park Night Club, one-off unannounced appearance. The band play a 45-minute set with resident pianist ex-Tornado Norman Hale. Numbers included old standards such as 'Blue Suede Shoes', plus their own material. Page débuts his Lake Placid blue Strat at this gig – 350 people witness the comeback.

1977

April 1 – Dallas Memorial Centre (start of eleventh US tour; stage set includes improved lighting and an 80-foot stage platform and many shows employ the giant ephidor video screen).
April 3 – Oklahoma Myriad
April 6/7/9/10 – Chicago Stadium (the third show in this series was abandoned after an hour when Page went down with severe stomach cramp as they performed 'Ten Years Gone').
April 12 – Minneapolis Sports Arena
April 13 – St. Paul Memorial Coliseum
April 15 – St. Louis Blues Arena
April 17 – Indianapolis Market Square Arena
April 19/20 – Cincinnati Riverfront Coliseum
April 23 – Atlanta The Omni
April 25 – Louisville
April 27/28 – Cleveland Richfield Coliseum
April 30 – Pontiac Silverdome (the attendance of 76,229 at this show breaks the record for a single act concert – set by Zepp in Tampa in 1973; their fee is a cool $800,000).
May 18 – Birmingham Coliseum
May 19 – Baton Rouge State University
May 21 – Houston Summit
May 22 – Fort Worth Convention Centre (Bad Company's Mick Ralphs joins them for an encore of 'It'll Be Me').
May 25/26/28/30 – Largo Landover Capitol Centre
May 31 – Greensboro Coliseum
June 3 – Tampa Bay Stadium (this show was abandoned after 20 minutes and three songs – 'The Song Remains The Same', 'Sick Again' and 'Nobody's Fault But Mine' – when rain flooded onto the stage causing an electrocution hazard; a proposed replacement date for the next day was cancelled by the authorities when disappointed fans caused disturbances).
June 7/8/10/11/13/14 – New York, Madison Square Garden
June 19 – San Diego Sports Arena
June 21/22/23/25/26/27/ – Los Angeles Forum (Keith Moon jams with them on the June 23 date on 'Moby Dick' and the 'Rock And Roll'/'Whole Lotta Love' encore).
July 17 – Seattle Kingdome
July 20 – Tempe Activities Centre
July 23/24 – Oakland Coliseum The rest of tour is cancelled when news is flashed to New Orleans that Robert's son had died. The outstanding dates on the

1977 tour cancelled after Robert Plant's tragedy were as follows:
July 30 – New Orleans Superdome
August 2/3 – Chicago Stadium
August 6 – Buffalo Rich Stadium
August 9/10 – Pittsburgh Arena
August 13 – Philadelphia JFK Stadium

1979

July 23/24 – Copenhagen Falconer Theatre (warm-up dates; on the first date, a power failure delays proceedings and the group eventually appear with only half their lighting rig in action).
August 4 – Knebworth Festival (full line-up: Fairport Convention, Commander Cody, Chas And Dave, Southside Johnny And The Asbury Jukes, Todd Rundgren's Utopia; official attendance was 110,000, however an aerial photo commissioned by Peter Grant proved that 210,00 were actually inside the arena; the fee the group picked up for this appearance was reputedly then the highest ever in the history of rock entertainment; the set includes a backdrop video screen and the introduction of Ramport/holo lasers for Jimmy's solo).
August 11 – Knebworth Festival, (full line-up: Chas And Dave, Commander Cody, Southside Johnny And The Asbury Jukes, Todd Rundgren's Utopia, The New Barbarians; att: 90,000).

1980

June 17 – Dortmund Westfallen Halle (start of fourth European tour for which they resort to a simple stage set up with black backdrop and a reduced scale PA; the set excludes marathons such as 'Dazed And Confused' and 'No Quarter'; the venues are the smallest Zepp have played since 1973).
June 18 – Cologne Sporthalle
June 20 – Brussels Forest National
June 21 – Rotterdam Ahoy
June 23 – Bremen Stadthalle
June 26 – Vienna Stadthalle
June 27 – Nuremburg Messezentrum Halle (this show was abandoned after three numbers – 'Train Kept A Rollin'', 'Nobody's Fault But Mine' and 'Black Dog' due to Bonzo suffering physical exhaustion)
June 29 – Zurich Hallenstadion
June 30 – Frankfurt Festhalle (Atlantic's Phil Carson jams with them on bass for an encore of 'Money').
July 2/3 – Mannhiem Eisstadion
July 5 – Munich Olympiahalle (Bad Company drummer Simon Kirke jams with them on 'Whole Lotta Love').
July 7 – Berlin Eissporthalle A proposed date at the Berlin Eissporthalle on July 8 was withdrawn from the itinerary.

POSTSCRIPT:

On September 11, 1980, Peter Grant announced full details of 'Led Zeppelin: The Eighties Part One', a touring campaign due to commence in America in the fall, with plans for further dates in the US and UK to follow in 1981. The following dates were scheduled:
October 17 – Montreal Forum
October 19/21 – Landover Capitol Centre
October 22 – Philadelphia Spectrum
October 23 – Landover Capitol Centre
October 26/27/29 – Cleveland Richfield Coliseum
October 29/30 – Detroit Joe Louis Stadium
November 1 – Buffalo War Memorial Auditorium
November 3/4 – Philadelphia Spectrum
November 6/7 – Pittsburgh Civic Arena
November 9 – St. Paul Civic Centre
November 10/11/12/13/15 – Chicago Stadium.

After the events of September 25, 1980, all the dates were cancelled.

LED ZEPPELIN
EQUIPMENT FILE

Appendix 4

JIMMY PAGE
GUITARS

Grazzioso – first guitar acquired when he was 14.

Fender Stratocaster – used with Neil Christian and The Crusaders.

From sessions through The Yardbirds to Led Zeppelin and beyond:

Gibson 'Black Beauty' Les Paul Custom – bought in 1962 for £185 on HP; used extensively during the session era and with The Yardbirds; custom wired with Bigsby 06130 tremolo arm. Also used in the early Zepp days, it was stolen on a tour flight change en route to Canada. In the July 19, 1973, issue of *Rolling Stone* Page placed an advert offering a reward for its recovery. There were no takers.

Vox 12-String – used with The Yardbirds and on 'Beck's Bolero'.

Fender 1958 Telecaster – given to Jimmy by Jeff Beck, this guitar was used during The Yardbirds era. In 1967 Page had it painted in psychedelic colours. It was this guitar Page employed for recording most of the first Zepp album and on their early tour dates, before he switched to the Les Paul. The solo on the studio version of 'Stairway To Heaven' was played on this guitar. Trouble with the pick-ups rendered this model difficult to use.

Fender 1966 Telecaster – a modified cream model was used by Jimmy on Led Zeppelin's European tour in 1980 and subsequently with The Firm and with Roy Harper at the Cambridge Folk Festival in 1984.

Gibson 1958 Les Paul – a main component of Page's guitar army, used with Zeppelin from the second album onwards in the studio, and from the second American tour on stage.

Gibson 1959 Les Paul (serial number: 91703) – Page's second string Les Paul, a gift from Joe Walsh. This model includes a modified coil splitting switch and an in/out switch located underneath the switchplate.

Gibson Seventies Les Paul – a resprayed cherry red gold top reworked by Clarence White and fitted with a Parsons/White B-string bender.

Gibson ES 1275 6/12-String Double-neck (serial number: 911117) – the famous Page trademark double-neck. This was custom built for live performances of 'Stairway To Heaven' in 1971. Also used on live versions of 'The Song Remains The Same', 'Tangerine', 'Sick Again', 'Celebration Day' and 'The Rain Song'. Rarely employed in the studio, 'Carouselambra' being a notable exception.

Dan Electro – black and white guitar used for performing live versions of 'White Summer/Black Mountain Side' and 1977/80 era versions of 'Kashmir' employing modal tunings.

Fender Sixties Stratocaster – Lake Placid blue model with tremolo arm first used on 'Presence' ('Hots On For Nowhere'). Also used on the live versions of 'In The Evening' 1979/80. Went on to be a popular Page guitar in The Firm days.

Fender 1959 Telecaster – Botswana brown model with a Rosewood neck and fitted with the Parsons/White B-string bender; first appeared on stage with Zeppelin in 1977. On the final tour in 1980, Page used it for 'Hot Dog' and 'All My Love'. Has become one of Page's favourite guitars, being extensively used on the ARMS dates, with The Firm and on the 'Outrider' tour.

Rickenbacker 12-String – used in the studio circa 1969/72.

Harmony Acoustic – used in the studio.

Martin D28 Acoustic – employed for the Zepp acoustic set.

Yamaha Acoustic (serial number: 40607660 0540968) – this guitar was offered as a prize by Jimmy for the Golden Lion Roadies Charity in December 1981.

Gretsch Chet Atkins Hollowbody – given as a prize in a 1974 Guitar competition in the *NME*.

Gibson RD Artist – used on stage with Zeppelin at Knebworth for 'Misty Mountain Hop'.

Fender Late Fifties Stratocaster – Buddy Holly type guitar in two-tone sunburst finish. One of its rare outings was a jam with Bad Company in New York in 1974.

Gibson SG – taken on later Zepp tours but rarely used. Was used in 1977 when Page jammed at the Half Moon in Plumpton and at the Brighton WEA conference.

Vega Five-String Banjo – used on 'Gallows Pole'.

Gibson ES5 Switchmaster – the sunburst guitar featured in the well known fifties pastiche shot of Led Zeppelin taken at Manticore studios in early 1977. This guitar was used on the *Death Wish 2* album.

Gibson ES5 – a blonde model similar to the hollow body guitar used on *Death Wish 2*.

Cromwell Cello Guitar – produced under licence for Gibson in the twenties, also used on *Death Wish 2*.

Gibson Everly Brothers Acoustic – original all-black sixties model given to Page by Ron Wood. One of Page's favourites.

Unidentified acoustic – with cut away body, used during the Zepp acoustic set in 1972.

Roland GR 300 Guitar Synthesiser – used on *Death Wish 2*.

Roland GR 707 Guitar Synthesiser.

Gibson A4 Mandolin.

Fender Mandolin (serial number: 3611H35)

Gibson Twenties Harp Guitar.

KET Custom Guitar – as seen in the 'Wasting My Time' video 1988.

Melobar American Guitar.

Fender Precision Bass – used in the studio only.

Alembic Omega Bass – used in the studio only.

Effects units:
Echoplex unit.
Eventide H949 Clockwork Harmonizer.
Cry Baby Wah Wah.
Boss SD 1 Distortion.
Boss CE 2 Chorus.
Theramin unit.
MXR Phase 90.

Violin bow.

Amplifiers: Two Marshall 100 watt amps. Four Marshall 4 × 12 cabinets.
Two Orange 4 × 12 cabinets.
Supro amp (for recording).
Hiwatt 50 (for rehearsal).
Vox AC 30 (for rehearsal).
In early Zeppelin days, Page used Rickenbacker amps from The Yardbirds set-up.

Picks: Herco Flex 75.

Strings: Ernie Ball Super Slinky. Ernie Ball Earthwoods (acoustics).

JOHN PAUL JONES
BASS GUITARS

Dallas Solid Body Bass – JP's first ever guitar.

Fender 1961 Jazz Bass (serial number: 74242) – used with the Jet Harris/Tony Meehan band right up to 1975 with Zeppelin.

Fender Precision Bass (serial number: 338826) – five string fretless.

Fender Precision Bass.
Gibson Violin Bass – pictured on the wheel sleeve of 'Led Zeppelin III', used for recording.

Fender 1952 Telecaster Bass – sometimes used on stage. Brought out for *Live Aid*.

Alembic Eight-String Bass – used for recording 'Presence' and on stage from the 1977 tour onwards.

Alembic Six-String Bass.
Alembic Four-String Bass.
Arco Stand-Up Electric Bass.
Framus Stand-Up Electric Bass.

Other Guitars
Custom built three-necked special electric/acoustic guitar with pedals – brought in for the live performance of 'Ten Years Gone' in 1977 and 1979.

Harmony Mandolin 3611H35.

Bass pedals: Bill Dunne Custom pedals. Taurus pedals.

Picks: Herco grey.

Strings: Rotosound wirewound.

Bass amplification: GMT 600B amp with two Cerwin Vega cabinets.

Keyboards:
Hammond C3 Organ with two R100 Hammond Leslie speakers – used on stage from the autumn 1969 tour.

Hohner Clavinet 771117 – brought in for 'Trampled Underfoot' in 1975.

Fender Rhodes – electric piano.

Melletron 216 – used from the Japanese tour in 1972 through to the 1975 dates.

Melletron 400.

Yamaha GX1 Organ – complete with infamous telephone. Used from the 1977 tour onwards. Later sold to Keith Emerson.

Yamaha GP 70B – electric grand piano used from 1975 to 1980.

Keyboard amplification: Mavis 15 × 6 paramatic desk. Crown power amps. Showco M4 cabinet.

JOHN BONHAM
PERCUSSION

John Bonham used various Ludwig kits throughout Led Zeppelin's career. On Zeppelin's first US tour he played a sparkle-tinted kit with 24-inch bass drum and two floor tom toms. During the tour Zeppelin played on the same bill as Vanilla Fudge and Bonzo was impressed with Carmine Appice's set-up and ordered a similar kit from Ludwig. This maple wood yellow kit with its huge 26-inch bass drum and additional Paiste gong and side conga drums saw action from the second US tour through to early 1970.
A metal Ludwig kit, again with 26-inch bass drum, in green finish was in use for the Bath Festival in 1970. Bonzo's fourth album symbol of three linked circles was added to the bass drum skin in late 1971. In 1972 Bonzo added two giant side kettle drums to his set-up. These were primarily brought in for the percussion employed on 'The Rain Song'.
For the 1973 US tour Bonzo invested in a stylish, all-perspex Ludwig kit that was used up to the Earls Court gigs in 1975. Mavis syn drum effects were employed on his 'Moby Dick' solo during this period. In 1977 Bonzo switched to a metallic finish kit minus the symbol on the bass drum skin. This model stayed with him through to the final tour in Europe 1980.
A Ludwig practice kit in black and white hooped design was installed in his home music room.

Specific technical details of John Bonham's late seventies set-up are as follows: 26-inch bass drum (a pre-tuned spare was always on hand for live gigs). Speed King foot pedal.
6 × 14 Supra Phonic snare drum with 42 strand snares.
16 × 16 top mounted side tom tom drum.
Two 16 × 18 deep floor tom tom drums.
29-inch machine tympani drum.
30-inch pedal tympani.
Paiste 15-inch Sound Edge hi-hats.
Paiste 24-inch ride cymbal.
Paiste 16-inch, 18-inch, 20-inch and 22-inch crash cymbals.
36-inch Paiste gong.
Natal conga drums.

Drum Effects: For the 'Bonzo's Montreux' recording in September 1976, Barcus Berry pick-ups were taped to his drum heads to create the various effects. Phasing effects were used for live work.

Drum heads: Bonzo originally used Remo Ambassador heads or the Ludwig equivalent. He later changed to Ludwig Silver Dots and Remo Back Dots. His choice of drumshells included wood, Vistalite and stainless steel.

Drumsticks: Ludwig 2A size.

Drum stage monitor system:
Mavis 15 × 6 inch paramatic desk.
Crown power amps.
Two Showco cabinets.
Two Showco F horn bass bins.

ROBERT PLANT

Shure microphone.
Harmonica.
Tambourine.
Vocal echo and harmoniser effects.

THE LED ZEPPELIN PA SYSTEM

As Led Zeppelin's live show evolved, so did their PA system. By the early seventies they had invested in their own custom built set up. A JBL system built by Univox in New York, it consisted of:

Crown 6DC 300 amps with 10 bass cabinets each containing four 15-inch JBL speakers.
10 JBL horns.

20 Shure microphones.
Two 12-channel mixers. This system was capable of producing 2,000 to 8,000 watts depending on the size of hall and was used extensively in Europe and the UK.

SHOWCO

The Showco lighting and sound company was founded in Dallas by Jack Calmes. A former booking agent (he put together the 1969 Texas International Festival with Zeppelin on the bill), he and partner Rusty Brutche pioneered the big arena PA systems that are now an accepted part of rock touring. Led Zeppelin employed the services of Showco for their US tours from 1972 and for every live date from 1975 onwards.
The Showco Sound City PA system Zeppelin used included:

Showco 30 × 8 superboard.
Crown power amps.
30 × 8 monitor desk.
Four Showco M4 cabinets.
Digital delay line unit. This system was capable of 100,000 watts maximum output.

Lighting/Laser effects: From 1973 Zeppelin's stage show was enhanced by an 80,000 watts lighting rig. Stage managed by Ian Knight, it included four Supertrouper spotlights, seven CSI spotlamps and 200

coloured spotlights. A Ramport/Holoco laser show with Krypton laser beams was also devised for use during Jimmy's violin bow solo.

Trucking: Led Zeppelin used Edwin Shirley Trucking to transport their vast array of equipment during their latter years.

TECHNICAL STAFF

Led Zeppelin's road crew during their reign included the following people: Richard Cole (road manager), Clive Coulson, Kenny Pickett, Henry Smith, Sandy Macgregor (early road crew members), Jo Jammer, Raymond Thomas, Tim Marten (guitars), Brian Condliffe, Andy Ledbetter (bass and keyboards), Mick Hinton (drums and percussion), Benji Le Fevre (vocal technician), Donny Kretzchmar (Showco monitor mixing), Rusty Brutshe (Showco sound), Kirby Wyatt (Showco lights), Allen Branton (Showco), Joe Crowley (Showco).

Personnel and PR staff: Bill Harry (publicist circa 1969/70). BP Fallon (publicist circa 1973/74). Rex King (Bonzo's assistant circa 1978/80). Rick Hobbs (Jimmy's assistant). Phil Carlo (Europe 1980 tour).

Legal representatives/Accountants: Steve Weiss, New York attorney. Joan Hudson Associates London.

POSTSCRIPT

Peter Grant: The Man Who Led Zeppelin

There may have been many contenders for the title of fifth Beatle . . . but there was only ever one contender for the title of fifth Zepp. His name was Peter Grant, their notorious manager and the man who led Zeppelin.

Mighty in stature, Peter Grant was the kind of manager that every artist seeks – immensely loyal, unstinting in his efforts on behalf of his clients and fully prepared to eradicate problems by whatever means necessary. This attitude ensured that Led Zeppelin earned *and retained* more money than any band before them. Thanks to Peter, no-one ever messed with Zepp.

Raised by his mother in London's East End, Grant has made little secret of the poverty in which he was raised. Evacuated during the war, he had little formal education but his early jobs as a stage hand, Fleet Street runner, army corporal, entertainment manager, bouncer, film extra and tour manager to visiting US rock stars, schooled him in ways that no teacher ever could. By the time he took on the management of Led Zeppelin, he was as experienced in the ways of the music industry as any manager in London. He was also tenacious about collecting all monies owed to him, in full, without delay.

Grant's style always belied the extraordinary success of Led Zeppelin. He never owned a suit and was always dressed in jeans and an open neck shirt, and he worked out of unassuming offices with a minimum of staff and office furniture. ''I think people spend too much time and money making offices swell,'' he once said. ''Why should I sweat it out to look ritzy. It's the personal touch that counts.''

Whatever tales have been told about the manner of his handling of the group's interests, both physical and otherwise, it's clear that without Grant's guidance, it is unlikely that Led Zeppelin would have attained their phenomenal success. His understanding of the American touring scene, picked up first-hand with The Animals and The Yardbirds in the mid-sixties, was a key ingredient in the almost instant success Zeppelin enjoyed from their first tour onwards. And once Led Zeppelin struck gold it was Grant's ability to develop their mystique that enhanced their appeal to an ever more devoted following.

That there were no TV appearances or singles, that he would keep them off the road for months on end, that he never pushed them to deliver an endless stream of product, were all carefully measured management decisions that ensured Zeppelin sustained their popularity throughout their 12-year reign.

Unpopular as his strategies undoubtedly were among American booking agents and promoters, Peter Grant was the principal architect of the shift in power from businessmen to artists during the seventies. By promoting his own Led Zeppelin concerts, he ensured that a far greater proportion of the receipts from those concerts wound up in the hands of Led Zeppelin, rather than in the hands of promoters and booking agents.

Following Led Zeppelin's demise, the eighties were a very quiet period for Grant. Although he did negotiate Robert Plant's initial solo deal, after the winding down of Swan Song, Grant relinquished his management ties and went into semi-retirement. Heart trouble also kept him inactive, but at the turn of the decade he emerged healthier than he had been in years.

Although not directly involved in management, he is still involved with Bad Company and has lent his vast experience in an advisory capacity to various projects.

At the time of writing, Malcolm McLaren, no stranger to the management game himself, is planning a feature film based on the life of Peter Grant. With a script written by Barry O'Keefe (*The Long Good Friday*), it's due to be filmed in London and Los Angeles in 1991. It will be interesting to see how this movie evolves.

Peter Grant remains immensely proud of his achievements with Led Zeppelin. It's a tribute to the respect he earned through those often crazy years that Jimmy Page, Robert Plant and John Paul Jones readily acknowledge the debt they owe to his shrewd handling of their careers during the Zeppelin era.

As Robert once explained to 18,000 people from the stage of the Earls Court arena:

''Now I'm not going to go into too much spiel tonight, because we normally leave all the spieling to our manager Mr Peter Grant over there in the wings . . . spotlight on Mr Grant! . . . spotlight on Peter Grant over on the left of the stage . . . the man who made it all possible. Let me tell you, he never likes to be in group pictures, he doesn't like playing soccer with us . . . but what a manager . . . what a member of the group in fact.''

4/93 (15191)